The
OSWALD
CHAMBERS
Collection

The OSWALD CHAMBERS *Collection*

• Biblical Psychology •
Studies In The Sermon On The Mount •

ISBN: 978-1-6673-0618-6 paperback
ISBN: 978-1-6673-0619-3 hardcover

Table of Contents

Contents

Studies in the Sermon on the Mount

Biblical Psychology

STUDIES
IN THE SERMON
ON THE MOUNT

By
OSWALD CHAMBERS

OSWALD CHAMBERS

Author of "Bible Psychology" "The Cure of t Souls' etc.
Principal of London
Bible Training College.

"We may all be disciples; why should we not be scholars of
the one Teacher? Come, let Him lure thee – give up all other
teachers and hear this Teacher sent from God."

J. PARKER

God's Revivalist Press
Cincinnati, Ohio.

FOREWORD

In his Sixth Study our author says, "Jesus warns His disciples to test preachers and teachers by their fruit. There are two ways of testing by fruit – one by the fruit in the life of the preacher, and the other is by the fruit in the life of the doctrine." It is a genuine joy to be able to apply these touchstones of character and teaching to the life and words of Oswald Chambers.

It was the writer's rare privilege to be in the same home with him and to sit under his ministry for a number of months; to see him daily and to find in him a patient counselor, an exemplary as well as trustworthy teacher, and a Christlike friend. The following words are none too vividly descriptive of this modern prophet teacher:

> "Who never sold the truth to -serve the hour,
> Nor paltered with eternal God for power,
> Who let the turbid stream of rumor flow
> Thro' either babbling world high or low;
> Whose life is work, whose language rife
> With rugged maxims hewn from life,
> Who never spoke against a foe"

And as to the second test proposed, "the fruit. . . of the doctrine" – will there be found in all the Church of Christ of today one whose words are more weighty with spiritual values? "But," says some simple soul, "I don't understand him." The more is the pity. Leave then the evening newspaper, the book of religious wonder-tales, the high-flown writings "watered" with adjectives, but empty of thought or power, and read these pages again and again until the truth "soaks" through to your innermost consciousness. There is about us a flood of profession, but a failure in possession; a torrent of criticism for those who "follow not us," but a trickling rivulet of sound advice to ourselves. To heed the words of our Lord's Sermon on the Mount as interpreted by Oswald Chambers will transform holiness people into holy people, and faithless verbosity into Christian humility. Unto which glorious result, God speed the day!

– J. F. K.

Study Number One

N. B. (1) Introductory note on the Gospel according to St. Matthew and St. Luke respectively.

(2) The student is advised to get a copy of Dr. Gore's "The Sermon on the Mount."

ST. MATTHEW: COLLECTION OF DISCOURSES.

1. Address to the Twelve.
   Matthew 5: 1-16, 39-42, 44-48; 7:1-6; 12:15-17.

2. Address on Prayer.
   Matthew 6: 9-15; 7: 7-11.

3. Answer to a Theological Question.
   Matthew 7: 13, 14; 8: 11, 12.

4. Address on Worldly-mindedness.
   Matthew 6: 19-34.

5. Address in the Synagogue of Capernaum.
   Matthew 5: 17-39, 43; 6: 1-8, 16-18.

ST. LUKE: CHRONOLOGICAL DIVISIONS.

1. Address to the Twelve.
   Luke 6: 20 : 20-28, 41-49; 11 : 32.

2. Address on Prayer.
   Luke 11:1-13.

3. Answer to a Theological Question.
   Luke 13: 23-30.

4. Address on "Worldly-mindedness.
   Luke 12: 13-34.

5. Address in the Synagogue of Capernaum.
   Luke 4: 31-37; (Mark 1: 21-28).

STUDY NUMBER ONE

In order to understand the Sermon on the Mount, it is necessary
to know the mind of the Preacher, and this knowledge
can be gained by anyone who will receive the Holy Spirit.
(Luke II: 13; John 20: 22; Acts 19: 2.)

Beware of placing our Lord Jesus as a teacher first instead of a Savior. We must first know Him as a Savior before His teachings have any meaning for us, or before they have any other meaning than that of an ideal which leads to despair. There are some people who take up this attitude: "I do not believe there is any necessity to preach an atonement through Jesus Christ, I do not believe it is necessary to say He died for our sins, I believe that Jesus is a teacher only." That attitude is very prevalent to-day, but it is a very absurd as well as dangerous one, for if He was only a teacher, His teaching would produce despair. Fancy coming to men and women with defective lives and defiled hearts and wrong mainsprings and telling them to be pure in heart! What would be the good of His giving us an ideal that we could not possibly come near? we are happier without knowing it. If Jesus is only a teacher, then all He can do is to tantalise us, to erect a standard we cannot attain to; but if we know Him first as Savior, if we are born again of the Spirit of God, we know that He did not come to teach us only, but that He came to make us what He teaches we should be.

The Gospel according to St. Matthew, in its original state in the early Church, was in two sections. One section was composed of five great discourses of our Lord's with no historical narrative at all. This was transcribed by Matthew himself. The second section has the five discourses fitted into the historical narratives of our Lord's life. The latter was compiled by a student-evangelist of Matthew's, and it is this latter Gospel that we know.

Matthew wrote his Gospel according to topics; Luke, a cultured physician, an evangelist and disciple of Paul's, wrote his Gospel in the perfect manner of the Greek historians, so that the student who wants to know where the various teachings of Jesus are to be placed in our Lord's life must turn to Luke's Gospel.

"The Sermon on the Mount" is the title given by Matthew to a collection of discourses by our Lord, only one of which was literally preached on the mountain, the others were preached in the mountainous district. The evangelists Matthew, Peter, Paul and John took incidents out of the life of our Lord on which they based their doctrines, and the four Gospels are simply the records of their preaching under the guidance of the Holy Spirit. It sounds very precarious to us to say that it was all trusted to memory and oral transmission, but when we remember there was a kind of curse given by the rabbis to anyone who put anything in writing, and if a student in a rabbinical school made a slip in memory he was supposed to be worthy of death, it alters our too hasty first conclusions about the matter. These early disciples were brought up in that school, and when Paul talks about the "deposit" that Timothy had, this is what he is alluding to. They were all trained to retain accurate details and descriptions of our Lord's life; and in the year 62 or 65 Matthew wrote his Gospel. The four Gospels are four contrasted views of our Lord's life, not contradictory views. The astute mind behind the Gospels is not a human mind at all, but the Holy Ghost. "Holy men wrote as they were moved by the Spirit of God." A "harmony of the Gospels" is a rather mistaken idea; harmony must imply discord as well as accord. The very same principle holds in understanding the unity of the Gospels as in understanding our Lord's teachings, viz., a personal knowledge of the mind of the Lord, which can he obtained by receiving the Holy Spirit. Peter says that holy men wrote as they were moved, he did not say holy machines. You will find that God the Holy Ghost instead of effacing the individuality of these men did exactly the opposite, He lifted their personality to a point of "white heat," so to speak, and used it as the means of presenting the Gospel of God. The more you brood over that line of things the more you will be able to discard the cheap and hasty criticism which is honeycombing so much of the teaching nowadays. You will find as many points in the Gospel that won't fit into another as you find points that will. The word we need is not harmony in the Gospels, but unity, and the unity is by the Holy Ghost.

(1) Address to the Twelve.

When our Lord ordained twelve men out of the multitude that followed Him He preached to them what we have in Matthew 5 and 7, and He began by saying, "Blessed are," and then He must have staggered them by what followed. They were to be blessed in every particular which they had been taught from their earliest childhood was a curse. The statements of Jesus seem so wonderfully simple, but in reality they are like spiritual torpedoes, they explode and burst in the unconscious mind, and they come up to our conscious mind and we say, "What a startling statement that is I" Our Lord was talking to Jews, and the Jews believed, down to their joints and marrow, that the sign of the blessing of God was material prosperity in every shape and form, and Jesus says, "Blessed are ye" for exactly the opposite.

We must remember that Jesus wrote nothing, He spoke everything, and to look upon His teachings as a written act of Parliament is absurd, and to look upon His statements as isolated texts to be mechanically followed is equally misleading. Our Lord expects that these statements of His will be carried out in the lives of these men in the power of the Spirit He is to give them. There are two ways of looking at the Sermon on the Mount: a number of teachers to-day say that it was a forecast of what is going to be during the Millennium and it has no application whatever to us now. There are others who say that it has only an application to us now and has no reference to any other time. Now both those views are right, but either alone is wrong. In this present dispensation, Jesus says the kingdom of God is inside men, and men are called upon to live out His Spirit and His teaching in an age that will not recognize Him. That spells limitation and very often disaster. In the next dispensation the kingdom of God will be established outside as well as inside men. These two points of view are always put together in the New Testament.

(2) Address on Prayer.

Our Lord begins His teaching about prayer with a little playful irony in which He tells them to watch their motives (Matt. 6:5), "Why do you want to pray? Do you want to be known as a praying man? Well, verily that is your reward, you will be known as a praying man, but there is no more to it, there is no answer to your prayer." The next thing He told them was to keep a secret relationship between themselves and God (Matt. 6:6), and in verse 7 He told them not to rely on their own earnestness when praying. These three statements of Jesus, which are so familiar to us, are revolutionary. Call a halt one moment and ask yourself, "Why do I want to pray, what is my motive? Have I a personal, secret relationship to God that nobody knows but myself? And what is my method when I pray, am I really relying on God or on my own earnestness?" These sayings of Jesus go to the very root of all praying. The majority of us make the blunder of depending on our own earnestness and not on God at all. It is confidence in Him. (1 John 5:14,15.) All our fuss, all our earnestness, all our "gifts of prayer" are not the slightest atom of use to Jesus Christ, He pays no attention to them. Our Lord gave His disciples the pattern prayer and supplied in that prayer their want of ideas and words and faith. Then He taught them the prayer of patience. Our Lord's instruction about patience in prayer conveys this lesson: "If you are right with God, and God delays the manifested answer to your prayer, don't misjudge Him, don't think of Him as an unkind friend, or an unnatural father, or an unjust judge, but keep at it. Your prayer will certainly be answered," says Jesus, "for everyone that asks receives," and "men ought always to pray and not faint." Your Heavenly Father will explain it all one day, He cannot just now because He is developing your character.

(3) Answer to a Theological Question.

Our Lord in His answers very rarely, if ever, appears to deal with the questions asked. In Luke 13 a very devout, pious individual asks Him if there be many saved or few, and Jesus gave him a reply in an Oriental proverb, the effect of which is, "See that your own feet are on the right path." At another time, the disciples said, in a really earnest mood, "Lord, increase our faith," and Jesus quoted them an Oriental proverb about a grain of mustard seed and a mountain, which if you watch the setting, undoubtedly conveys this: "Get personally related to me, and lack of faith will never bother you." Whenever we lack faith, it is simply that we do not trust Him; faith must be the result of a personal understanding. Our Lord's answers seem at first to evade the point, but instead of evading it, He goes underneath the questions and puts something in that will solve every question. He never answers our shallow questions, but He deals with the great, unconscious need that made them arise. One class of questions our Lord never answered, those that come from the head, the reason being that no question from the head is ever original.

(4) Address on Worldly-Mindedness.

Our Lord in this discourse and in many others, was strong on the necessity of a line of demarcation between worldly-mindedness and spirit-mindedness while we are in the world. We are most of us certain that we can serve two masters with a little skill and tact, but we sooner or later come to the conclusion that Jesus knows best. (There is all the difference between Heaven and Hell in that simple phrase, "Jesus knows best." Think what it means in your personal life, in your business life. Some of us are uncommonly like the disciples when Jesus was with them in the fishing boat, they thought in effect, "He is a carpenter, and doesn't know anything about fishing; He can go to sleep, He does not know anything about managing boats;"but when the storm comes on, Jesus is the only one who can manage the boat, the fishermen are terrified out of their wits. It is a great moment in a man's life when he realizes that Jesus knows more about his business than he does himself.)

Take our attitude to our Lord's statement that everyone that asks receives, the majority of us think we believe it, but our attitude really is, "I'll ask, but it may not be His will to answer," meaning that I have no confidence in Jesus further than my common sense allows me to go. We call ourselves Christians, but where do we place Jesus? We limit Him on the right hand and on the left, by trusting to ourselves. The man or woman who trusts Jesus in a definite, practical way ought to be freer than anyone else to do his or her business; free from fret and worry, they can go with absolute certainty into the daily life.

Jesus also taught that if men were to be spiritual, they must sacrifice the natural, that the only ground of the spiritual is on the basis of the sacrifice of the natural. One of the greatest principles – which we do not seem to grasp, but which was very evident in our Lord's life – is that the natural life is neither moral nor immoral. I make it moral or immoral. Jesus says the natural life is meant for sacrifice, we can give it as a gift to God, that is the way to become spiritual. Jesus says if we do not do that, we must barter the spiritual. That is where Adam failed, he refused to sacrifice the natural life and make it spiritual by obeying God's voice in it, consequently he sinned, the sin of his right to himself. If we say, "I like this natural life, I do not want to be a saint, I do not want to sacrifice the natural life for the spiritual," then Jesus says you must barter the spiritual. It is not a punishment, it is an eternal principle. If you are going to be spiritual, you must barter the natural, sacrifice it. Spirituality is not a sweet tendency towards piety in people who have not enough life in them to be bad; spirituality is the possession of the Holy Spirit of God which is, as it were, masculine in its strength, and that will make the most corrupt twisted,. sin-stained life spiritual if He be obeyed

(5) Address in the Synagogue.

Jesus distinctly says here that He is the meaning and the fulfillment of all the old commandments, and if any man says it does not matte whether you heed those commandments or not Jesus says that He condemns him. If the old commandments were difficult, our Lord's princi ples are fathoms deeper and more difficult. He actually says that unless the men who were His disciples exceeded all the good doings of the good people Who are not His disciples, they will in no case enter the kingdom of Heaven. Think of the best men and women you know who have never received the Spirit of God and who make no profession – they are upright, sterling, noble and Jesus says in effect, "If you have received my Spirit and are my disciples, you have to exceed everything they do and are, or you will never see the kingdom of Heaven." Instead of the criticism of Christians being wrong, it is absolutely right; we have to *produce our goods up to* and have the life in us that Jesus said we would *sample.* If we are born again of the Holy Ghost, have by means of His cross, we have to show it by the way we talk, the way we act and transact our business.

The teaching in the Sermon on the Mount produces despair in the natural man, the one thing Jesus wants it to do, because immediately we get to despair we come to Jesus Christ like paupers, and are willing to receive from Him. "Blessed are the paupers in spirit" – that is the very first principle of the kingdom. As long as we have some conceited, self-righteous notion of our own – "Oh, yes, I can do this" – God has to allow us to go on until we break our ignorance over some obstacle, then we realize that, after all, Jesus knew best – "Blessed are the poor in spirit." It is receiving all the way along.

Jesus spoke these things openly to all men, not to a special clique, and if they are binding on any man they are binding on all equally.

This is a brief introduction to our more detailed study of the Sermon on the Mount. Pray that God's Spirit will illuminate these studies to you.

Study Number Two

MATTHEW FIVE.

A. DIVINE DISPROPORTION.
1. The "Mines" of God.
    Luke 6:20-26.
2. The Motive of Godliness.
    Matthew 5 : 11, 12.

B. DIVINE DISADVANTAGE.
1. Concentrated Service.
    Matthew 5:13.
2. Conspicuous Setting.
    Matthew 5:14-16.

C. DIVINE DECLARATION.
1. His Mission.
    Matthew 5:20.
2. His Message.
    Matthew 5 : 20.

N. B. A working exposition of the subconscious mind will be given in this- lecture.

STUDY NUMBER TWO

MATTHEW 5.

We will take the note at the foot of the outline first. N. B. Every mind has two compartments: a conscious and an unconscious compartment. Subconscious simply means under consciousness. The things we hear and read slip away from our memory; we say, they do not really, they go into the unconscious mind. The work of the Spirit of God in a Christian is to bring back into our conscious mind the things that are stored in the subconscious. So in studying the Bible never go on the line that because you do not understand what you are reading just now it will be of no use; you find the habit of Bible study is to store the mind with Bible knowledge, and then perhaps after years when you come across something in your circumstances, the Spirit of God will bring back to your conscious mind something you never remembered you had, and you say, "I wonder wherever that came from!"

Always bear in mind this twofold aspect of the mind. There is nothing supernatural or marvellous in it in the sense of being uncanny, it is simply a knowledge of how God has made us. So it is foolish to estimate only by what we consciously understand at the time; we may not see any meaning in it for our lives, but if we store it away the Spirit of God will bring it back to our remembrance.

The Sermon on the Mount lays down the principles at the basis of our Lord's kingdom, and it is by these principles, which are purposely veiled as laws and conduct, that we understand the nature of the Kingdom. A principle is something that explains, and the principles of the Sermon on the Mount explain the character of our Lord's kingdom. It is by these principles alone that we understand His kingdom, but when it comes to personal conduct we find instantly God veils them.

The two methods of applying these principles to the conduct of individual Christians to-day – both of which are wrong – are first, the lax method, which makes out that these principles are mere poetry and nothing more. The other method is the literal one whereby the statements are applied literally. The first method makes out that society, as it is, is all right; the latter method makes out that it is all rotten. The one abiding method of interpretation is the Spirit of Jesus Christ in the heart of a believer bringing His principles to apply in the particular circumstances in which he is placed. (See Rom. 12 :2.) The methods we have mentioned are dodges to get away from the sternness of Jesus Christ's requirements. If the Sermon on the Mount is to be applied literally, then any fool can do that, we do not need to be born again to do that. But Jesus Christ insists that if any man is going to partake of the character of His kingdom, he must have His nature, all we understand by being born again and sanctified. Then we have the responsibility, God does not take it, we have the responsibility of walking in the light and applying His principles to our circumstances. The whole thing is put in a nutshell by the apostle Paul: "Be renewed in the spirit of your mind, that you may prove what the will of God is, the thing that is acceptable and right and perfect."

A. Divine Disproportion. (Matt. 5: 1-12.)

(1) The "Mines" of God. (Luke 6 120-26.)

(2) The Motive of Godliness. (Matt. 5:11, 12.)

The Sermon on the Mount is quite unlike the Ten Commandments, in the sense of its principles being absolutely unworkable unless Jesus Christ can remake us.

(I) The "Mines of God." (Luke 6:20-26.) I mean by "mines" an under-working charged With explosives. The first time you read the Beatitudes they appear beautiful and simple and unstartling, and they go unobserved into your subconsciousness.

Then you come across something in your practical life whereby the Holy Ghost brings back one of these Beatitudes, and you find, to your astonishment, that it is like a spiritual torpedo, it "rips" and "tears" and revolutionizes everything you ever knew. The Beatitudes spring from the life blood of Jesus Christ, that is they contain all His meaning, and when we read them first they seem merely mild and beautiful precepts for all unworldly, useless people, and of very little practical use in the stern, workaday world in which we live. However, we soon find that these Beatitudes contain the dynamite of the Holy Ghost. In Luke's account (Luke 6: 20:-26) the Beatitudes are paralleled by the "Woes," which is an indication of how these principles of Jesus work. They explode, as it were, when the circumstances of life require them to do so. For instance, when you find yourself suddenly faced by circumstances that praise you for your spiritual possessions, Beatitude 3 emerges into the conscious life like a veritable spiritual torpedo; or again, when your circumstances are finding you full of ecstacy and delight over spiritual service, Beatitude 4 comes into the life with staggering amazement. You cannot apply them literally. You allow the life of God, first of all, to invade you by regeneration and sanctification, and then as you have been soaking your mind in the teaching of Jesus, and it has been slipping down into the unconscious mind, then a set of circumstances arises where suddenly one of them emerges, and instantly you have to ask yourself, "Will I walk in the light of it? Will I accept the tremendous spiritual tornado which will be produced in my circumstances if I follow this teaching of Jesus? I have the power to follow it if I will!" That is the way the Spirit of God works. It always comes with astonishing discomfort to begin with, it is all out of proportion to our ways of looking at things, and we have slowly to form our walk and conversation in the line of His precepts.

(2) The Motive of Godliness. (Matt. 5: II, 12.) The motive at the back of the precepts of the Sermon on the Mount is, first and

foremost, love for God. Not that the Beatitudes have no meaning in our relationship to men, that relationship is so obvious it scarcely needs noting, but the Godward aspect is not so obvious. Read the Beatitudes with your mind fixed on God, Put His name after every one of them, and you will realize the neglected side of the Beatitudes. "Blessed are the poor in spirit," towards God. "Blessed are the meek," towards God's dispensations. "Blessed are the merciful," to God's reputation. "Blessed are the pure in heart," that is obviously Godward. "Blessed are the peacemakers" (exactly the note that was struck at the birth of Jesus, a peace-making relationship between God and man). Is it possible to carry out the Beatitudes? Never! unless God can do what Jesus Christ says He can, give us the Holy Spirit, who will remake us and put us in a new realm. The Sermon on the Mount is a statement of the life we will live when the Holy Ghost is getting His way with us.

Our Lord says that His disciples are to rejoice on one condition, when they are reviled and persecuted and slandered for His sake. That is left out in modern Christian teaching, we are told that if we suffer for "conviction's sake," for "conscience's sake," it is all that is necessary. Peter says you do not do any more than other people if you only suffer that way. We have to suffer for "Jesus' sake:" that is, the whole motive underneath is to be well pleasing to God. The true blessedness of the saint is in determinedly making and keeping God *first*. Herein is the disproportion of Jesus Christ's principles and moral teaching, the reason being that Christ bases everything on God-realization, while other teachers base their teaching on self-realization. Whenever the Holy Ghost sees a chance of glorifying Jesus, He will take your heart, your nerves, your whole personality, and simply make them blaze and glow with a personal, passionate devotion and love to the Lord Jesus Christ; not devotion to a cause, not a devotee to a principle, but a devoted loveslave of the Lord Jesus

Christ. No man on earth has that love unless the Holy Ghost has imparted it. (Rom. 5: 5.) We may admire Him and respect Him and reverence Him, but we cannot love Him; the only lover of the Lord Jesus Christ is the Holy Ghost.

B. Divine Disadvantage. (Matt. 5: 13-16.)
(1) Concentrated Service. (5:13.)
(2) Conspicuous Setting. (5:14-16.)

The disadvantage of a saint in the present condition of things is that he has to make the centre of his life, confession of Jesus, not in secret, but glaringly public. The tendency to be holy and say nothing about it is right from every standpoint but from the standpoint of the Holy Spirit. It is doubtless much to the advantage of Christian men and women in this age to keep quiet (that is, advantage from the self-realization standpoint), and the tendency is growing stronger, "Don't say anything about it; be a Christian, live a holy life, but do keep quiet."

(1) Concentrated Service. (5:13.) "Ye are the salt of the earth." Our Lord's picture of salt is terse and concise, for the most concentrated thing known to human beings is salt, it tastes like nothing else but salt every time and all the time. That is our Lord's illustration of a disciple. Salt preserves wholesomeness and prevents decay. The disciples of Jesus in the present dispensation preserve society from corruption. Some modern Christian teachers would like us to believe that Jesus said, "Ye are the sugar of the earth," meaning that gentleness and winsomeness without curativeness is the idea of a Christian. How are we to maintain the healthy, salty tang of saintliness? By remaining rightly related to God through Jesus Christ.

(2) Conspicuous Setting. (5:14-16.) The things our Lord uses as illustrations, viz., light and a city set on a hill, are the most conspicuous things known to us, there is no possibility of mis-

taking them. Jesus says, "Be like that, in your home, in your business, in your church, conspicuously a Christian for ridicule or for respect according to the moods of the people you are with." Our Lord taught His disciples, in Matthew 10:1628, the need to be conspicuous proclaimers of the truth, and not to cover it up for fear of wolfish men. Our Lord will have nothing of the nature of a covert disciple. These three things, salt, light and a city set on a hill, are things among men that cause the most annoyance as well as those that attract the vilest things. Salt, to preserve from corrupion, has very often to be placed in the midst of it and before it can do its work it causes excessive irritation, which spells persecution. Light attracts bats and hideous nightmoths and points out the way for burglars as well as other people. Jesus would have us remember that men will certainly defraud us. A city is the gathering place for all the human driftwood that will not work for its own living, so the Christian will have any number of parasites and ungrateful "hangers-on." All these considerations form a powerful temptation to pretend we are not salt, to put our light under a bushel, and cover our city with a fog. You cannot soil light; you may attempt to grasp a beam of light with the sootiest hand, but you leave no mark on the light. You can soil a moral man or an innocent man, but you cannot soil a man or woman who is made pure by the Holy Ghost and who remains there; they are light. A sunbeam may shine into the filthiest hovel in the slums of a city, but it cannot be soiled. Thank God for the men and women who are spending their lives in the slums of the earth, not as moral characters to lift their brother men to cleaner styles, but as the light of God, pure and unspotted from the World, shining a way for the men to get back to God!

If we have been covering our light, uncover it! The light always reveals and guides and blazes, and men dislike it when their deeds are evil and prefer darkness.

C. Divine Declaration. (Matt. 5:17-20.)

(1) His Mission. (5:17-19.)

(2) His Message. (5:20.)

Here our Lord places Himself as the exact meaning and fulfillment of all the Old Testament commandments and prophecies. He says that His mission is to fulfill the law and the prophets, and further that any teacher in this present era that breaks the former laws and teaches men to do so because they belong to a former dispensation shall suffer severe impoverishment. All not ignored. There are teachers who say that former Old Testament laws are fulfilled in Christ, the Sermon on the Mount supersedes the Ten Commandments, and that because we are not under "law but under grace," it does not matter whether we honor our father and mother, whether ue covet our neighbor's possessions, etc. Beware of statements like this: "There is no need now-a-days to observe giving the 'tenth,' either of money or of time, we are under a new dispensation and it ail belongs to God." That, in practical application, means sentimental "dust-throwing." The giving of the tenth is not a sign that it all belongs to God, but a sign that the "tenth" belongs to God and the rest is ours, and we are held responsible for what we do with it. It is surprising how easily we can juggle ourselves out of Jesus Christ's principles by one or two pious principles repeated often enough. The only safeguard is to keep personally related to Him. 1 John 1:7 is the great safeguard for all spiritual understanding. "Walk in the light" – not the light of my convictions or theories, but the light God is in. Literal interpretation of the Sermon on the Mount is child's play; the interpretation by the Spirit of Christ is the stern work of a saint, and it requires all that the Lord kept teaching His disciples – Spiritual Concentration.

(2) His Message. (5: 20.)

Our Lord's message here is that the righteousness of the scribes and Pharisees was right, not wrong, and that His disciples were to exceed that righteousness. That the Pharisees did much more and other than righteousness is obviously clear, but our Lord is here talking of their righteousness. What is it that exceeds right doing if it be not right being? Right being, without doing anything, is possible, but it cannot exceed the righteousness of the scribes and Pharisees. The way I can stop right doing is by refusing to enter into relationship with God, both by His words and providences. This is an aspect of things continually overlooked in Christian morality. The statement we so often hear, "If I were in your circumstances, I could be as good as you are," is perfectly true, but in your own circumstances you can do much better if the Spirit of God dwells in you. We are apt to think the charge is not true that, if they were in the circumstances we are in, they would be as good as we are. Of course they would, in all probability much better, but let us get hold of the secret that the harder the circumstances God's providence has brought around you, the brighter and grander does your light shine; the more difficult and perplexing the surroundings, the more difficult the people you have to deal with, the more God-glorifying is the exhibition of Christ's life in you. The monks in the Middle Ages refused to take the responsibilities of life; all they wanted was to be and not to do. They could not exceed the righteousness of the scribes and Pharisees; they shut themselves away from the world, and people to-day want to cut themselves off from this and that relationship. But Jesus Christ's message is that unless we exceed in *doing* (the Pharisees were nothing in *being*), we shall never enter the kingdom of God.

Verse 16 brings out the same meaning, "When men see your good works, they will glorify your Father in Heaven." If our Lord had meant in being only, He would not have used the word exceed, He would have said, "Except your righteousness be otherwise than."

Study Number Three

MATTHEW FIVE.

A. THE ACCOUNT WITH PURITY.

1. Disposition and Deeds.
   Matthew 5: 21, 22.

2. Temper of Mind and Truth of Manner.
   Matthew 5: 23, 26.

3. Lust and License.
   Matthew 5: 27, 28.

4. Direction of Discipline.
   Matthew 5: 29, 30.

B. THE ACCOUNT WITH PRACTICE.

1. Scandal.
   Matthew 5: 31, 32.

2. Irreverent Reverence.
   Matthew 5: 33-36.

3. Integrity.
   Matthew 5: 37.

C. THE ACCOUNT WITH PERSECUTION.

1. Toward Insult.
   Matthew 5: 38, 39.

2. Towards , Extortion.
   Matthew 5: 40.

3. Towards Tyranny.
   Matthew 5: 41, 42.

STUDY NUMBER THREE

MATTHEW 5.

Our Lord here is laying down this principle that, if these disciples are going to follow Him and obey His Spirit, they have to lay their account with purity, with practice, and with persecution. Now purity is an intensely difficult thing to define. Purity is a state of heart on the inside which we can best define as being just like Jesus Christ's heart. You cannot make yourself pure by obeying laws. Our Lord shows how this heart purity works out. He takes, first of all, a parallel picture from the old law, and then shows how He interprets it from the pure-heart standard. It is not only a question of doing the things rightly, but of the doer on the inside being right.

(1) Disposition and Deeds. (5:21,22.) Our Lord here is alluding to something that was quite familiar to the disciples. It was customary for some people to totally disregard what was known as the common judgment, what we would call the ordinary law courts, and if they went too far they got into danger of an inner court (we have nothing quite like it in our law), and if they insisted on being contemptuous with that one, they were in danger of the final judgment, which meant they were flung out as wastrels and anarchists. Jesus uses that as a spiritual illustration, He puts it this way, that our disposition has to be like His, that our motive, i. e., the place we cannot get at ourselves, must be right. Read Psalm 139 with this idea in mind. The Psalmist is realizing he is much too big for himself, that there are things he cannot get at, but that, just as God can understand the big world outside, He can understand the bigger world inside him. To the Psalmist the world is bigger on the inside than on the outside, and he says, "Now, Lord, search me out and see if there be any way of grief in me," and the Hebrew words mean, "Trace me out; the dreams of my dreams, the motives of my motives,

make those right." That is what Jesus is alluding to here, the motives of my motives and the springs of my dreams must be so right that right deeds will naturally follow. Other teachers tell of certain things to suppress, certain rules and regulations to obey; Jesus Christ never gives us rules and regulations. Try, for instance, to use the Sermon on the Mount as a series of rules and regulations and you find you cannot do it. They are truths that can only be interpreted by a new spirit which Jesus Christ puts in. Jesus teaches that He can alter our mainspring of action. He does not teach us to curb or suppress the wrong disposition, He does not even give us something to counteract it, He gives us a totally new disposition. Every now and again that aspect of Jesus Christ's teaching which is so radical is being refined away by Christian teachers, they tell us that Jesus Christ cannot do what He says He can. They say, "Of course what the Lord meant was not what He said, but what I tell you," that He does not alter our disposition, but He puts something in us that counteracts the old disposition. That is a compromise with something Jesus never compromised with. The only way in which a Christian knows that Jesus has given him a pure heart is by trying circumstances. This is the way it works; you are brought under trying circumstances, people imply wrong motives to you, and if the Lord has made your heart pure, you are the most astonished person in the world, because, instead of feeling resentment, you feel exactly the opposite, you feel a most amazing difference inside. That is the only proof we have according to the Sermon on the Mount that God has altered the. heart, not that we persuade ourselves He has done it, but that we prove it. When circumstances put us to the test, we say, "Why, bless God! this is a marvelous alteration, I know now He has altered me because before I would have got sour and irritable and sarcastic and spiteful." Our Lord goes behind the old law to the disposition.

(2) Temper of Mind and Truth of Manner. (5:23-26.) The spiritual lesson there is the difference between reality and sincerity.

The thing that Jesus alters is the temper of our minds, so that we are no longer in bondage to rules and regulations, but find when the difficulties come that we obey our Lord's rules easily. (See Matt. 11: 28-30.)

The illustration is of a man in the old Jewish order going to take a paschal lamb to the priest to be slain, and, remembering he had leaven in his house, he had to go back and take the leaven out before he took his offering. Jesus applies it spiritually. If you are going to the altar and you remember someone has something against you, first go and put that right, and if you are a saint, you will find you have the power to do it. A disciple of Jesus has no difficulty in doing what, to worldly people, would be an impossible humiliation. Many of us have sincere manners toward one another, but the test Jesus gives is not the truth of your manner, but the temper of your mind. When you come to the altar, you have something brought to your memory – Jesus does not say when you "rake up something," that is where Satan gets hold of embryo Christians and makes them hyper-conscientious. Jesus says if at the altar there you remember, the inference is that the Spirit of God brings it to your memory, and when He does, never check it. Say, "Yes, Lord, I recognize it," and obey Him at once, no matter what the humiliation is. That is impossible in a worldly person and impossible in you and me till God has altered us. Suppose I do remember something at the altar, and I was in the right and they were in the wrong, and the Spirit of God says to me, "You go and obey;" if I have not had the temper of my mind altered by Jesus, I will say instantly, "No, indeed, do you think I am going to tell them, when I was in the right, that I have to make it up? Immediately they will say, 'I knew I would make you say you were sorry!' " That is the temper of mind in all of us till we have been altered. Immediately we are altered the other temper of mind is there and, to our astonishment, we find we do things we never could do before. Jesus Christ brings men to the practical test, it is not that I say I am pure in heart, it is that I prove I am in my deeds, that the attitude is right, that I am not only sincere in my manner and talk, but I am sincere in the attitude of my mind.

One of the points we do not realize sufficiently is the influence of what we think over what we say. We may say wonderfully truthful things, but what we think is the thing that tells. It is quite possible to say truthful things in a truthful manner, and tell a lie all the time by thinking. I can repeat exactly what I heard you say to Mr. Somebody-else, word for word, every detail scientifically truthful, and yet I can convey a lie by it because the temper of my mind has been a different one to yours when you said the things.

Jesus says be truthful in manner, and the one thing He is "going for" here is to prove that the disposition must be altered. All through the Sermon on the Mount the same thing comes out. Jesus is dealing on the inside, the old law dealt with the outside. Jesus said you have to exceed that, do all the old law, but do much more, and "the only way you can do the much more is by letting me have my way with you, letting me give you my Spirit, by letting me alter you from the inside, and when you come into the different circumstances and I say to you, 'Do this,' don't remember what you were before I altered you, but remember that everything I tell you to do you can do, and the only knowledge you have that you can do it is that you discover you can, immediately you try. Don't say, 'I cannot do that, I tried it before and could not.'" The whole point of our Lord is, "Obey me, and you will find you have a wealth of power inside."

Instantly you obey, you find the temper of your mind is real. The great thing about Jesus is that He makes us real, not only sincere. Remember, the people who are sincere without being real are not hypocrites nor shams, they are perfectly earnest and honest and desirous of fulfilling all that Jesus wants, but they really cannot do it, the reason being they have not received the Person who makes them real, viz., the Holy Spirit.

(3) Lust and License. (5:27,28.) Our Lord teaches here what the apostle Paul reemphasizes in Romans 6: 12, viz., that sin is not in the mortal flesh, but in the principle that rules the mortal flesh: "Let not sin therefore reign in your mortal body that ye should obey it in the lusts thereof." The "it" he is referring to is the sin that dwells in your mortal body. Our Lord says by implication that what He alters is the principle of desire in our mortal bodies. "Lust," which means "I must have it at once," is the very nature of sin. Jesus alters that and puts love in its place, which is the opposite of lust. Esau and his mess of pottage are a picture of lust; Jacob serving for Rachel is a picture of love. Our Lord in this illustration puts lust and license on the grossest, vilest ground, but remember, it applies all through, from the very lowest basis of immorality. Our Lord puts it on here right up to the very height of spiritual life. Our Lord says that He alters the mainspring of "I must have it at once," the impatience of desire. Never confine lust to the vile, gross elements only, it goes right through. It is that principle Jesus alters. He does not alter our human nature, that does not need altering; He alters the mainspring, and the great marvel of the salvation of Jesus is that He alters heredity. License means, "I will do what I like and care for nobody." Liberty means, "I have the power to do what is right."

Do you see how we are growing? The disciples were taught to lay their account with purity, purity is too deep down for us to go to, our only exhibition of purity is the purity that was in the heart of our Lord, and that is the purity He implants in us. Now He says that is deeper down than you can go, but you will know whether it is there by the disposition that works in circumstances. You will know whether it is there by the temper of mind you exhibit in trying circumstances, and you will know it is there when you come up against circumstances that would have awakened in you in the previous time lust and self-desire, but now they awaken the opposite. It is not a question of a possibility on the inside, but of a possibility that shows itself in performance. That is the only test there is. "He that *doeth* righteousness is righteous, even as he is righteous." (1 John 3:7.)

(4) Direction of Discipline. (5:29,30.) If Jesus can alter our disposition, what is the need of discipline? Yet in these verses our Lord puts very stern discipline, to the parting with the right arm and the eye. The reason is this, that our physical cases, *i. e.*, mortal bodies, have been used by the wrong disposition, and when the new disposition is put in, the old physical case is not taken away, it is left there for us to discipline and make it an obedient servant to the new disposition. When God alters a person by regeneration or sanctification, you will always notice the characteristic is a maimed life to begin with, as Jesus describes here. In 5:48, Jesus describes an absolutely different life, not a maimed life, but a perfect life, but in the beginning it is maimed, meaning by that there are a hundred and one things you dare not do and you do not want to do when you are introduced to the new disposition, things that are to you and also in the eyes of the world that knew you, as your right arm and your eye, and the worldly person comes to you and says, "What an absurd idea! Whatever is there wrong in that? What can be wrong in a 'right arm'? It is the best thing you have; how absurd you are, why do you want to go to the extreme swing of the pendulum?" God will make you go to the extreme swing of the pendulum at the beginning. There never was a saint yet who did not have to start with Jesus a maimed life. Jesus says it is better that you should enter into this life, this Christian life, maimed, lovely in God's sight and lame in man's, than that you should be lovely in man's sight and lame in God's. You will find that principle runs all through, and at the beginning Jesus Christ, by His Spirit in you, has to check your doing a great many things that are perfectly right for everybody else but you. Paul mentions the same thing when he says, "Now

do not use your limitations to criticize someone else." The world calls you a fanatic and a crank, personally I have no respect for a person who has not been a crank or a fanatic, because it is a sure sign that he has never begun to seriously consider life.

Jesus, when He alters our disposition, takes us back to the first beginning of our physical life, and He teaches us to take our body and put it in harmony with the new disposition, and we have to do it in stern discipline and get the body to express the new disposition, and it can only be done as we obey. The idea Jesus conveys here is that the discipline is to cut off a great many things for your own spiritual life's sake. People say, "Well, I don't see any harm in that, why should I not do it?" Immediately a person argues like that, the proof is as strong as it can be that Jesus Christ is not first. If I am only willing to give up wrong things for Jesus Christ, never let me talk about being in love with Him. Anybody will give up wrong things if he knows how to, but will I give up right things for Him? A Christian is the only person who has the right to give up his rights. You will notice the big difference there is between everyone else's idea of purity and the Lord Jesus Christ's. Our idea of purity, where it does not come from Jesus Christ, is that of according obedience to certain laws and orders; that is not purity, that is apt to be prudery. Read the bald, shocking statements of the Bible, there is nothing prudish about the Bible. The Bible insists on purity, not prudery; that is, you are capable of facing the vilest scenes in life, unspotted. That is what Jesus Christ wants. If He can only make us prudish, why, we would be horrified if we had to go and work for Him in the slums and in the moral abominations in heathendom, we would be shocked all to pieces; but with Jesus Christ's purity, He can take us where He went Himself – in the face of the vilest moral corruptions, the most hideous diseases – and keep us as pure as He kept Himself. The purity Jesus Christ teaches is the purity of His own heart which He puts into you and me. It is always a bad sign when a skeptic says, "There are things in the Bible I would not allow my daughter to read." What is that the evidence of? A vilely impure heart, that is all. The Bible, from cover to cover, will do nothing in the shape of harm, but only good. It is to the impure in heart that these things are corrupting.

B. THE ACCOUNT WITH PRACTICE.
(Matt. 5-' 31-37-)

Practice means what I am continually doing that no one sees or knows but myself.

(1) Scandal. (5:31, 32.) Our Lord taught, by example and precept, that no man should stand up for his own honor, but only for the honor of another. You can easily see in a hundred ways how it worked in the life of our Lord. They called Him a glutton, a winebibber, devil-possessed, a sinner, a madman, and He never opened His mouth; but immediately they said a word against His Father, He not only opened His mouth, but He said some of the most terrible things the world ever heard. Jesus teaches us that by His Spirit He alters the standard of honor in the disciples. Jesus made Himself of no reputation, and the disciples don't bother their heads about what people say about them, but they do bother themselves tremendously about what people think of Jesus Christ. The disciple realizes that his Lord's honor is at stake in his life, not his own honor. The more you meditate on that principle, the more opposed you find it is to the principle of the world, even the Christian world. The best illustration for scandal is that of mud on your clothes. If you try and touch it while it is wet, you will rub it into the texture, but if you leave it till it is dry, you can flick it and it is gone without a trace. Leave scandal alone, never touch it.

(2) Irreverent Reverence. (5:33-36.) In our Lord's day the habit of backing up ordinary assertions with an appeal to the name of God was as bad, if not worse, than in our own day. It is not the question of an oath in a law court, Paul took the oath, our Lord said something very like it before Caiaphas. Nowadays we

talk most irreverently about the most reverent things. Many of us speak glibly and familiarly about the Holy Ghost, about Jesus and about God. Irreverent reverence, that is what our Lord checks. Do not flippantly talk about those things and those terms which ought to be mentioned with the greatest reverence. I remember an Indian zenana woman who got saved, she could not say many words of English, but I will never forget the way she said the words "Jesus Christ"! She was a very ugly woman, but at the pronouncement of those words her face became transfigured; the whole soul of the woman was in reverent adoration for the Lord Jesus Christ. Jesus here checks us and says, "Never you call anything in the nature of God or the Holy Ghost to attest what you are saying, speak simply and humbly, realizing that truth in a man is the same as truth in God," and to call in God as a witness to back up what I say is nearly always a sign that what I am saying is not true. If you submit children for a long while to a skeptical atmosphere and call in question all they say, it is that, that first of all instils the habit of swearing. I do not mean using profane language, but it makes children say, "Well, ask him." Such a thought never occurs to a child naturally, it only occurs when the child has to talk to suspicious people, who are continually saying, "Now I do not know whether that is true," and the child gets the idea that it cannot speak the truth unless some one else backs it up. Many of us are responsible for making people call in another witness which they have no right to do.

(3) Integrity. (5:37.) Integrity means the unimpaired state of a thing. Suspicion is of the devil, and is the greatest cause for making people say more than they need to. In that aspect it "cometh of evil." In the other aspect when I know of eight or ten reasons for the truth of what I am saying, it is a proof that what I am saying is not strictly true. If it were, we would never have to think of the reasons. Our Lord gets us back to the one sim-

ple point, "If I have altered your disposition you will talk like I do; let people do anything they like with your truth, but never explain it." There is a great difference between Jesus Christ and those of us who are His modern followers. Jesus never explained anything, we are always explaining, we are always saying, "Well, I do not mean that, I mean something else." We get into tangles by not leaving the thing alone. If people have made mistakes, leave them alone, let mistakes correct themselves. Our Lord never told His disciples when they made mistakes. They made any number of blunders about Him, but He went quietly on planting the truth. It comes out also with regard to the question of praise. I always like to find out what people think of what I have done when I am not sure of having done well, but when I am certain I have done well, I don't care an atom whether folks praise or not. We have to live on the line of integrity. We find the same thing with regard to fear and courage. We all know the kind of men who say they are not afraid, but the very fact that they say it proves they are. Jesus Christ puts in a truthfulness that never takes knowledge of itself. It never occurs to a pure, honest heart to back up what it says. It is a wounding insult to be met by suspicion; that is why from the very first we ought never to submit children to suspicion; if we do, we find what Jesus said, that what is more than simple, direct talk comes from the evil one, either in you or in any other person, is true.

C. ACCOUNT WITH PERSECUTION. (Matt. 5:38-42.)

(1) Insult. (5: 38, 39.) The picture given in 5: 38, 39 is not very familiar to us. In the East a slap on the cheek is the grossest form of insult, its only equivalent with us is spitting in the face. Epictetus, a Roman slave, said a slave would rather be thrashed to death than flicked on the cheek. Jesus says, "Now if you are flicked on the cheek as my representatives, pay no attention," that is, show a disposition that is equivalent to turning the other cheek, which

will paralyze them with amazement. Personal insult will be the occasion in the saint of revealing the incredible sweetness of the Lord Jesus Christ.

(2) Extortion. (5:40.) Another picture that is unfamiliar to us. According to the Jew- ish law, and the law of other countries in our Lord's day, if a man's cloak and coat were taken from him as the result of a lawsuit, he could get back the loan of his cloak to sleep in. Jesus taught His disciples that, "If people extort things from you when you are in my service, let them have the things, but go on with your work."

(3) Tyranny. (5:41,42.) Under the Roman dominance, the Roman soldiers could compel anyone to be a baggage carrier for a mile. (Simon, the Cyrenian, is a case in point; the Roman soldiers compelled him to be baggage carrier for Jesus.) Jesus says, "If you are my disciple, you will always do more than your duty, you will go the second mile." There will be none of the spirit of, "Oh, well, I cannot do any more, they have always misrepresented and misunderstood me." Jesus says if you are His disciple, you will always do more than your duty. It would have been a sad outlook for us if He had not gone the second mile.

Verse 42 is the most radical of all. The fact that modern Christians wiggle, twist, compromise about this verse springs from infidelity in the ruling providence of our Heavenly Father. Modern people say, "It is absurd. Do you mean to tell me I have to give to everyone that asks? if I do, every beggar in the place will be at my door." Will they? Try it. I have yet to find a person who has fulfilled Jesus Christ's command who did not find that God restrained the people who beg. You will find at the very heart of that modern wiggle is infidelity – "I do not believe God can control the beggars; if once I am known to give to everybody that asks, then they will come." Try it. I tell you they will not. If ever God's ruling is seen, it is seen when once a disciple obeys what Jesus Christ says.

Another thing, Jesus Christ never taught this: give because they deserve it; He says, "Give because I tell you." You can always find a hundred and one reasons why you should not obey our Lord's statements, the reason being that we are always more apt to trust reasonings than reason, and reasonings always mean we do not take God into calculation at all. "Does this man deserve what I am giving him?" Why, immediately you say that before Jesus Christ, the Spirit of God says to you, "Who are you? Do you deserve all you have? Do you deserve the salvation you have? Do you deserve all the blessings I have given you more than the other man?" The great motive of all giving is Jesus Christ's command. Tolstoi applied the principles of Jesus without the Spirit of Jesus; he. applied the statements of Jesus literally, but he absolutely disbelieved in being born again, consequently there was no restraining hand of God, no proof that God was with him or in him in those particulars. But once let a disciple get rightly related to Jesus Christ, and let the Spirit of God alter the disposition, then as circumstances arise obey His principles, and you will find exactly what Jesus teaches: "God is your Father, He loves you, you will never think of anything He will forget, therefore you have no business to worry."

Study Number Four

A. DIVINE RULE OF LIFE.
1. Exhortation.
   Matthew 5:45-47.
2. Example.
   Matthew 5: 46.
3. Expression.
   Matthew 5: 48.

B. DIVINE REGION OF RELIGION.
1. Philanthropy.
   Matthew 6: 1-4.
2. Prayer.
   Matthew 6:5-14.
3. Penance.
   Matthew 5:16-18.

C. DIVINE REASONINGS OF MIND.
1. Doctrine of Deposit.
   Matthew 6: 19-21.
2. Doctrine of Division.
   Matthew 6: 22, 23.
3. Doctrine of Detachment.
   Matthew 6: 24.

D. DIVINE REASONINGS OF FAITH.
1. Careful Carelessness.
   Matthew 6: 25.
2. Careless Unreasonableness.
   Matthew 6: 26.
3. Careful Uselessness.
   Matthew 6:27-29.
4. Careful Infidelity.
   Matthew 6:30-32.
5. Concentrated Consecration.
   Matthew 6: 33, 34.

STUDY NUMBER FOUR

MATTHEW 5 AND 6

A. DIVINE RULE OF LIFE. (Matt. 5: 45-47.)

Our Lord concludes by a divine rule which we by His Spirit ought to apply to every circumstance and condition of our lives. Our Lord does not make statements which we have to follow literally; if He did, we would not grow in grace. He gives us a principle and a rule of conduct, and we have to rely upon His Spirit to teach us to apply them to the various circumstances in which we find ourselves.

(1) Exhortation. (5:45-47.) Our Lord's exhortation here is to be generous in our behavior to all men, whether they be good or bad. The marvel of the divine love is that God exhibits His love to bad people whom we desert. For instance, in Luke 15, we can understand after a bit how God is represented as the Father loving the prodigal son, but He also exhibits His love to the elder brother, to whom we feel a strong antipathy. Beware of walking in the spiritual life according to our natural affinities. We all have natural affinities which we bring with us to the world, that is, people we like and others we do not like, some people we get on well with and others we do not. Never let those likes and dislikes be the rule of your Christian life. God says through John, "Walk in the light as He is in the light," and God gives you communion with people you have no natural affinities for.

(2) Example. (5:46.) Woven into the words of our Lord's exhortation is His reference to our Example, and our Example is not a good man, or even a good Christian, but God Himself. (See 5: 45 and 48.) I do not think we allow the big surprise of that to lay hold of us. Jesus never says anywhere, "Follow the best example you know, follow good Christians you know, watch the

people who love me and follow them." He says, "Follow your Father which is in Heaven."

(3) Expression. (5:48.) The expression of Christian character is not good doing, but Godlikeness. In verse 48 there is a re-emphasis of verse 20. The perfection of verse 48 refers to the disposition and temper of God in us. The Revised Version reads, "Ye shall be perfect," but that does not mean in a future state, it means, "You shall be perfect if you let me work in you what I have been describing." The whole point is, if the Spirit of God has transformed you on the inside, you will exhibit not good human characteristics, but good divine characteristics in a human being. In verse 48 our Lord completes the picture He began to give in verses 29, 30. In the former He pictures a maimed life; here He pictures a well-balanced life, for holiness means a perfect balance between my disposition and the laws of God. In verses 29, 30 our Lord pictures the maimed life, which is the characteristic of everyone of us at the beginning, and if we have never had that characteristic, the question is very open whether we have received the Spirit of God, because if the Spirit of God has regenerated us He makes us take the opposite extreme to everything we have been doing. He makes us what people call "fanatics." So you very often find in our own case and in others that, if we are to obey the Spirit of God, we have to live a limited and maimed life. But in verse 48 Jesus gives the picture of a perfectly full-orbed life, not hereafter, but here. It is only as we walk in the light as He is in the light, that we begin to understand the example Jesus gives us – God, not men. It is not sufficient to be good, to do the right thing; you must have your goodness stamped by the image and superscription of Jesus. It is supernatural all through. The whole secret of a Christian, according to Jesus, is the supernatural made natural in us by the grace of God. The way it works out is not in having times of communion with God, but the expression of it works out in the practical details of our life. If we have been regenerated, the proof of it is when we come in contact with the things that

create a "buzz." We find, to our great astonishment, we have a power we never had before, a power to keep wonderfully poised in the center of it all, a power that God explains only by the cross of Jesus Christ. It is not a question of putting statements of our Lord's in front of us and trying to live up to them, it is receiving His Spirit and finding we can live up to them with little, effort.

B. DIVINE REGION OF RELIGION. (Matt. 6: 1-18.)

The region of religion means the domain of my life lifted to God before men; the other region of our natural life lived to men before God. In Matthew 5 our Lord demands that our dispositions be all right in our ordinary calling before Him. Now He says you have to live to me before men. The main idea in the region of religion is, "Your eye on Me, not on men."

(1) Philanthropy. (6:1-4.) This corresponds to verse 42 of chapter 5, with this difference, that Matthew 5: 42 refers to the life lived with the eye on God. Briefly summed up, it means this: "Have no other motive in giving than to please God." Our Lord allows of no other motive, but you find when you look at modern philanthropy it has every other motive but that. The motive we are continually being *egged* on with, is, "It will do them good, they need the help, they deserve it." Jesus never brings that aspect out in the whole of His Sermon. In chapter 5 it is, "Give because I tell you," and here it is, "Don't have mixed motives." Our Lord is picturing in chapter 6 something the Jews were familiar with. The Jews used to put their money in the boxes in the woman's court of the Temple, and the Pharisees put their money in with a great clang which sounded like a trumpet. Jesus was standing in the Temple and heard the clanging sound of the gifts of the Pharisees, and He said, "Now don't do that sort of thing, their motive is to be known as generous givers; if you are my disciples, never give with any other motive than that you are pleasing God." It is a very penetrating thing to ask yourself this question before God, What was my motive in doing that kind act? You will be

astounded how rarely the Spirit of .God gets a chance to fit our motives on to be right with God, we mix them with a thousand and one other motives, which Jesus steadily makes simple, one motive only, "your eye on me." That is the way we become children of God.

(2) Prayer. (6: 5-14.) Prayer here is looked at in the same way as philanthropy, with the one motive, viz., to please God. "Your Father knoweth what things ye have need of before ye ask Him." (Verse 8.) Then common sense says, "Why ask Him?" Because the whole idea of prayer in this chapter is that Jesus is saying, "Watch your motive before God, have no other motive as Christians than to know your Heavenly Father." Notice all through this chapter the essential simplicity of our Lord's main principle – right towards God, right towards God, no matter what people think.

(3) Penance. (6:16-18.) Penance is putting myself into a physical strait-jacket for the sake of disciplining my spiritual character. Penance is the great note in the Roman Catholic religion, and it is altogether omitted in Protestantism, and we have been the losers in the consequence. We have been so full of antipathy to Roman Catholic doctrines that we have missed altogether what our Lord and also St. Paul said about the need to have penance. You will find that physical sloth will upset spiritual devotion quicker than anything. If the devil can't get at us by enticing to sin, he gets in by "sleepingsickness," spiritually. "Now you can't possibly get up in the morning to pray, you are working hard all day, and you can't give that time to prayer, you must not do this and that, God doesn't expect it." Jesus says, "God does expect it."

In verse 16 our Lord says when you do fast don't make cheap martyrs of yourself, pretend by a joyful face that you are not putting yourself through the stern discipline that God knows you are. The pictures were familiar to Jews, they were commanded to pray several times a day, and the Pharisees took care that they happened to be in the midst of a city when the hour for prayer came, and they would jump down, and in an ostentatious manner give themselves to prayer in public. Jesus says, "Don't be like that. That is their motive, they want to be known as praying people and verily they have their reward." And the same with their times of fasting, they looked so sad and miserable that everyone knew they were fasting. Jesus says when you have to go through a period of discipline before God, pretend you are not going through it. (Verse 17.) If ever I can tell to others the discipline I put myself through in order to further my life with God, the discipline from that moment becomes useless. Our Lord repeats over and over again, You have to have a relationship between you and God which nobody knows and nobody dare know; you must have something between you and God that the dearest friend on earth never guesses; if you have a life of discipline with God, don't say a word about it, appear not unto men to fast. The Spirit of God will apply it to each of us, and we will see there are lines of discipline, lines of limitation, physical and mental, which the Spirit of God says, "Now you must not allow yourself." When you fast, fast to your Father in secret, not before men. The ostensible fasts on the outside are of no use; it is the fasts on the inside that God knows.

C. DIVINE REASONINGS OF MIND. Matt. 6: 19-24.)

We mean by divine reasonings, the way a Christian thinks about everything. Until this is learned by our obedience to God, the majority of us drift in Christian experience without any thinking. One of the most fruitful things is to find out what the New Testament says about the mind. The Spirit of God comes through Paul and Peter and John with the one steady appeal to stir up our minds. The only way Satan can get in as an angel of light is to those Christians whose hearts are right, but whose minds are not stirred up. Our Lord here deals with the question of the mind, how I am to think and reason about things.

(1) Doctrine of Deposit. (6: 19-21.) In thinking as a Christian, every effort to persuade myself that the real treasure of my heart and mind is with God is a sure sign that it is not. If I have to reason with myself, and say I am perfectly certain that my treasure is in Heaven, and my motives are right with God, then you may be sure it is not so. The first thing Jesus says is, "Lay up for yourselves treasures in Heaven." Spiritual experience means that the Spirit of God in our hearts teaches us to fasten our eyes and our thinking on God, and when in practical life we come to deal with money matters and matters of earth, the Spirit of God reminds us, to our great peace and delight, that our treasures are in Heaven, and we find we begin to do the right thing with our property and money and everything that has to do with this earth in a way that astonishes us. The ideal is not to make out that my motive is right, but that the motive has been put right, and therefore it begins to put my thinking right. All the confusion and conflict arises when people try to be Christians without the Spirit of God; they try to reason it out. The first thing we have to do is to be born again of the Spirit of God, and obey Him as He begins to explain to our mind that the real motive at the heart of it is all right.

(2) Doctrine of Division. (6:22, 23.) We have to learn from this that the correct understanding of all physical and mental things is by a single eye. That is the symbol for the conscience of a man being put right with God by the Holy Spirit. One idea runs all through our Lord's teaching: "Right with God, right with God!" First, second and third! The proof that we are right with God is that we never try to be right, because the Spirit of God has put us in the right relationship. That is a roundabout way of saying that if I have been born again of the Holy Ghost, I am right with God, then if I keep in the light as He is in the light, that keeps my eye single, and slowly and surely all my bodily actions begin to be put into the right relationship, and

everything becomes full of harmony and simplicity and peace. To rightly divide material matters and interests, a man must be born from above.

(3) Doctrine of Detachment. (6:24.) This is a fundamental and favorite theme of our Lord's: you cannot be good and bad at one and the same time, and you cannot serve God with an eye on successful service; and you can never make "honesty the best policy," a motive. These thoughts run all through Jesus Christ's teaching. If I am to be holy, there is one consideration, I have to stand right with God, and see that that relationship is the one thing that is never dimmed in my practical life, and all other things will right themselves. Jesus says you cannot serve God and mammon. What we mean by a worldly Christian is one who frankly disbelieves that statement of our Lord's, and says, "Oh, yes, with a little more skill and subtlety and wisdom (we call it diplomacy), a little more compromise, we can serve both." The devil's temptation to our Lord to compromise is repeated over and over again. The doctrine of detachment means that I must realize that a division is made between the Christian and the world, as high as Heaven and as deep as Hell. That is the reason Jesus says, as He did in chapter 5 (also in 1 Peter 4:4), that when you get right with God you become what the world calls "a fanatic." When you get right with God you become something that is contemptible in the eyes of the world. Try to put into practice any of the principles of the Sermon on the Mount and you will be treated, not with indignation, but with amusement, and if you persist in it you will find the world gets annoyed and detests you. In the beginning of the Christian life always make allowance for the swing of the pendulum. It is not an accident, it is the set purpose of God that we go to the extreme reaction from what we were before. He sees that we do the exact opposite of all we did before, God does not gradually overcome it, He violently breaks

us from it, and only brings us back into the domain of men when we are perfectly right with Him, so when we get back into the domain of men we are among them, yet not of them. (John 17.) When we are matured in godliness and have proved to Jesus that we do not compromise between mammon and godliness, then He trusts us and trusts His own honor in placing us where the world, the flesh and the devil may try us, knowing that "He that is in us is greater than he that is in the world."

C. DIVINE REASONINGS OF FAITH. (Matt. 6:25-34.)

The reasonings of faith mean the practical working out in my life of my implicit, determined confidence in God.

(1) Careful Carelessness. (6:25.) Jesus does not say that a man who doesn't think about anything is blessed; that man is a fool. Jesus says you must be carefully careless about everything but one thing: "Your right relationship to me." Our Lord teaches here the complete reversal of the reasonings of a practical, sensible person who has no faith in God whatever. Our Lord tells the disciples that they have to be studiously careful that they are careless about how they stand to self-interest, to food, to drink and to personal property, because they are set on minding the right relationship to God. I have to be carefully careless for one reason. Ever so many people are careless over what they eat and drink, and they suffer for it; they are careless about what they put on, and they look as they have no business to look; they are careless about property, and God will hold them responsible for it. What Jesus is saying is that the great care of the life is to make the relationship to God the one care, and everything else secondary. Immediately you look at that you find it is the most revolutionary statement human ears ever listened to. You will find our arguing is exactly the opposite, even the most spiritual of us. We say, "I must live, I must make so much money, I must be clothed, I must

be fed," that is how it begins; that is, the great concern of the life is not God; the great concern of the life is how I am going to fit myself to live. Jesus says, "Reverse the order, get rightly related to Me first, see that you maintain that as the greatest care of your life, never put the concentration of your care on the other things." You will find, if you read the Old and New Testaments, the reason God allows "dry rot," bankruptcy, disease and upset, is that His children will not obey Jesus Christ on that line. It is one of the severest disciplines, to allow the Spirit of God to bring us into harmony with Jesus on these concluding verses of Matthew 6.

(2) Careful Unreasonableness. (6:26.) To be careful of all that the natural man says we must be careful over, Jesus declares unreasonable, because the natural man says to think about the means of living in order to live. Picture to yourself all the sparrows and blackbirds and thrushes sitting on hedges in the early spring, thinking and worrying their heads about how they would stick their feathers in. Jesus says they don't bother themselves at all. The very thing that makes them what they are is not their 'thought, but the Father's which is in Heaven. Jesus says, "You maintain obedience to the Holy Spirit, who is the real principle of your life, and He will supply the feathers for you. You are much better than a sparrow." Our Lord uses that illustration more than once. He does not use it by accident, He uses it purposely to show us the utter unreasonableness, from His standpoint, of being so anxious about the means of living.

(3) Careful Uselessness. (6:27-29.) Our Lord says that it is utterly useless to mistake careful consideration of circumstances for that which produces character. "Consider the lily," it obeys the law of its life in the circumstances it is placed in. As Christians, consider your hidden life with God, *i. e.,* pay attention to the source, and God will look after the outflow. The hardest working thing is a bird, but it does not work to stick feathers on itself; it

obeys the law of its life and becomes what it is. Jesus Christ's argument is, "You are the men and women who are the fittest to do the work of the world, the other people are not, because the other people have the ulterior motive of looking after circumstances in order to produce a fine character. It cannot be done. If you will concentrate on the life I give you, make that your business, you are perfectly free for all the other things because you know your Father is watching the life on the inside." You cannot produce the life on the inside by heeding the outside all the time. Imagine a lily doing what some of us want to do spiritually. "Oh, I must give up this, I must go here and there" – quick-silver Christians. Imagine a lily hauling itself out of a pot and saying, "Well, I don't think I smell nice here, I don't think I look exactly right." The lily's duty is to do what it does – obey the law of its life where it is placed by the gardener. Paul says, "All these things work together for your good." Watch your life with God, see that that is right and you will grow all right.

(4) Careful Infidelity. (6:30-32.) Jesus tersely sums up common-sense carefulness, if it is in a person without the indwelling Spirit of God, as infidelity. Since you received the Spirit of God and obeyed Him, Whenever you try to put other things first, you find confusion, you find the Spirit of God presses through and says, "No, this first, where do I come in this new relationship, in this mapped-out holiday, in these new books you are buying?" The Spirit of God always presses that point till we learn to obey the first consideration; knowing that God is my Father, He loves me, I shall never think of anything He will forget; why should I worry? It is not only wrong to worry, it is real infidelity, because it means, "God cannot look after my practical little details" (and it is never anything else that worries us). Did you ever notice what Jesus says (in Matthew 13) will choke the life He puts in? The devil? No, "The cares of this world." It is the little foxes, the

little worries, always, and that is how infidelity begins. The great cure for infidelity is obedience to the Spirit of God. . If once we get into our hearts and lives in thinking, what God has put in us spiritually, we would find that the men and women who are rightly related to God are the men and women who carry in them heaven on the way to Heaven, that is, they are free to do the work of the world like no one else. A business man with the Spirit of God in him can do the work of a business man ten thousand-fold better than a man without the Spirit, because the responsibility of his life is of! him and on God.

(5) Concentrated Consecration. (6:33,34.) Our Lord teaches that the one great secret of Christian health and prosperity is concentration on God and His purposes.

Study Number Five

MATTHEW SEVEN.

A. CHRISTIAN CHARACTERISTICS.
1. The Uncritical Temper.
    Matthew 7: 1.
2. The Undeviating Test.
    Matthew 7: 2.
3. The Undesirable Truth-Teller.
    Matthew 7: 3-5.

B. CHRISTIAN CONSIDERATENESS.
1. The Need to Discriminate.
    Matthew 7: 6.
2. The Notion of Divine Control.
    Matthew 7:10.
3. The Necessity for Discernment.
    Matthew 7: 11.

C. CHRISTIAN COMPREHENSIVENESS.
1. The Positive Margin of Righteousness.
2. The Proverbial Maxim of Reasonableness.
3. The Principal Meaning of Revelation.

STUDY NUMBER FIVE

MATTHEW 7.

A. CHRISTIAN CHARACTERISTICS. (Matt 7:1-5.)

A characteristic is something which steadily prevails, not something that occasionally manifests itself. It is what people do steadily and persistently that makes their character. This chapter indicates the steady characteristics of a Christian, not what a Christian is occasionally; that is a spasmodic thing which God mourns over, "Thy goodness is as a morning cloud," He says.

(1) The Uncritical Temper. (7:1.) Our Lord says regarding Critical judgment, "Abstain!" This sounds very strange, because the characteristic of the Holy Spirit in a believer is to reveal to him the things that are wrong; but the strangeness is only on the surface, the discernment of the Holy Spirit is not for purposes of criticism, but for purposes of conversion. The Holy Spirit reveals to you something of the nature of unbelief and sin perhaps in other people, perhaps in yourself. His purpose is not to make you feel the smug satisfaction of a critical spectator, "Well, thank God I am not like that," but exactly the opposite, to make you turn clean round from the whole thing, or, if it is in someone else, to make you lay hold of God so that God enables him to turn away from the wrong thing. (See 1 John 5:16.) Criticism is not possible to a wholesome spiritual life, for when criticism becomes a habit it destroys moral energy, kills faith, and paralyzes spiritual force. The critical faculty is an intellectual one, not a moral one. A critic must be removed from what he criticizes. The only person who can criticize human life is the Holy Ghost. No human being dare criticize another human being, because immediately he does, he puts himself in a different place altogether to the one he criticizes. Our Lord allows no room for criticism; He makes any amount of room for discrimination. When a man crit-

icizes a work of art or a piece of music his information must be complete, and he stands away from the thing he criticizes, and is able to criticize it as superior to it. Jesus says you can never take that attitude, and if anyone does take that spirit of criticism he grieves the Spirit of God and instantly puts himself in the wrong position. Criticism when it decomposes becomes deadly. If you are criticized much, it has the effect of decomposing you, you become good for nothing. After a good dose of criticism all the gumption and power and spiritual life is knocked out of you for a time. That is never the work of the Holy Ghost and never the work of the saint; it is the work of the devil always. Whenever criticism is used, it is Jesus saying, "Apply that to yourself," but never apply it to anyone else. Any point of view that makes me decompose other persons, makes me lynx-eyed to see where they are wrong, and the effect of my seeing where they are wrong is to paralyze them; it does not do them any good, which shows that criticism never came from the Holy Ghost. If I come and say, "Well, I love you, but I must tell you so and so/' I simply am an unreal fraud, I do not love you, I have put myself into a position far superior to you, I am in the position of a critic of a work of art; but Jesus says a disciple can never stand off from another life and criticize it. So He advocates here to be of an uncritical spirit. Let that maxim of the Lord's sink into your heart and you will see how it hauls you up, "Judge not;" why, we are always at it. Any power in me that separates the set of powers in another soul and prevents it from being one force is critical and bad. The effect of criticism is always to divide the powers of the other person. You know some simple, honest soul who is doing things you know to be wrong, now be careful, if you take the part of the devil and become a critic, you will divide the powers of that soul and prevent it being a force for anything. You will knock it all to pieces. Take Jesus Christ's way, tell Him, and "I will give you life for him that sins not unto death." You will find when the Holy Ghost discriminates, He criticizes in the true position of a critic, that is, He is able to show what is wrong without wounding and hurting; when we criticize we wound in such a way that the powers never get back to their right purposes. Jesus says to be uncritical in your temper. It is not done once and for all, we have to be always remembering that that is our Lord's rule of conduct. Beware of anything that puts you in the superior person's place.

(2) The Undeviating Test. (7:2.) That verse is not a haphazard guess, it is an eternal law of God. A scriptural case in point: when Mary of Bethany broke the alabaster box of ointment, the disciples said, "What a waste." John says that one disciple in particular said the words, viz., Judas. When Jesus referred to Judas in John 17, He called him a "son of waste." Whatever judgment I give, it is measured to me again. "I am perfectly certain Mrs. So-and-so has been criticizing me." Well, what have you been doing? You will never find it fail, and Jesus puts it here in connection with criticism, if you have been shrewd in finding out defects in others, remember that will be exactly the measure given to you, that is the way people will judge you, and in Psalm 18 the Psalmist says that is how God is to us, if we are "froward" to God, He is "frowar d" to us; if we are pure towards God, He is pure towards us. It works from God's throne right down; life serves back in the coin you pay.

Romans 2:1 applies it in a still more definite way, and says that the person who criticizes another is guilty of that very thing, not only in possibility but in actuality. We do not believe the statements of the Bible to begin with, for instance, do we believe that statement that what I criticize in another I am guilty of myself? God does not look at the act, He looks at the possibility. The consequence is this, we can always tell sin in another, why? Because we are sin- ners and the great danger is mistaking carnal suspicion for the conviction of the Holy Ghost. The fact that I can see hypocrisy and fraud and unreality in other people is because they are all in my heart, and if I put myself in a superior position and tell them of it, I have put myself in the place of the Holy

Ghost. Take that idea and see what Jesus says, "Out of the human heart proceed," and then follows the catalogue. When the Holy Ghost convicts He convicts for conversion, that they might turn round and be put in another place and have different characteristics. The great characteristic of a saint is humility, that is, feeling the full realization of, "Yes, all those things and all the other evils would have been manifested in me but for the grace of God, therefore I have no right to judge." Jesus says, "Don't," for if you do, it will be measured to you exactly as you have judged. Which one of us would dare stand before God and say, "My God, judge me as I have judged my fellowmen?" We have judged our fellowmen as sinners; if God judged us like that, we would go to Hell. God judges us through the marvelous atonement of Jesus Christ.

(3) The Undesirable Truth-teller. The kind impudence of the average truth-teller is inspired of the devil when it comes to pointing out the defects of other people. Watch, for instance, the characteristics of the devil in the Bible. The devil is lynx-eyed for things he can criticize, and we have all had part and parcel with him in times past; we have all been shrewd. "I just want to tell you, my friend, you have something in your eye that is very objectionable, let me take it out and you will feel better;" that puts me in a superior position to you. I am further on than you, a finer spiritual character. Where do you get that characteristic? In the Lord Jesus Christ? Never, He took on Himself the form of a servant, – "I speak the words my Father would have me speak." How did He do it? By submitting His intellect to His Father, and when the Spirit of God works through His saints He works through them unbeknown to them; He works through them like light; He concentrates His light on them, and you know what is wrong with you, and if you do not understand the principle, you will say, "That person is always criticizing me." He is nothing of the sort; it is the Spirit of God through him that has discerned in you what is wrong. But what Jesus is pointing out is, "Beware of

taking the place of the Holy Spirit; beware of putting yourself in the superior person's place."

The last curse in a Christian's life is the other person who becomes a providence to you, quite certain you cannot do anything without him, and if you do not heed him it will be very bad for you and very risky. The position is one Jesus has ridiculed here with terrific power. He actually says in verse 5, "Thou hypocrite." The word hypocrite does not mean a person who is playing two parts consciously for his own ends; the word hypocrite is literally, play-actor, one whose reality is not in keeping with sincerity. When we begin to find fault with other people, we are not hypocrites; we are perfectly sincere, and say, "All I desire is their good," but Jesus says in reality you are a fraud; you are a play-actor. "Thou hypocrite, first cast out the beam out of thine own eye, and then shalt thou see clearly to cast out the mote out of thy brother's eye." If I have let God remove the beam from my own outlook on life by His mighty grace, I will carry with me the sunlight confidence and hope that God can easily do for my brother what He has done for me, because he only has a splinter; I have had a log of wood ! Look for a moment in your own heart and you find this is the confidence God's salvation gives you, "I am so amazed that God has altered me that I can despair of nobody." When anyone comes across you after you have been marvelously saved by the grace of God, you have the sunshine confidence that inspires him, and you say, "Oh, yes, God can undertake for you; you are only a little bit wrong, but I was wrong down to the remote attitude of my mind; I was a mean, prejudiced, self-interested, self-seeking person, and God altered me, and therefore I can never despair of you." Beware of the unconscious twist that makes you feel like pious Christians, who can talk well; but by laying to heart these sturdy rules of our Lord's, let us grow up into Him in all things. Reflect on the first five verses of this chapter, and you will see at once why a man like Daniel had to bow his head in vicarious humiliation and intercession. "I have sinned," he said, "with Thy people," and the call every now and again comes to communities and nations as it came to Daniel. These statements of Jesus save us from that fearful peril of spiritual conceit, "Thank God, I am not as other men."

B. CHRISTIAN CONSIDERATIONS. (7:7-11.)

Consider how God dealt and deals with you, says our Lord, and then consider again that you do likewise to others. "Never believe that thing that ought not to be true."

(1) The Need to Discriminate. (7:6.) In this verse Jesus inculcates the need to carefully examine what you present in the way of God's truth to other people. If you present, He says, the perils of God's revelation to unspiritual people, they will trample the pearls under foot and turn again and make a havoc of you. Jesus does not say they will turn and trample you under their feet; that would not matter so much, but they will trample the truth of God under their feet and rend you. The Holy Spirit alone can teach any one of us what that means. There are some truths of God that God will not make simple, and that is why Jesus said, "I speak in parables." The only thing God makes plain in the Bible is the way of salvation and the way of sanctification; after that it depends entirely on my walking in the light. Over and over people "water down" the Word of God to suit those who are not spiritual, the consequence is the Word of God is trampled under the feet of swine, and the people of God are being rent in pieces. What we have to ask ourselves is, "What way am I flinging God's truth before unspiritual swine?" The words are not mere human words, they are the words of Jesus Christ.

When Jesus talks about our confession before men, He never says to confess anything but Himself ("He that confesseth Me before men"), and you will find every time you give a testimony on another line, what Jesus says here is true, the testimony on other lines is for saints, for those who understand and are spiritual; your testimony to the world is Jesus Christ, confess Him. "He saved me, He sanctified me, He puts me right with God." Jesus says if you do that, "I will glorify you before my Father in Heaven. On the other hand, be careful how you give my holy things to dogs." Dogs are a symbol of the folks who live on the streets, the outside people who say there is nothing mysterious in the Bible, it is not inspired, it is simply an ordinary book; don't cast your holy things before them, and be careful that you don't give the pearl of God's truth to men who are swine. Paul gives illustration after illustration, as our Lord does, of the pearl of sanctification being dragged in the mire of fornication. It all comes through people not revering and not respecting the mighty caution of our Lord Jesus Christ.

(2) The Notion of Divine Control. (77-10.) Our Lord, by the simple argument of these verses, urges us to keep our minds filled with the notion of God's control behind everything, and that means that the disciple must always maintain an attitude of perfect trust and an eagerness to continually ask God for things and for answers to questions; those things are not spontaneously given us by the Holy Spirit. Paul makes a big distinction between being possessed of the Spirit and forming the mind of Christ. Jesus is laying down rules for conduct of those who have the Spirit. *Notion* your mind with the idea that God is there. If once all the mind is notioned along that line, when you are in difficulties it is as easy as breathing to remember, "Why, my Father knows all about it." It is not an effort, it comes naturally when perplexities are very pressing; before you have gone and asked this and that person, now the notion is forming so powerfully in you that you simply go to God about it. You will always know whether the notion is working by the way you act in difficult circumstances. Who is the first one you go to? What is the first thing you do? What is the first power you rely on? It is the rule that works on the principle we indicated in Matthew 6, God is my Father, He loves me, I shall never think of anything He'll forget, why should I worry? There are times when God cannot lift the darkness from

you, but trust Him; Jesus said He will appear to you like an un-kind friend, but He is not; He will appear to you like an unnatural father, but He is not; He will appear to you like an unjust judge, but He is not. Keep that notion strong. If we let these searchlights go straight down to the root of our lives, we shall find why Jesus said, "Don't judge," we won't have any time to; the whole of our time will be taken up living in the life and power of God so that He can pour out through us rivers of living water; some of us are so concerned about the outflow that it dries up. We continually ask, "Am I of any use?" Jesus tells us how we are to be of use: "If you believe on me, out of you will flow rivers of living water." Keep the notion strong and growing, of the mind of God behind all things. Nothing happens in any particular unless God's will is behind; therefore I rest perfectly confident. And remember, prayer is not only asking, it is an attitude, an attitude that pro-duces an atmosphere in which asking is perfectly natural.

(3) The Necessity for Discernment. (7:11.) The discernment here needed is the reasoning fa- culty of the saint's mind applied to the saint's self. If you, an evil being, saved by grace, can have such wonderfully kind thoughts and do such wonderfully kind things, how much more will your Heavenly Father give good things to those who ask Him? Probably one of the things that most scares the average evangelical Christian is when he hears some of us saying to an ordinary sinner, "If you ask God for the Holy Spirit, He will give Him you." How shocking! Fancy telling a sinner to ask God to give him the Holy Spirit! They give the old reasoning, "But I thought the Bible said, if I regard iniquity in my heart the Lord will not hear me." Certainly He won't, but that is when you are a Christian; if you are rightly related to God and regard iniquity in your heart, God won't hear your prayer; but Jesus is speaking of the time before that. "If you, being evil."

We put ourselves in God's place, in the place of the supe-rior person; Jesus says, "Get this reasoning incorporated into you. How much have you deserved? Nothing, everything has been given you by God." We find, over and over again, by our actions and sympathy to certain people, we blame God for His neglect of them, and God never says a word; we never say a word against God, but by our attitude we say that we are filling up what God forgot to do. Jesus says. "Never have that notion, never allow it to come in." In all probability the Spirit of God will begin to show that because we have neglected what we ought to have done they are where they are.

Take the great craze of what is called "Socialism," which is getting into the very churches. The Church is saying that Jesus Christ came to be a social reformer. A ridiculous notion. We are to be social reformers, not God. God came to alter us, and we are trying now to shirk our responsibility and put it on God and say God does that; the thing He does is to alter our disposition and put us right. These rules of Jesus would instantly make social reformers, it would begin straight away where we live. What am I like in my relationship to my father and mother, to my brothers and sisters, my friends, my employers, my employees? Have I this habitual spiritual discernment of understanding that all the good things that have been given to me have been given by the sheer sovereign grace of God?

Then God save me from the mean, accursedeconomical notion that I must only help the people who deserve it! Sometimes one can almost hear the Spirit of God shout in the heart, "Who are you, that you talk like that? Did you deserve the salvation of God; did you deserve the sanctification that God has given you; did you deserve to be filled with the Spirit?" It is all done out of the sheer sovereign mercy of God. "Then be like your Father in Heaven," says Jesus; "have a perfect disposition like His." Again Jesus puts it, "Love as I have loved." That is not done once and for all; it is a continual, steadfast, growing habit of life.

Humility and holiness always go together. You find, whenever the hardness and the harshness begin to creep into personal actions toward one another, no matter what the preaching is like, the preaching may be as stern and true as God's Word, but if the harshness and hardness come into our actions, we may be certain we are swerving from the light. Never "water down" God's truth, and never forget when we deal with one another that we are sinners saved by grace, no matter where we stand. If we stand in the fulness of the blessing of God, we stand there by no other right than the sheer sovereign grace of God.

C. CHRISTIAN COMPREHENSIVENESS. (7:12.)

Christian grace comprehends all the man. (See Mark 12: 30, 31.) It is not that you will be pure in heart only, not only that you will have a mind enlightened, not only a soul put right, not only divine strength given, but the whole lot comprehended by the marvelous power and grace of God. That is what Jesus is referring to in verse 12 – the whole man, body, soul and spirit being brought into fascinating captivity to the Lord Jesus Christ. An illustration is that of the gas mantel; if it is not rightly adjusted, it does not glow rightly, only one bit glows, but get it adjusted exactly, then when the light comes the whole thing is comprehended in one great blaze of light. That is what Jesus indicates here, that every bit of the nature (not parts of it, some of us have goodness in spots) has to be absolutely absorbing till we are one glow with the comprehensive goodness of God. Paul puts it this way, "If ye are children of light, walk in the light, and ye shall have your fruit in all righteousness, in all goodness and in all truth." (See Eph. 5:8,9.)

(1) The Positive Margin of Righteousness. The limit to the manifested grace of God in me is my body, and the whole of my body. Some of us can understand having a pure heart, having minds rightly adjusted to God, being indwelt by the Spirit, but what about the incandescent body, what about the finger tips what about the bodily organs, what about the bodily relationship, what about the eyes and the mouth and the ears? That is the margin of righteousness in me.

You will find that there is a divorce possible in our outlook that is not possible in Jesus Christ. We make a divorce between the clear intellectual understanding of things and the practical outcome. Jesus has nothing to do with it, He won't estimate our fine intellectual conception unless the practical outcome is shown in reality. There is no estimate ever given by our Lord of an eloquent, sincere prophet or preacher. He sums such up in Matthew 7. They were sincere, and were honoring the Word, so the devils were cast out, but Jesus said, "Depart from me."

We have a very great snare in our capacity to understand a thing clearly with our minds and exhaust it by stating it, and you will often find that overmuch earnestness blinds the life to reality. When once you begin to get in earnest, you will find that becomes your god, it is the earnestness and zeal with which things are said and done, and you find after awhile the reality is not there; the real, wonderful power and presence of God are not manifesting themselves through the body; there are relationships at home, or in business, or in private that show when the veneer is taken off, that you are not real. The great thing for us all in this study of the Sermon on the Mount is to allow the principles and rules of Jesus to soak right straight down into our very makeup. It would be like a baptism of light to let these teachings of Jesus soak us through and through until we are incandescent.

(2) The Proverbial Maxim of Reasonableness. Our Lord's use of this proverb is positive, not negative. He said, "Do to men what you would like them to do to you." A very different thing from, "Don't do to other people what you don't want them to do to you." What would I like other people to do to me? Jesus says, "Well, don't wait; do it to them." I would like people to think of me as I really am before God. Well, think of them like that. I would really like people to give me credit for the generous motives I have. Well, give them credit for having them. I would really like that people should not pass harsh judgments on me, but that they should always understand that the one great motive of

my life is to do them good. Well, have that attitude towards them. That is a maxim that Jesus wants us to have by us.

It is commonly used the other way, you find it even in newspapers, "Don't do to others what you don't want them to do to you." But look at it the other way, "Do to other people as you wish them to do to you." If I have a feeling that I would like that person to pray for me; well, pray for that person. The measure of my growth in grace is my attitude towards others, and the Holy Ghost will kindle my imagination to picture many things I would like them to do to me; that is His way of telling you what to do to them. "Love your neighbor as yourself."

The devil comes as an angel of light and says, "You must not think about yourself." Well, if you don't, what can you make of that statement? The Holy Ghost will make you think about yourself. His only way of educating me when I am right with Him as to how to deal with other persons is making me picture what I would like those other persons to do to me, and then I go and do it to them. That is our Lord's measure for practical ethical conduct all through the Sermon on the Mount. No wonder men want to say His principles don't apply to this life, but to a future dispensation; but let us begin to work them out now.

(3) The Principal Meaning of Revelation. The principal meaning of revelation is that the law of God may be incarnated in the believer – "Written epistles known and read of all men." This is the law that came through the prophets; for what purpose? That it might be manifested in your lives.

Jesus Christ came to make the great laws and principles of God incarnated in human life; not in good human life, but in bad human life. That is the miracle of Jesus Christ's grace, He did not put these things up as standards for us to come up to; He puts us in the place where He can remake us, and put the principles in us, and enable us to work them out by His guidance.

Study Number Six

MATTHEW SEVEN.

A. TWO GATES, TWO WAYS.

Matthew 7:13, 14.

1. "All Noble Things are Difficult.'
2. "My Utmost for the Highest."
3. "A stoot heart tae a' stae brae.'

B. TEST YOUR TEACHERS.

1. Possibility of Pretense.
   Matthew 7: 15.
2. Place of Patience.
   Matthew 7:16.
3. Principle of Performance.
   Matthew 7: 17, 18.
4. Power of Publicity.
   Matthew 7: 19, 20.

C. APPEARANCE AND REALITY.

1. Recognize Men Without Labels.
   Matthew 7: 21.
2. Remedy Mongers.
   Matthew 7: 22.
3. Retributive Measures.
   Matthew 7: 23.

D. THE TWO BUILDERS.

1. Spiritual Castles.
   Matthew 7: 24.
2. Supreme Crisis.
   Matthew 7: 25.
3. Suspicious Conditions.
   Matthew 7:26.
4. Supreme Catastrophe.
   Matthew 7: 27.
5. Scriptural Concentration.

STUDY NUMBER SIX

MATTHEW 7

The vital distinction between warning and threatening is just the difference between God and the devil. God never threatens, the devil never warns. Warning is a great, arresting statement of God's, inspired by His love and patience. The more you brood over that, the more you will find it throws a flood of light on the passages of the Old Testament in which God's warnings seem to be very strange, and of the New Testament where the statements of Jesus are so vivid, such as in Matthew 23.

Always remember that both the voice of God and of Jesus are divine voices, not human; there is no element of personal vindictiveness in them, no question of holding it, "If you don't do this, the consequences will fall on you." It is the great, patient love of God that puts the warnings, as much as to say, "Not this way." "The way of transgressors is hard," go behind that statement in your imagination, God is almost tender as He cannot make it easy; and God has made it difficult to go wrong, especially for His children.

A. TWO GATES, TWO WAYS. (Matt. 7:13, 14)

Our Lord is using here an allegory that was perfectly familiar to all the people of His day, and He lifts it by His inspiration to embody His patient warning. Our Lord continually used proverbs and sayings that were familiar to His hearers, and put an altogether new meaning into them; and we now take three phrases that are quite familiar to us and which embody our Lord's thought.

(1) "All Noble Things are Difficult." Our Lord warns, in Matthew 7:13,14, that the devout life of a disciple is not a dream, but a decided discipline which calls for the use of all our powers. Note that no amount of determination can give me the new life

of God, that is a gift; but the point of determination comes in letting that new life work itself out according to Christ's standard. We are always in danger of confounding what we can do and what we cannot do. At the beginning we try to save ourselves, we try to sanctify ourselves, we try to give ourselves the Holy Spirit; all those things are utterly impossible. The only way we can get salvation, get sanctification, and get the Holy Spirit is by receiving them as gifts. The other snare is that we try to make out that God must make us "walk in the light." God does not, I must do the walking, He gives me the power to walk, but I must see that I use the power. So you find the confusion continually recurs, our trying to do what God alone can do, and then trying to make out that God will do what only we can do. Our Lord here in these warnings has indicated what we have to do, He has put the power and the life in us, He fills us with the Holy Spirit, now we have to work it out; that is, we have to realize that this noble life is gloriously difficult, not a difficulty that makes us faint and cave in, but a difficulty that rouses us up to overcome it.

(2) "My Utmost for the Highest." Our Lord emphasizes the need for us to keep our minds fixed on the straight way, *viz.*, as a disciple I will do my utmost as a proof that I appreciate God's utmost for me. How did Jesus live a holy life? He lived it by sacrificing Himself to His Father. How did He talk holy talking? By sacrificing His intellect to His Father. How did He work holy working? By submitting His will to His Father. I have to use my utmost endeavors to do the same thing, and if I have the life of God I can do it. The motto over our side of the Gate of Life is, "All God's commands I can obey." Jesus, in John 14, puts that as the test of discipleship, "If you love me, you will keep my commandments," and you learn never to allow *I cannot* to creep in. "Oh, I am no saint, I cannot do this," – those things must never come in, because if they do, we are a disgrace to Jesus Christ. "My utmost for the highest." Do I so appreciate the marvelous salvation of

Jesus in saving and sanctifying me and filling me with the Holy Spirit that I do my utmost to be worthy of Him?

(3) "A stoot heart tae a' stae hrae" (a strong heart to a difficult hill). In these verses our Lord warns us that the Christian life is a holy life, and that means we must not substitute the word *happy*. (Happiness we certainly will have, but it is a consequence of holiness.) Our Lord continually warns, without putting it in so many words, that we must never get off on the idea, which is exceedingly prevalent nowadays, of what we may safely call "the gospel of temperament," *viz.*, that we have to be happy and bright. All those are effects, they are not causes. Immediately you make that the dominant characteristic of your life, "I am determined I will be happy and joyful," it will all go from you, because those things are not causes, they are not objects, they are consequences, things that follow without striving after them. Our Lord insists that we keep at one point, our eyes fixed on the one place, the strait gate and the narrow way, which means in my life, pure, holy living, and I will have happiness.

Note what our Lord says in the way of warning about worry in John 14; for instance, the words "Let not" are a command, and the words in practical Christianity mean "Worry is wicked." If you are going to keep this strong heart that God has given you to the difficult braes in life, you have continually to watch that one thing. You remember in the first parable our Lord gave, He said that "the cares of this life will choke my word in you," and you will find it is not the devil that first switches folks off Christ's way, it is the ordinary, steep difficulties of daily life; difficulties connected with money, with food, with clothing and situations. Remember Jesus Christ's warning that these things will choke all He puts in.

Look back on your own life, we have each had a place where the little worries have blotted God's face out, enfeebled our hearts and made us sorry and humiliated before Him, much more so than the times when we felt the temptation to sin. The temptation to sin finds something that makes us face it with vigor and earnestness, but the cares of this life, the *braes*, or difficulties, require the stout heart that God gives.

The whole summing up of this first great warning is twofold: it is easy to drift a little way, but it is easier to direct our steps in His way. Our Lord uses the illustration in Matthew it, "Take my yoke upon you, and learn of me, for my yoke is easy and my burden is light," It Seems amazingly difficult to put the yoke of Christ on, but immediately you do, it makes everything easy. It is much easier at the beginning apparently just simply to drift and say, "Oh, I can't"; but immediately you do, you find, blessed be the name of God, your heart and body and soul say. "I have the easiest way after all." Happiness and all these things attend, they are not my aim, my aim is the Lord Jesus Christ, and He has showered the *hundredfold* more on me all the way along.

B. TEST YOUR TEACHERS. (Matt. 7:15-20.)

Jesus warns His disciples to test preachers and teachers by their fruit. There are two ways of testing by fruit, one is by the fruit in the life of the preacher, and the other is by the fruit in the life of the doctrine. I may have a perfectly beautiful life in its fruits, but I may be teaching a doctrine which, if logically worked out, will produce the devil's fruit in other lives. Jesus says, "Test your teachers."

Without His warnings we are always captivated. It is the easiest thing in the world for us to be captivated by a beautiful life and say, "Now what that beautiful life teaches must be right." Jesus says, "Be careful, test your teacher by the fruit." The other side is just as true, that you may have teachers teaching beautiful truth whose doctrine in its fruit will be magnificent, but the fruit in their own lives is rotten. If we see a man with a beautiful life, we say his doctrine must be right, but not necessarily so; then we say because a man teaches the right thing, therefore his life is all right, not necessarily so. Test the doctrine by its fruit, and test the teacher by his fruit.

(1) Possibility of Pretence. (7:15.) Jesus would have us know that there are people who come clothed in the right doctrine, but inwardly their spirit is the spirit of Satan. The very allowing of my mind to think that it is possible to pretend is quite sufficient warning. Jesus says, "Beware of the possibility of pretence." Immediately the disciples' eyes are off Jesus, pious pretending follows instantly. I John 1:7 is the essential condition for all saints. You find, as you study the Sermon on the Mount, that you are *badgered* by the Spirit of God from every standpoint but one, and it is the standard of a child depending on God. Immediately we depend on anything else, there comes in this possibility of pretence, pious pretence, not hypocritical; we are dealing with pretence, the desperately sincere effort to be right when we know we are not. A hypocrite is something infinitely more than that, a hypocrite is one who tries and succeeds in living a twofold life for his own ends. Our Lord is describing dangerous teachers here.

(2) Place of Patience. (7:16.) Our Lord in some cases would have us *bide our time.* This warning is against over-zealousness on the part of heresy-hunters. An incident in the life of our Lord points out what I mean. John and another disciple came to Jesus and said: "We saw a man casting out devils, and as he did not come with us we forbade him." Jesus said, "Don't, no man can do these things and speak lightly of me." Take heed that we do not make carnal suspicion take the place of the discernment of the Spirit. Fruit, and fruit alone, is the test, not the disciples' fancy. If I see distinctly in a minister or a Sunday-school teacher or a fellowChristian the fruit in the life showing itself like thistles, then Jesus said, "Now you know perfectly well there is the wrong root there, you do not gather a thistle off any other root than a thistle-root"; but it is quite possible to mistake in the winter time a rose tree for a weed, unless you are thoroughly expert in judging, so there is a place for patience, and the Lord would have us' heed it.

Wait for the fruit to manifest itself and don't be guided by fancy. It is an easy business to get alarmed and to persuade myself that my conviction is the standard of Christ. Immediately I do, I condemn everyone to perdition who does not agree with me, I am obliged to, because my conviction has taken in me the place of Jesus Christ. God's Book never says, "Walk in the light of my conviction," but "Walk in the light of the Lord." You have to make a vital distinction between the people who object to my way of presenting God's Gospel and the people who object to God's Gospel. There are ever so many people who object to my way of presenting the truth, but they certainly do not object to God making them holy, and I have to make the distinction clear, I have to remember that the difficulty in presenting the truth has been with me, not with God.

(3) Principle of Performance. (7:17,18.) If I wish the performances of my life to be steadily holy, I must be holy in the principle of my life. If I am to bring forth good fruit, I must have a good root. Just as it is possible for a man in a flying-machine to imitate a bird, so it is possible to imitate the fruit of the Spirit. The vital difference is the same in both, the aeroplane cannot persist, it can only fly spasmodically, there is no principle of life behind; and my imitation of the Spirit requires certain things that keep me from the public gaze and then I can imitate fairly well; but if I am going to bring forth the performance and fruit that is right, I must have the principle inside right. I must know what it is to be born again of the Holy Ghost, and sanctified, and filled with the Holy Spirit, then my performance will bring the fruit. Fruit is clearly expounded in the Epistles and is quite distinct from gifts or from the manifest seal of God on His own Word.

(4) Power of Publicity. (7: 19, 20,) Our Lord in His own life lived most publicly. When standing before Caiaphas He said, "I spake nothing in private" (John 18: 20), and our Lord here applies the same test of publicity to His disciples. All through the life of our Lord the one thing that made His enemies mad was the manner in which He did things, they were annoyed at His miracles because they manifested His public power. People are

annoyed at the same things to-day, they are annoyed at public testimony. Jesus makes publicity the test, that is, there is no use saying, "Oh, yes, I live a holy life, but I don't say anything about it"; then you certainly don't, for the two go together. Our Lord warns that the men who won't be conspicuous as His disciples will be made to be conspicuous as His enemies.

Whenever a thing has its root in the heart of God, it wants to be public, it wants to get out, it must do things in the external and the open, and Jesus Christ not only encouraged it, but He insisted on it, both for bad and for good. Things must be dragged out, it is God's law, men cannot hide what they really are, and if they are His disciples, it will be publicly portrayed.

Our Lord said, in Matthew 10, that men like wolves will want to devour you if you publicly perform or testify, but do not hide your light under a bushel for fear of wolfish men who can only destroy your body, but be careful that you do not go contrary to your duty and have your soul destroyed; be as "wise as serpents and harmless as doves." That warning of the Lord needs to come back here, that we have simply to wait in patience; if there are certain men and women who are not living in the public, conspicuous lives as the saints of God, as sure as God is on His throne, the inevitable principle must work, the public exposure of them. If we are not publicly conspicuous in the good, we will be publicly conspicuous in the bad.

C. APPEARANCE AND REALITY. (Matt. 7: 21-23.)

Our Lord here makes the test of goodness not only good intention but carrying out God's will. (1) Recognize Men Without Labels. (7:21.) Human nature is very fond of labels, that means the counterfeit of confession. It is so easy to be branded with labels, so easy in a certain stage to wear a *bonnet* or a *ribbon*, it is much easier to do that than to confess. Our Lord Jesus never used the word *testimony*, He used a much more testing word, He used the word *confess.* Our Lord said that the test of goodness was confession by doing the will of God. Therefore if the disciple is to discern between the man with the label and the man with the goods, he must have the spirit of discernment, *viz.,* the Holy Spirit. The label and the goods ought to go together, but our Lord is warning His disciples that there are times when they do not. A good many of us before we get right with God like to say, "Oh, yes, I quite agree with that, I don't think anyone ought to wear a badge." Jesus says, "If you don't confess me before men, I will not confess you before my father," and immediately you confess you must have a badge, and if you don't put one on yourself, they will put one on you. Watch what Jesus says about discipleship, you must be conspicuous, and the old cunning, carnal mind comes in and says we must live the holy life and say nothing about it. That is absolutely contrary to the spirit of the New Testament. Our Lord here is warning that it is possible for a man to carry the "label" without the goods, that is, it is possible for men to wear the badge of being "my disciple" while they are not.

(2) Remedy Mongers. (7:22.) Our Lord here warns against those who utilize His words and His ways to remedy the evils of men while they are disloyal to Jesus. "Many will say to me in that day, Lord, Lord, have we not prophesied in Thy name? and in Thy name have cast out de- vils? and in Thy name have done many wonderful works?" Not one word of confession of Jesus, one thing only, and that is, we have preached Him as a remedy, like quack preachers. The test of discipleship, as Jesus is dealing with it in this chapter, is fruit in goodly character, and the disciple is warned not to be blinded by the fact that God honors His Word even when it is preached from contention and the wrong motive. (See Phil. 1:15.) We have all had puzzles with the thing that is indicated in this statement of Jesus, we start out with the honest, plain, simple truth that the labels and the goods must go together, they ought to go together, but Jesus is warning here

that sometimes they get severed, and you sometimes find cases in which God honors His Word and the people who preach it are not living a right life. Now He says if you are going to judge the preachers, judge them by their fruit. He gave the same warning in Luke 10 to His own disciples. They were delighted because the very devils were subject to them, and Jesus said, "Don't rejoice in that I gave you power, but rejoice that your names are written in the Book of Life." We are back to the one point – right relationship to Jesus Christ, unsullied in every way, in every detail, private and public.

(3) Retributive Measures. (7:23.) In these solemn words Jesus states that He has to confess to some Bible expositors, some prophetic students, some workers of miracles, that they must depart from Him for they have twisted the ways of God and made them unequal, that is the meaning of the word "iniquity" (twisted out of the straight). We are continually perplexed by people who are preaching the right thing and who are proving that God is blessing the preaching, and yet all the time the Spirit of God is warning, "No! No!! No!!!" Only as we rely on and recognize the Spirit of God do we discern how Jesus Christ's warnings work. Never trust the best man or woman you ever met, trust only the Lord Jesus Christ. That holds good all the way along, "Lean not to your own understanding, put not your trust in princes, put not your trust in anyone." Have you ever noticed that every (not some) character in God's Book, when that character is taken as a guide, leads away from God? We are never told to follow in all the footsteps of the saints, we are only told to follow in the footsteps of the saints in so far as they have obeyed God. "Keep right with me, keep in the light," says Jesus, and you have fellowship with one another, that is with everyone else in the light. All our panics, moral, intellectual and spiritual, come just on that point, whenever we take our eyes off Jesus Christ, we get startled. "There is another one gone down, I did think he would stand right." "Look at Me," says Jesus.

D. THE TWO BUILDERS. (Matt. 7:24-29.)

The emphasis of our Lord is laid here on hearing and doing these sayings of mine. It would be a profitable study if we would hunt up what Jesus has to say about hearing. "He that hath ears to hear" – it would throw an amount of light on how I have heard what He said.

(1) Spiritual Castles. (7:24.) Our buildings must be conspicuous, and the test of the spiritual building is not its fair beauty but its foundation and bulwarks. Look at the most beautiful spiritual fabrics which are raised in the shape of books and lives, beautiful and full of the finest diction and statements spiritual and good; but when the test comes, down they go. What is the test? They have not been built on "these sayings of mine," that is, they are built altogether in the air, with no foundation.

(2) Supreme Crisis. (7:25.) Every spiritual castle will be tested by a threefold storm: rain, flood and wind – the world, the flesh, and the devil, and it will only stand if it is founded on these sayings of mine.

(3) Suspicious Conditions. (7:26.) Every spiritual fabric that is built with the sayings of Jesus instead of being founded on them, Jesus calls a building by foolish men. "He that heareth these sayings of mine and doeth them." There is a tendency in everyone of us to appreciate with our intellects and even with our spirits and hearts the teachings of Jesus, but if we refuse to do them, everything we build will go by the foundation when the test comes. Paul applies this when he says, "If I build hay, wood or stubble, gold or silver, it has all to be tested by the supreme test"

(4) Supreme Catastrophe. (7:27.) All that I build will be tested supremely and it will tumble in a fearful disaster unless it is built on the sayings of Jesus. It is an easy business to build with the sayings of Jesus, to sling texts of Scripture together and build them into any kind of fabric you like. Jesus did not say he that builds with my statements, but he that builds on them the charac-

ter of home life, of business life. Did you ever notice the repulsion that the healthy saint and the healthy worldling have against any man or woman who tries to build with the statements of Jesus? You will find that God brings the pagan and the saint before this tremendous standard, "What about your actions?" These things are quoted in your office, in your homes, but how do you work them out? That is what Jesus is saying, it is only when it is built on my statements, that is, our Lord makes no allowance for having some compartments holy and other compartments not, the whole thing must be radically built on the foundation.

(5) Scriptural Concentration. (7:28,29.) The summing up is a descriptive note inspired by the Spirit of God on the way in which people who heard Jesus had forgotten everything else but His doctrine. Its application for us is not what would Jesus do, but what did Jesus say. As I concentrate on what He said, so I can stake my immortal soul on those statements.

THE END.

BIBLICAL
PSYCHOLOGY

By
OSWALD CHAMBERS

OSWALD CHAMBERS

Biblical Psychology

A Series of Preliminary Studies

By OSWALD CHAMBERS

Principal, Bible Training College
London, England

God's Revivalist Office

Ringgold. Young And Channing Sts.

Cincinnati, Ohio

PREFATORY NOTE

This book is simply compiled from verbatim reports of my lectures on Biblical Psychology, delivered at the Bible Training College, 45 North Side, Clapham Common, London, England, during 1911.

The reports were taken by my wife and sent on to the editors of the "Revivalist," who now, out of the generosity of their hearts, are publishing them in book form.

May this "Introduction to the Study of Biblical Psychology" stir up the minds of the saints, lest Satan as an angel of light instil error. (2 Pet. 1 : 12, 13.)

Oswald Chambers.

CHAPTER I.

MAN: HIS CREATION, CALLING AND COMMUNION.

(Although the passages quoted appear as "texts,"
they are really portions of connected revelation.)

1. CONDITIONS BEFORE MAN'S CREATION. Gen. 1:1.
   (a) Celestial Creations. Job 38: 4-7.
   (b) Celestial Catastrophe, Isa. 14: 12; Luke 10: 18.
   (c) Celestial Condemnation. John 8: 44; Jude 6.

2. CONDITIONS LEADING TO MAN'S CREATION. Neh. 9: 6.
   (a) Terrestrial Chaos. Gen. 1: 2.
   (b) Terrestrial Creations. Gen. 1: 2-25.
   (c) Terrestrial Cosmos. Gen. 1: 4, 10, 12, 18, 21, 25, 31.

3. CLIMAX OF CREATION. Gen. 1: 26, 27.
   (a) The "Son of God." Gen. 1: 27; Luke 3:38.
   (b) The Six Days' Work. Gen. 1:28-31.
   (c) The Sabbath Rest. Gen. 2: 1-3.

1. Conditions Before Man's Creation.

Between Genesis 1, verses 1 and 2, there is a great hiatus. Verse 1 refers to an order of things before the reconstruction referred to in verse 2. I mean- by (a) celestial creations, the creations that were before men and our system of things as we understand them. These celestial creations all belong to the period before man. The creations first alluded to then are not men, but something other than man. Job 38, verses 4 to 7, has a distinct reference to such a time when the "sons of God shouted for joy." Who were these sons of God? They were certainly not men; they were un-questionably angels and archangels, and you will find that the indirect inference from the Bible is that God had put that former world under the charge of an archangel "Lucifer."

The Bible also alludes to (b) a catastrophe before man, was created, which makes the first and second verses of the first chapter of Genesis understandable. God gave the rule of this universe to Lucifer, and he opposed himself to God's authori-ty and rule, and dragged everything down with him, and con-sequently called forth on this earth a tremendous judgment, which resulted in chaos "and the earth was without form and void." You will find this catastrophe referred to in such passag-es as Isaiah 14:12, and Luke 10:18, "I beheld Satan as lightning fall from Heaven." When did out Lord behold this? Surely it is legitimate to suggest that it refers to the period before our Lord's incarnation, when He was with God, in the very begin-ning, before all things. (This particular verse is frequently taken to refer to the time yet to be, and that our Lord is annihilating time in His forelook.) These verses are like mountain peaks re-vealing a whole tableland of God's revelation of the order of things before man was created.

Then comes (c) the condemnation of the "angels," a celes-tial condemnation, nothing whatever to do with man, but the condemnation of Lucifer and all his angels. (Jude 6.) When Jesus Christ alludes to the beginning, He does not mean the beginning of man; He means the beginning of the creation of God which was long enough before man was created. (See John 8:44.) ("Hell" has nothing whatever to do with man primarily.) Hell is a place of angelic condemnation. You will never find that God says Hell was made for man. It is true that it is the only place for a man who rejects God's salvation. Hell was the result of a distinct condemnation that was passed by God on celestial beings, and is as eternal as those celestial anarchists.

There are three amazing episodes that indicate the conditions before the creation of man, viz.: that the archangels and the angels governed a wonderful world which God created in the beginning, and which God's Spirit is alluding to by that phrase in Job, "The sons of God sang together." Lucifer fell, and with him all his angels in a tremendous ruin (clearly mentioned in Genesis 1:2), and "the earth was without form and void, and darkness was upon the face of the deep, and the Spirit of God moved upon the face of the waters." Without some such indication, the second verse would be unintelligible, for to say that "in the beginning God created the Heaven and the earth," and then to say that "the earth was without form and void" is a confusion and a confounding. The inference is that between the epochs referred to in the first and second verses there has occurred this catastrophe which the Bible does not say much about. The evident purpose of the Bible is to tell us what God's purpose is with man. Roughly outlining that purpose, we might say that God created man to counteract the devil.

2. Conditions Leading to Man's Creation.

(a) Terrestrial Chaos. (Gen. 1:2.) Satan has been the means of the ruin of the first created order, and now God begins to create another order out of the confusion of ruin. "Void" means the aftermath of destruction by judgment, or the result of Divine judgment.

(b) Terrestrial Creations. God began to create things. Genesis 1: 2-25, gives a detailed account of the creation of the earth and the life on it. The Bible nowhere says that God set processes at work, and out of these processes were evolved the things which appear. The Bible says the things of this world were created by a distinct "fiat" of God. If the Bible entirely agreed with modern science, it would soon be "out of date," because modern science is in the very nature of things bound, to change. Genesis

1 indicates that God created the earth and the life on the earth to fit the world for man.

(c) Terrestrial Cosmos. The order and beauty of this world were created by God for man. Genesis 1, verses 4, 10, 12, 18, 21, 25 and 31, all say that "God saw that it was good." After the judgment by God on the previous order, God created "a new thing," to fit all for a totally new being whom no angel had ever seen before. He was to be a man, and he was to stand at the end of the six days' work as a creation of earth, and at the threshold of God's Sabbath day. God created man, not an angel, and not God Himself. He created him to be a unique being. Man was related to this earth, created out of this earth, and yet he was created in the image of God, whereby God could prove Himself more than a match for the devil by a creation a little lower that the angels (the order of beings Satan belongs to). This is, as it were, God's tremendous experiment in this creation. He puts man at the head of the Terrestrial Creation. The whole meaning of the creation of the world is to fit and prepare it for this wonderful being called Man that God had in. His mind. There is nothing in the Bible about evolving and developing man as a "survival of the fittest," or the "process of natural selection." The Bible reveals that we are earth and spirit, a combination of the two. The devil is spirit, just as God is; the angels are spirit; but when we come to a man, man is to be earth and spirit.

3. Climax of Creation.

(a) "Son of God!" -(Luke 3: 38.) Adam' was a son of God. As far as the terrestrial is concerned, there is only one other primal "Son of God" in the Bible, and He is Jesus Christ. This is an important point. Yet we are called "sons of God," but how? By being reinstated through the atonement of Jesus Christ. We are not the "sons of God" by natural generation. Have you noticed that Adam did not come into the world as we do? Neither (lid Adam come into the world as Jesus Christ came. Adam was not

" begotten;" Jesus Christ was. Adam was "created," God created Adam, He did not beget him. We are all "generated," we are not created beings. Adam was the "son of God," and God made him as well as everything else that was created.

In Genesis 1:27 we read, "So God created man in His own image, in the image of God created He him; male and female created He them." This is a point of importance. "Adam and Eve" are both needed before the image of God can be perfectly presented. God, as it were, is all that the best manhood presents us with, and all that the best womanhood presents us with. This aspect will be dealt with again in subsequent lectures.

(b) "The Six Days' Work." This word "day" unquestionably means roughly what we understand by twenty-four hours, and has no such meaning as "Day of Atonement" or "Day of Judgment." These terms do not refer to a "solar day," but to a "period of years of time." The devotion to the ephemeral scientific doctrine of evolution must be held responsible for the endeavor to make the Bible mean periods of years, instead of a solar day. The particular unparabolic use of the term "morning and evening" in Genesis distinctly indicates a solar day. Man was the end of the six days' work. In God's plan the whole of the six days' creation was meant for man. (The tendency nowdays is to put the six days' work of creation above man. Men and women are far more concerned about dogs and cats than about human beings. It is the reverse of what God made it. The whole purpose of creation in God's plan is man.)

There is not only the tendency to exalt animals above man, but there is the new speculation of the superman, i. e., a doctrine which holds that man, as we understand him and as the Bible reveals him, is not the climax of creation, but there is a higher race yet to be called "the superman," and that man is as inferior to this being that is going to be as the ape is to him. Now all through the New Testament Jesus Christ foretold, and the Spirit of God, foretold, that we were going to have the "worship of man" installed, and it has begun already, it is in our midst to-day. We are told that Jesus Christ and God are simply ceasing to be of importance to the modern man, and what we are worshipping more and more now is humanity, and this is slowly merging into a new phase. All the "up-to-date" minds are looking towards the manifestation of a "superman," a being much greater than the being we know as man. II. Thessalonians 2, gives us the picture of the head of this great expectation. He is to be the darling of every religion; there is to be a consolidation of religions, and races and everything on the face of the earth, a great socialism. The ethical standard for the superman claims to be higher than Jesus Christ's. The tendency noticeable already is that people object to some of Christ's teaching, such as "Loving your neighbor as yourself;" they say, "That is selfish, you must love your neighbor and not think of Yourself." The doctrine of the superman is absolute sinless perfection. We are going to evolve a being, they say, who has got to the place where he cannot be tempted. This is all an emanation from Satan. Man is the climax of creation. He is on a stage a little lower than the angels, and God is going to overthrow the devil by this being who is less than angelic. God has, as it were, put him in the "open field," and He allows the devil to do exactly what he likes up to a certain point, because God says, "I know that He who is in you is greater than he that is against you." That is the explanation in our own spiritual life-setting. Satan is to be humiliated by man, by the Spirit of God in man, and by poor fallen beings, too, like we were, but all by the wonderful regeneration through Jesus Christ.

Man is the head and the purpose of the six days' creation. Man's body has those constituents in it that connect it with the earth; it has fire and water and all the elements of the life of animals, and consequently, God keeps us here. It is man's domain, and we are going to be here again after the terrestrial cremation. "Hereafter" without the devil, without the sin and without the wrong. We are going to be here marvelously redeemed in this wonderful place which God made very beautiful, and which has been, played havoc with by sin, and creation is waiting for the "manifestation of the sons of God."

Not only is man the head and the climax of the six days' work, but he is the beginning of, and stands at the threshold of (c) the very Sabbath of God. God's heart is, as it were, absolutely at rest now that He has created man, even in spite of the fact of the fall, and all else; God is absolutely confident that the whole thing will turn out as He said it would. The devil has laughed at God's hope for thousands of years and has ridiculed and scorned that hope. God is not upset or alarmed about the final issue. He is certain that man will bruise the serpent's head. This refers to those of us who are born again through Jesus Christ's amazing atonement.

The first condition was chaos, God created angels and they fell and there was ruin; than God remade the void into a new creation, and by making a being never existent before, a being a "little lower than the angels. "

CHAPTER II.

MAN: HIS CREATION, CALLING AND COMMUNION.
MAN'S MAKING.

4. THE MAN OF GOD'S MAKING. Gen. 2: 4-25.

    (a) The Image of God. John 4: 24.

    (b) The Image of God in Angels. Gen. 6: 2; Ps. 89: 6; Job 1: 6; 38: 7.

    (c) The Image of God in Man. Gen. 1:26; Ps. 8:4, 5.

5. THE MANNER OF MAN'S MAKING. John 1: 3.

    (a) Man's Body. Gen. 2: 7.

    (b) Man's Soul. Acts 17: 28.

    (c) Man's Self -Consciousness. Prov. 20: 27; 1 Cor. 2: 11.

N. B. Visible creations that surround man are not in the image of God.

    Some notes will be given on the appearances of angels in our material universe.

    Some notes also on the human representations of God.

4. The Man of God's Making.

God's heart, so to speak, is at rest now that He has created man. (Gen. 2:4-25.)

(a) The Image of God. (John 4:24.) "God is spirit." This is a mountain-peak text which reveals a whole tableland of God's revelation about Himself.

(b) The Image of God in Angels. The phrase "sons of God" in the Old Testament always refers to angels, and we have to take from the context whether they are "fallen angels" or not. Angels have no physical frame, they are not like man, and they are not manifested after this order of things. If, however, they are called "sons of God," the inference is clear that they bear the image of God.

(c) The Image of God in Man. The image of God in its primary reference to man must refer to the hidden or interior life of man.

From these three revelation facts in God's Book, men have reasoned backwards. They have said that because men have bodies, God has a corporiety, too. This mistake began centuries ago and it is continually being revived, the reason being that the Bible does refer to the form of God. For instance, the Old Testament alludes over and over again to what is called the "anthropomorphic" view of God. God is represented as having hands and limbs and looking like a man, and from this the inference is easy that surely God has a body like man. The answer is that all the Old Testament pictures of God are forecasts of the Incarnation, and have nothing to do with stating that God is in the form of a man. Read the passages in Isaiah alone, and they will reveal the apparently conflicting statements about God; He is represented in many contradictory phrases, yet immediately you read the life of Jesus Christ in the New Testament, all these contradictions blend in that unique Being, Jesus Christ, the second Adam. However, the Bible does speak of a "form of God" (Phil. 2:6), but the error arises from our too readily inferring that form" means physical body. The great Triune God has "form" and the term used for that form is "glory." Our Lord refers to this in John 17: 5. Our word "Trinity" is an attempt to convey the externally disclosed divine nature itself, and "glory" is the Bible term for conveying the idea of the external (so to speak) form of that Triune Being. This will be alluded to several times in the course of our studies in Biblical Psychology, and we will thus get familiar with this profound revelation.

(Sometimes God is referred to as the sun, but the sun is never stated to be made in the image of God, though there are illustrations in God's Book drawn from the sun to illustrate Him. But nowhere has it ever been stated that God made the sun in His own image.)

Angels in the Bible record certainly do appear to men. You may take this as a correct inference from the revealed facts in

God's Word, that angels have the power of will to appear to human beings, when those human beings are in suitable, subjective conditions. That power is given to "good" and "bad" angels alike. You will find this inference a great guide regarding "Spiritualism." Spiritualism is not a trick, according to the Bible; it is a fact. Man can communicate with beings of a different order from his own, and he can put himself into a state of subjectivity in which angels can appear. Angels may thus be said to have a power of will to materialize themselves. It is probably to this that Paul refers in Romans 8:38 and Ephesians 6 : 12.

The Image of God in Man. The image of God in man is primarily spiritual, yet it has to be manifested in the body of a man also. We read in Psalm 8:5 that God made man a "little lower than the angels," that might as well be translated a "little lower than God and the angels." You will find that man's chief glory and dignity is that he was made of the earth to manifest the image of God in that substance. We are apt to think because we are made of earth that this is our humiliation, but it is not so. It is the very point that God's Word makes most of. He made man of the dust of the ground, and the redemption of Jesus Christ is for the dust of the ground as well.

Man's body before he degenerated, must have been dazzling with light. (We get this by direct inference from Genesis 3:7.) Man was obviously naked before his disobedience, and the death of his union with God instantly revealed itself in his body. (See next chapter.)

5. The Manner of Man's Making.

God did not create man by direct fiat but by His own deliberate power He moulded him. (See Gen. 1:26, 27.) The first mistake we must note is the inference that the soul was made along with the body; the Bible does not say it was. The Bible says that the body was created prior to the soul. Man's body was made by God, and it was built out of the "dust of the ground," that means that man is constituted to have affinity with everything on this earth. This is not his calamity, it is his peculiar dignity. (We dot not further our spiritual life "in spite of our bodies" but in and by means of our bodies.) Then we read that God breathed into man's nostrils the breath of life, and man became a "soul-enlivened nature." There is another breathing mentioned in John 20:22, when our risen Lord breathed on the disciples and said, "Receive ye the Holy Spirit." This is not exactly the same thing as Genesis 2:7. In the latter reference God breathed into man's nostrils the breath of life which became man's spirit, not God's; but in the former reference in John, Jesus Christ breathed into His disciples Holy Spirit. "When God breathed into man's nostrils the breath of life, man did not become a living God, man became a "living soul." Thus in man, degenerate or regenerate, there are three aspects, spirit, soul and body. The uniting of man's personality, body, soul and spirit, may be brought about in various ways. The Bible reveals that sensuality will do it (Eph. 5:5); that drunkenness will do it (Eph. 5:18); and finally that the devil will do it (Luke 11:21); but the Holy Ghost alone through Jesus Christ will do it rightly, this is the only at-one-ment. When our personality is sanctified, it is not God's Spirit that is sanctified, it is out spirit (1 Thess. 5:23), and cleansing from filthiness of the spirit refers to man's spirit. God's inbreathing into man's nostrils called into actual existence his soul, which was potentially in the body (potentially means existing in possibility, not in actuality). So man's soul is not his body or his spirit, but is that creation which holds his spirit and his body together, and is the medium of expressing his spirit in his body. It is not true to state that man's soul moulds his body; it is his spirit that moulds his body, and his soul is the medium the spirit uses to express itself.

It is absolutely impossible for us to conceive what Adam was like as God, made him, his very material body instinct with spiritual light, his very flesh in the likeness of God, his spirit in the image of God, and his soul in absolute harmony with God. In the personal life of a man who has fallen away from God, his soul and his spirit gravitate more and more to the dust of the earth, more and more to the brutish life on one side and the Satanic life on the other. The marvelous hope before us is that in and through Jesus Christ, our personality in its three aspects is sanctified and preserved in that condition blameless in this dispensation, and that in another dispensation body, soul and spirit will be all instinct with the glory of God, (Whenever an Old Testament character succeeded in doing God's will perfectly, earth seemed to lose its hold on him, e. g., Enoch, Elijah. Again, why did not Jesus Christ go straight back to Heaven from the Mount of Transfiguration? He emptied Himself a second time of the glory of God and came back again for the humiliation of the Cross. Then when Jesus Christ comes again, those who are saved and sanctified will be changed "in the twinkling of an eye," all the disharmony will cease and a new order begin.)

What does glorification mean? Adam is never spoken of as being glorified in the first decades of creation. Glorification is Christ enthroned in fulness of consummating power, having subdued all things unto Himself, and then finally entering back into the final being of the original Triune God as "in the beginning" before any first creations were.

In conclusion, God made man in His own image and breathed into his nostrils the breath of life and man became, not a living God, but a living soul, a soul-enlivened nature, and this whole bodily temple, every corpuscle of blood, every nerve, every sinew, every muscle was the temple that could manifest an exact harmony with God and manifest the image of God in the very form of man in perfect faith and love. The angels can only manifest the image of God in what we call bodiless spirits, there is only one being who can manifest God on this earth, and that is man. Satan thwarted that purpose, and then laughed his devilish laugh against God, but the Bible says that God will laugh last.

CHAPTER III.

MAN: HIS CREATION, CALLING AND COMMUNION. MAN'S UNMAKING

1. THE PRIMAL ANARCHY. Gen. 3; Rom. 5: 12.
   (a) The Serpent. Gen. 3: 1.
   (b) The Serpent and Eve. 2 Cor. 11: 3.
   (c) The Serpent, Eve and Adam. 1 Tim. 2: 14.
   ORIGINAL SIN is – Doing without God.

2. THE PRE-ADAMIC ANARCHY. Ezek. 28: 12-15.
   (a) Satanic Pretensions. Implied, Matt. 4: 8; 2 Cor. 4: 4.
   (b) Satanic Perversions. Gen. 3:5; implied, Job 1: 9.
   (c) Satanic Perils. Jude 6; Matt. 16:23; 2 Thess. 2:9.
   ORIGINATOR OF SIN – Dethroning of God.

3. THE PUNISHED ANARCHISTS. Gen. 3: 23, 24.
   (a) Destitution and Death. Gen. 2: 17.
   (b) Division from Deity. Gen. 3: 8, 13. *
   (c) Divine Declaration. Gen. 3: 15.
   ORIGIN OF SALVATION – Dating way back to God.

Now we come to the revelation statement as to how sin was introduced into this world.

1. The Primal Anarchy.

(a) The Serpent. (Gen. 3: 1.) This creature was evidently a beautiful creation of God, and we must beware of imagining that is was in the beginning as it was after God's curse. God, after the fall of Adam, cursed this beautiful creature into the serpent, to feed on dust and to crawl; and consequently the serpent in the physical domain is the picture of Satan in the spiritual domain.

In our universe of physical things, we will find many which represent spiritual things; they are, as it were, pictures of them. The serpent is the physical picture from man's standpoint of what Satan appears in the spiritual domain from God's standpoint. However, this line of thought properly belongs to Biblical Philosophy, so we will only thus allude to it in passing.

(b) The Serpent and Eve. (2 Cor. 11:3.) Why did Satan come via the serpent, and to Eve, why did he not go to Adam direct? In talking about man and woman as they were first created, it is exceedingly difficult to present that subject without getting introduced to all sorts of small, petty and disreputable ideas, especially nowadays, relative to the distinctions between man and woman. In Adam and Eve we are dealing with the primal creations of God. Adam was created immediately by the hand of God, and Eve was created mediately. Eve stands for the soul side, the psychic side, of the human creation, all her sympathies and her affinities are with the other creations of God around. Adam stands for the spirit side, the kingly, Godward side. Adam and Eve are together the likeness of God, for God said, "Let us make man in our image, male and female created He them." Woman stands not as inferior to man; the revelation made here is that she stands in quite a different relation to all things, and both are required to make the complete, rounded creation of God referred to by the big general term MANKIND. Eve having affinity and sympathy with the creation round about, would naturally listen with very much more unsuspecting interest to the suggestions that came through the subtle creature that talked to her. The Bible says that Eve was deceived; the Bible does not say that Adam was deceived; consequently Adam is far more responsible than Eve, for Adam sinned deliberately. There was not the remotest conscious intention in Eve's heart of disobeying, she was deceived by the subtle wisdom of Satan via the serpent. Adam, however, was not deceived in any shape or form; when Eve came to him he understood it was disobedience, and he sinned with a deliberate understanding of what he was doing, so the Bible associates sin with Adam (Rom. 5: 12) and transgression with Eve. (1 Tim. 2: 14.) [In this connection it is of importance to note that the Bible reveals that our Redeemer entered into the world by the woman. Man as man had no part whatever in the redemption of the world; it was "the seed of the woman." In Protestant theology and in the Protestant outlook we have suffered much from our opposition to the Roman Catholic Church on one point, viz.: our intense antipathy to Mariolatry, and we have lost the whole meaning of the woman side of the revelation of God. All that we understand by womanhood and by manhood, all we understand by fatherhood and motherhood is embraced in the term "El Shaddai." (Gen. 17:1.) This is a mere hint at a line of thought we cannot take up here.]

Perhaps one may legitimately make a distinction between transgression and sin in human conduct. (See Matt. 6: 12-15.) Transgression is nearly always an unconscious act, there is no conscious determination to do wrong. Sin is never an unconscious act, as far as culpability is concerned, it is always a conscious determination. Adam was the introducer of sin into this order of things. Original sin is doing without God. A noticeable feature in the conduct of Adam and Eve is that when God turned them out of the Garden they did not rebel. The characteristic of sin in man is "fear and shame." Sin in man is doing without God, but it is not rebellion against God in its first stages, there is no rebellion anywhere in Adam and Eve against God.

2. The Pre-Adainic Anarchy.

(a) Satanic Pretensions. The pretensions of Satan are very clear. He is the "god of this world," and he will not allow any relationship to the true God. Satan's attitude of pretence is the same as the attitude of a pretender to a throne – he claims it as his right. "Wherever and whenever the rule of God is established and recognized as such by man, Satan at once proceeds to instil the tendency of mutiny and rebellion and lawlessness.

(b) Satanic Perversions. Satan ever perverts what God says. Genesis 3: 5 is one of the revelation facts concerning Satan. Remember the characteristics of union with God are faith in God and personal, passionate devotion and love for God. The first thing Satan aims at in Adam and Eve is that, by perverting what God says. (In Job 1:9 Satan goes the length of trying to pervert God's idea of man. There is an amazing revelation of power in Satan! He is represented as presenting himself with the "sons of God" in the very presence of God and trying to pervert God's mind about man. You may apply personally not exegetically such a statement as the following in Isaiah: "He will not quench the smoking flax, nor break the bruised reed." Satan is also called the "accuser of the brethren." He not only accuses and slanders God to us, but he accuses us to God, and it is as if he looks down and points out a handful of people and insinuates to God, "Now; that woman is a perfect disgrace to you, she has only one spark of grace amongst all the fibres of her life, I advise you to stamp out that spark." What is the revelation? "He will raise it to a flame." Or, Satan points out a man and says, "That man is a disgrace to you, he is a 'bruised reed,' I wonder you build any hope whatever on him, he is a hindrance and an upset to you, break him!" But no, the Lord will bind him up and make him into a wonderful instrument. The old reeds were used as wonderful musical instruments, and instead of crushing out the life that is bruised and wrong, He will heal it and discourse sweet music through it.)

In the Genesis revelation Satan says that God is jealous – "God knows if you disobey Him, you will become like God." He perverted God's statement, he did not say that God had said it. Satan is too wise for that, he said, "Has God said it?" insinuating, "You do not know what He meant, but I do; He meant that if you eat of that tree and disobey Him, you will become like He is." I do not think that Eve accepted that statement about God, because when you watch, it worked as a deception, unconsciously, and what she saw was that it was remarkably delightful to take that fruit; but the discerning and understanding of it is given us by God. No wonder Paul says, and the Spirit says through the Epistles, that we are not "ignorant of the devices of Satan." Remember, Satan's pretension is that he is equal with God. His perversion is twofold: he perverts what God says to us, and tries to pervert God's mind about us.

(c) Satanic Perils. What are the Satanic perils? In Matthew 16:23 we come to the location where we live. The perils spring straight out of the way we are made. Have you ever noticed the remarkable identification Jesus Christ makes in that passage? What is it Peter had said? "Pity Thyself, Lord." "Get thee behind Me, Satan." Then He tells Peter that he is saying the thing that belongs to the wrong disposition of man which is identified with Satan. Beware of Satanic perils where you take them to be natural tendencies. Remember Satan is an awful being, he is able to deceive us on the right hand and on the left, and the first beginnings of his deceptions are along the line of self-pity. Self-pity, self-conceit and self-sympathy will make us accept slanders against God. Satan's perils arise out of the wrong disposition that Adam intraduced us to, and that wrong dispositon shows itself in self-pity and self-sympathy. (Beware of slandering the "old man," as is very often done. I mean, making the "old man" appear ugly. The "old man" does not appear ugly to anybody but the Holy Ghost. The "old man," i. e., this disposition that connects me with the mystical "body of sin," is the most highly desirable thing on earth to me till I am quickened by the Spirit of God and born from above. It makes me consider "my rights"; it makes me look after myself and consider what is good for me.)

Then another peril. (2 Thess. 2: 9.) That means that there are tremendous and appalling external manifestations of Satan, and the curious thing is that nowadays people are paying much more attention, and watching out more eagerly for these great manifestations of Satanic power while they allow the other Satanic peril to have its way. Spiritualism is child's play compared to this other thing. Once you get the disposition altered, you will never be deluded by any of the Satanic powers that manifest themselves in spiritualisms in the external world. The peril is the inside peril which men never think of as a peril. "My right to myself," my "self-pity," my "self-conceit," my "consideration for my progress," my "ways of looking at things," that is the Satanic peril in me that will keep me in perfect sympathy with Satan's ideas.

Satanic anarchy is conscious and determined opposition to God. Wherever there is a law of God, Satan will break it. Wherever God's rule is, Satan will put himself alongside and oppose it. As we said in the last chapter, Satan's sin is at the summit of all sins; man 's sin is at the foundation of all sins, and between them there is all the difference in the world. Satan's sin is conscious, emphatic, and immortal rebellion against God. He has no fear, no veneration, and no respect for God's rule. "Whenever God's law is stated, that is sufficient, Satan will break it, and his whole purpose through the disposition of sin in you and me is to get us to the same place. The anarchy in Satan is, then, a conscious, tremendous thing. Satan in the Bible is never represented as being guilty of "sins," never represented as being guilty of doing wrong things. He is a wrong being. Men are responsible for doing wrong things, and they do wrong things because of the wrong disposition that is in them, and sometimes you will find that the moral cunning of your own nature makes you blame Satan, when you know perfectly well you ought to blame yourself. The true blame for sins lies in the wrong disposition in you and me, and I think it right to say that Satan in all probability is as much upset as the Holy Ghost, when men go into external sins, but from a different reason. When men go into external sins and upset their lives Satan knows perfectly well that they will want another ruler – a Savior, a Deliverer – but as long as he can keep us in peace and unity and harmony apart from God, he will do it. Remember, then, that Satan's sin is dethroning God. **3. The Punished Anarchists.**

We found in a previous chapter how God punished Satan. He has reserved for him what is revealed as the eternal Hell. Now we come to the punishment of Adam and Eve. (Gen. 3:23, 24.) This is an old familiar revelation fact to us, but if we get the truth of it we see that there is no rebellion in Adam and Eve. They did not fight against God, they simply went out covered with fear and shame. Satan was the originator of sin; Adam was not. Adam accepted the way his wife had been deceived and sinned with his eyes open, and instantly an extraordinary thing happened: "They knew they were naked." The more you meditate on the verse, the more will you find in it, and there is quite sufficient to indicate this – that when Adam's spirit, soul and body were in perfect faith and love to God, united to God, his soul was the medium which brought down the marvelous life of the Spirit of God, the very image of God, into his material body and clothed it in inconceivable splendor of light, until the whole man was the likeness of God. Instantly he disobeyed, that went, the connection with God was shut off, and spirit, soul and body tumbled into death that instant. The question of dissolving Into earth in a few years time, is nothing more than death visible. Do not bring in the idea of time at all, death happened instantly in spirit, soul and body – spiritually and psychically. He tumbled into ruin because the connecting link with Deity was gone, and his spirit, soul and body tumbled into disintegrating death, and when Adam and Eve heard of the "goings of God in the Garden," they were both terrified and hid. By the great term Dearth, the body crumbles back again into the dust, the soul disappears, and the "spirit goes back to God who gave it." "What does this latter statement mean? That the spirit is the immortal part of every man, and that the spirit goes straight back to God who gave it, it is not absorbed into God. The spirit of man goes back with the characteristics that he has made on it, for judgment or for praise from God. It goes back to God who breathed into man's nostrils the breath of life.

God turned man out of the Garden of Eden into destitution. By turning man out, He put him on the way to become an infinitely grander and nobler being than even Adam was in the first place. He put him out into destitution, and through the very worst onslaught of Satan, He made a better creature than the first Adam was. It seems to me that the whole Bible from Genesis to Revelation instead of being a picture of despair is the very opposite. The " worst" is always bettered by God. Let Satan do his worst; God has "staked" His all on the new creation. He took His hand off, as it were, and let Satan do the very worst that diabolical spiritual genius could do, and Satan did it. Satan knew exactly what would happen to man, viz.: that God would have to punish him, and God did punish him, with a perfect certainty that the being that was going to come out of the ordeal of the fall was going to be greater than the Adam He first made. Adam and Eve went from the Garden covered with fear and shame. What are the characteristics of the old disposition in the New Testament? "Fearfulness and unbelief." What does God's atonement do? It takes away ' tearfulness and unbelief" and gets us back again into ' 'faith and love" to God. What does regeneration mean? The Holy Spirit lifting man straight back again out of the slough he has got into by death and sin, into a totally new realm, and by sudden intuitions and impulses that new life is able to lift soul and body up for a time. If that soul will not obey the new union with God which the Spirit life has given, it will ultimately fall away from the new birth God has given it. The new birth God has given it is to get it to a place where soul and body will

be identified with Christ, until spirit and soul and body are sanctified here and now, and preserved in that condition not now
by intuitions, not by sudden impulses and marvellous workings
of the new life within it, but by a certain, conscious, superior,
moral integrity, transfigured through and through by the union
made by the Spirit with God through the atonement of Jesus
Christ. When Adam sinned, that cut off his union with God, and
God turned him out and kept the way open to the tree of life, i.
e., prevented Adam getting back as a fallen being; if Adam had
gotten back as a fallen being he would have become an incarnate
devil, and the devil would have thwarted God finally with man;
but God guarded the way to the tree of life in turning Adam out.
If Adam had been a, rebellious devil, there would have been the
same havoc on this earth that there was when the angels fell,
but Adam did not sin like Satan. Adam was covered with fear
and shame, and the light referred to just now that glistered all
through man's physical body, faded out by sin; but Christ will
change this "body of humiliation' ' and make it like His glorious
body, and it will result not only in an intuitive innocency, but
in a conscious manly and womanly holiness. Holiness is tested
innocence, holiness is really the outcome of the new disposition
God has given us maintained against every odd. It is militant,
Satan is continually pressing and ardent, but it maintains itself.
It is morality on fire and transfigured into the likeness of God.
Holiness is not only what God gives me, but what I manifest
that God has given me. I manifest by my reaction against sin,
the world, and the devil, this corruscating holiness. "Whenever
God's saints are about in the world they are protected by a "wall
of fire," they do not see it, but Satan does. "That wicked one
toucheth him not." Satan has to ask and plead for permission;
as to whether God grants him permission, has to do with the
sovereignty of God, and is not in our domain to understand. All
we know is that Jesus Christ taught us to pray, "Lead us not into

temptation."

Man was turned into destitution, and thus he was divided from Deity. God disappeared from him, and he disappeared from God. As we mentioned before, there are three false unities possible in man's experience, viz.: sensuality, drunkenness, and the devil, whereby man's spirit, soul and body are brought back again into harmony, quite peaceful, quite happy, no sense of death about him. A drunken man has no self-consciousness, he is perfectly delivered from all things which disintegrate and upset. Sensuality and Satan do the same thing, but each of them only for a time. "When Satan rules, men's souls are in peace, they are not troubled like other men, not upset, but happy and peaceful. But there is only one right at-one-ment, and that is in Jesus Christ. There is only one right unity, and that is when body, soul and spirit are united by God the Holy Ghost through the marvelous atonement of Jesus Christ.

The origin of salvation is a daring way back to God. How did Jesus Christ work a way back to God? Through every worst piece of Satan's work. The statement in God's Book is that Jesus Christ, by the sheer force of the tremendous integrity of His incarnation, hewed a way straight through sin and death and Hell right back to God; more than conqueror over all.

CHAPTER IV.

MAN: HIS CREATION, CALLING AND COMMUNION. READJUSTMENT BY REDEMPTION

1. INCARNATION. Word Made Weak. John 1: 14. God-Man.
    (a) Self -Surrender of Trinity. John 17: 5; Mark 13: 32; Eph. 4: 10.
    (b) Self -same with Trinity. Matt. 11:27; John 14:9.
    (c) Self-sufficiency of Trinity. Prov. 8: 22-32.

2. IDENTIFICATION. Son Made Sin. 2 Cor. 5: 20, 21. God and Man.
    (a) Day of His Death. Matt. 16: 21; Mark 9: 31; Rom. 6: 3.
    (b) Day of His Resurrection. Rom. 6: 5; Phil. 3: 10.
    (c) Day of His Ascension. Matt. 28: 18; 2 Cor. 5: 16.

3. INVASION. Sinner Made Saint. Gal. 2: 20. God in Man.
    (a) The New Man. 2 Cor. 5: 17.
    (b) The New Manners. Eph. 5: 22-32.
    (c) The New Mankind. Eph. 4: 13; 2 Pet. 3: 13.

1. Incarnation.

"Trinity" is not a Bible word. The Triune God is revealed over and over again in. the Bible, and the idea conveyed by the Trinity is a thoroughly Scriptural one. The following distinctions have existed from all eternity:

The Essence of Godhead (esse) usually known as God the Father;

The Existence of Godhead (existere) usually known as God the Son;

The Proceeding of Godhead (procedere) usually known as God the Holy Ghost.

One of the things we have to guard against is the teaching that God became incarnate to realize Himself. That statement is un-biblical. God was selfsufficient before the Son became incarnate.

The whole basis and kernel of what is known as New Theology is based on that one fundamental error – that God had to create something in order to realize Himself; and consequently we are told that we are absolutely essential to God's existence, that apart from us God is not. Once starting with that theory, all that is known as New Theology is as easy as A. B. C. The Bible has nothing to do with any such conception. The creation and the incarnation are the outcomes of the overflowing life of the Godhead. Immediately you start with "God is all, " you get another aspect of New Theology. The Bible reveals that God is not all. The Bible distinctly states that our universe is a pluralistic one, not a monistic one; that means that other forces are at work besides one, such as man and Satan. These are not God, and never will be. Man is meant to come back to God and to be in harmony with Him through Jesus Christ; Satan will forever be at enmity with God.

In Philippians 2: 6 the "form" of God is mentioned. What is the form of God? We touched on this point in dealing with the first subject. We found that men had reasoned that because the Bible said man was made in the image of God, therefore God had a body. We proved that it was not a "corporeal form," and that whenever God is mentioned as having human members, the Incarnation is referred to. The term "glory" when referred to the Godhead conveys the idea of "form." The Bible has revealed that the Godhead was absolutely self-sufficient. God did not need to be incarnated to satisfy Himself, nor was the creation needed. The Godhead had a form originally, and the reference* to the "form" of the Godhead may be best implied in the term, "glory."

Jesus Christ is not a Being one-half God and the other half man. That was the line on which George Eliot made shipwreck of her faith. She translated Strauss' life of Jesus Christ, and this impossibility to human reason was represented to her mind by him. The Bible reveals that Jesus Christ is God-man, viz.: God incarnate, the Godhead existing in flesh and blood. The Incarnation is part of (a) the Self -surrender of the Trinity. John 17:5 refers to this. Jesus Christ was not a being who became divine, He was the Godhead incarnated, the "Word became weak, and Jesus Christ emphatically alludes to His own limitations. St. Paul says that "He emptied Himself of His glory," i. e., He emptied Himself of the "form" of Deity and came right down here as a weak human being and took upon Himself "the likeness of sinful flesh."

Again in Mark 13:32 we get another indication of His limitations. I am aware of the danger of attempting to sketch out the self-consciousness of Jesus. We cannot do it; we must remember what the Scriptures say about Him, that He was the Godhead incarnate, and that He emptied Himself of His glory in becoming incarnate. It was not God the Son paying a price to God the Father; it was God the Father, God the Son and God the Holy Ghost surrendering this marvelous being who became the Lord Jesus Christ, for one definite purpose. Never separate the Incarnation from the Atonement. The Incarnation is for the sake of the Atonement. In dealing with the Incarnation, we are dealing with a revelation fact, not with a speculation. Another allusion to the limitation by incarnation is in Hebrews where the writer is referring to Christ's temptation. To say that Christ was not tempted, flatly contradicts the Word of God, the Bible says He "was tempted in all points like as we are, yet without sin."

(b) Self-same with Trinity. (Matt. 11:27.) This verse implies that Jesus says, in effect, " I am the only organ for revealing the Godhead; you cannot know God through nature, or through the love of your friends, you cannot know God any other way than through Me." Will you couple with that John 14: 9? There again is the same statement made clear that no one knows anything about Deity in the way of revelation unless he accepts that revelation as Jesus Christ. Such statements come over and over again in our Lord's teaching, and you will find the more you examine His teaching that He makes the final destiny of man depend on his relationship to Him.

(c) The Self-sufficiency of the Trinity. (Prov. 8: 2232.) That passage is amazing in the light of the Incarnation. The writer is referring to what he calls 11 wisdom," and if you connect wisdom with the first chapter of John, you will find the very same idea used. The word there is "Logos." The word Logos means God's Word expressing His thought. The Trinity was self-sufficient; the Incarnation was not meant to satisfy God, but for another purpose altogether. Instead of man and Jesus Christ being necessary to complement God so that He might realize Himself, the thought is exactly the opposite, viz.: that man might realize God and regain adjustment to Him. The whole purpose of the Incarnation is redemption, and to produce a being more noble than the original Adam by overcoming the disasters of the fall and curse. At the climax of everything the Son resumes the original position of the Trinity, the Trinity thus resolving itself into this absolute self-sufficient Deity again. The Son gives all up to the Father. These statements refer to the resumption of the Trinity to the original position of the Godhead.

2. Identification. Son made Sin. (2 Cor. 5:20, 21.)

This is an indication of why God became incarnate, why the "Word was made weak, why the Logos became possessed of a weak human frame. It was that the Son might be identified with sin. Remember the teaching here is not that Jesus Christ was punished for our sins, that is another and slighter aspect than the one we are dealing with. The statement here is astounding : that He was made sin for us. Jesus Christ became identified not only with the disposition of sin, but with the very "body of sin." He had not the disposition of sin, and He had. no connection with the body of sin in Himself; but He became identified with sin, "Him who knew no sin He made to be sin." Language can hardly bear the strain, but it may nevertheless convey the thought that

Jesus Christ went straight through identification with sin, so that every man and woman on earth may be freed from sin by His atonement. He went through the depths of damnation, through the deepest depths of death, and Hell, and came out more than conqueror; and consequently everyone of us who is willing to be identified with our Lord will find that he or she is freed from the disposition of sin, freed from their connection with the body of sin, and they can come out more than conqueror because of what the Lord Jesus Christ has done.

(a) The Day of His Death. I mean by "Day" the period of time covered by His life on earth. "Why did He come and live thirty years in Nazareth ? "Why was He born as the babe of poor people in such a condition that the mightiest empires of the world could simply not be able to detect His existence? "Why did He live three years of popularity, scandal and hatred, and why did He say, "I came here to be killed"? (Our Lord never presents His life as the life of a martyr. He said, "I have power to lay down my life, and I have power to take it again." "I lay down my life because of the great purpose behind in the mind of God.") The only way you can explain Jesus Christ is the way He explains Himself, (and He never explains Himself away). Why did He live and die? The Scriptures reveal that He lived and died and rose again that we might be readjusted to the Godhead, that we might be brought back into favor and love, and be delivered from sin. To teach that the Lord Jesus Christ cannot deliver from sin may end in nothing short of blasphemy. Present that line of thought before God, tell Him that the atonement cannot deliver us from sin, it can only give us a divine anticipation; and the danger and unscripturalness of it will soon appear. The Book reveals that He became indentified with sin that we might be "made the righteousness of God in Him." Forgiveness is the least outcome from God's standpoint; from my standpoint it is a tremendous thing, but that is not the whole meaning of the experimental part of that wonderful life to me. I have to get where I can be identified with the Lord Jesus Christ, where I know that my connection with the body of sin is severed, where I am "made the righteousness of God in Him," where I am readjusted to God, and free in this life to fulfill the commands of the Lord.

(b) The Day of His Resurrection. By the resurrection of the Lord Jesus Christ, He has power to impart to you and to me the Holy Spirit, which means a totally new life. The Holy Ghost is the Deity in proceeding power who applies the atonement of the Son of God to my experience. Jesus Christ laid all His emphasis on the Holy Spirit – "He will lead you into all truth;" "He will bring to your remembrance what I have said;" "He will not only be with you, He will be in you." We hear on the right hand and on the left that this is the age of the Holy Spirit. Thank God it is, and the Holy Spirit is with all men that we might receive Him. But God the Father was rejected and spurned in the Old Testament dispensation; Jesus Christ the Son was despised and spurned in His dispensation (He was flattered too); and God the Holy Ghost is despised, as well as flattered, in this dispensation. He is not given His right. "We praise Him and talk about Him and say we rely on His power, but the question of receiving Him in that He might make real in my life what Jesus Christ did for me, is too rare an experience nowadays to be formidable. Immediately the Holy Spirit does come in as light and as life, He will chase through every avenue of your mind, and His light will penetrate every recess of your heart; He will chase His light through every affection of your body and make you know what sin is. The Holy Spirit "convicts of sin," man does not. By His resurrection our Lord Jesus Christ can impart Holy Spirit. The Holy Spirit is that marvelous Spirit that kept our Lord while He was incarnate, spirit, soul and body in perfect harmony with absolute Deity, and Jesus said, "You have not that life in yourself," and you cannot have it unless you get it through Him. "He that

believeth on Him hath everlasting life," this is the life He is referring to – Holy Spirit life which will take your spirit, soul and
body and bring them back into communion with God, where if
you will obey the light the Holy Spirit gives, He will lead you
into this amazing identification with the death of the Lord Jesus
in a deeper sense, viz.: until you know experimentally that your
old disposition, your right to your self, is crucified with Him,
and that your human nature is free to obey the commands of
God. (The word "substitution" is never used in the Bible, but
the idea is Scriptural. Substitution is always two-fold, not only
Christ identified with my sin, but I am identified with Christ
so that the ruling disposition of Jesus may be put in me. Sin on
-the one side and righteousness on the other. The righteousness
there means the ruling disposition of the Lord Jesus Christ.)

(c) In the Day of His Ascension our Lord Jesus Christ became
omnipresent, omniscient, and omnipotent. That means this – all
that He was in Himself in the day of His flesh, all that He was
able to impart in the day of His resurrection, He now is almighty
to bestow without measure on all obedient children of men. He
makes us one in holiness with Himself, one in love with Himself,
and ultimately one in glory with Himself. He is the supreme Sovereign, and He is able to give unto His people a supreme sovereignty. In the days of our flesh as saints, He says, "Lo, I am with
you all the days, even unto the end." He is with us in all wisdom,
guiding, directing, controlling and subduing, and He is with us
in all power. He is King of kings and Lord of lords from the day
of His ascension until now.

3. Invasion. Sinner Made Saint. (Gal. 2:20.) By Jesus Christ
being identified with sin, I can get back again into perfect harmony with God. God does not remove our responsibility; He puts a
new responsibility on us. We are sons and daughters of God by
the atonement of Jesus Christ, and we have a tremendous dignity
to maintain, and we have no business to bow our necks to any

yoke but the yoke of the Lord Jesus Christ. There ought to be in us, the scorn of a holy meekness whenever it comes to being dictated to by the dispensation we live in. The dispensation we live in is governed by the "prince of this world," who hates Jesus Christ. His great doctrine is self-realization; while Christ's great doctrine is Christ-realization. We ought to be free from the yoke of the "prince of this world," only one yoke should be on our shoulders – the yoke of the Lord Jesus. He was meek towards all His Father did to and for Him, He let God Almighty do what He liked with His life and never murmured. He never brought sympathy down to Himself, and never awakened self-pity.

Galatians 2:20 is the Scriptural expression of identification with the Lord Jesus Christ in such a way that my whole life is changed. My old destiny was getting wonderfully like the destiny of Satan – self-realization; now Paul say's it is no longer that destiny for me, it is Christ-identity in me. "The life I now live in the flesh, I live by the faith which is in the Son of God." The very faith that governed Jesus Christ now governs me. He is not talking about the elementary faith in Jesus,, but the very faith that was in Jesus. Paul says also, "Let this mind be in you which was also in Christ Jesus." There is only one kind of holiness, and that is the holiness of the Lord Jesus; only one kind of human nature, and that is the human nature of us all, and Jesus Christ by His identification can give me exactly the same disposition He had, and I have to habitually see that I work it out through my eyes, and ears, and mouth, and all the organs of my body and life in every detail. Paul had been identified with the death of Jesus Christ, and his whole life was invaded by a, new spirit. His connection was with a totally new realm, the mystical body of Christ. He had been baptized by one spirit into one body, and had no connection now with the body of sin. The body of sin is that mystical body which ultimately ends with Satan. The mystical body of Christ is ours by sanctification, we are made part and parcel of it. The term "invasion" is used because it gives the idea better than that of marriage. Our Lord's description in John 15 of the vine and the branches is a much more satisfactory one in every way than the marriage relationship. The picture from the vine and the branches is that every bit of life in the branch that is bearing fruit is from an invasion by the parent stem; and so with us, the whole life is drawn from the Lord Jesus, not only the spring and the motive of it, but the actual thinking and living and doing. That is the Apostle Paul's meaning when he talks about the "new man in Christ Jesus." After identification and sanctification, that is where the life is drawn from, "all my fountains are in Thee." And have you noticed that God will wither up every other spring you have? He will wither up your natural virtues, He will break up confidence in your own power, and He will wither up your confidence in every respect, in brain, in spirit and in heart and body, until you learn by practical experience that you have no right to draw your life from anything else than the tremendous reservoir of the resurrection life of Jesus Christ. Thank God if you are going through a drying-up experience!

Our Lord never patches up our natural virtues, He replaces the whole man on the inside, until the new man can shew himself in the new manners. God does not give new manners, we make our own; but we have to make them out of the new life. (Eph. 4:22-32.) Every detail of your physical life is to be absolutely under the control of the new disposition that God Almighty has planted in you through identification with the Lord Jesus, and you will no longer be allowed to murmur "can't." There is no. such a word in the Christian's vocabulary when rightly related to God. There is only one word, and that is "I can." Paul says in Philippians, "I can do all things through Christ which strengthened me," and watch the kind of things he could do, "I know how to be abased; I know how to be exalted; I know how to be empty; I know how to be full."

The manners refer to Christian character, and we are responsible for that. God works the alteration on the inside, and now Paul says, "Work out what God works in," and you will find that God will use the machinery of your circumstances when you are right with Him. He is not after satisfying you and glorifying you. He is after manifesting in your edition what His Son can do. Paul says that Jesus is going to be "admired in them that believe." This invasion of the life of Jesus Christ makes us sons and daughters of God. These are things that the angels desire to look into. It is as if they looked down on us and said of that woman, "How wonderfully like Jesus Christ she is, she did not use to be like that, but look at her now. "We know Jesus Christ did it, but we wonder how?" Or, "Look at that man, he is just like his Master, how did Jesus Christ do it?"

Thank God we are not going to be angels, we are going to be something tenfold better. By the full redemption of the Lord Jesus Christ, there is a time coming when our bodies will be in the image of God. The bodies of our humiliation are to be changed to "glorified bodies," and they are to bear the image of God just like our spirits.

CHAPTER V.

SOUL: THE ESSENCE, EXISTENCE, AND EXPRESSION.

1. THE TERM SOUL. (Generally.)
   (a) Applied to Men and Animals. Gen. 1: 20, 21, 24, 30.
   (b) Applied to Men, not Animals. Gen. 2: 7; 1 Cor. 15: 45.
   (c) Applied to Men Individually. Gen. 12: 13; 1 Sam. 18: 1.

N. B. – (1) Never applied to angels or to God. (Comp. 2 Cor. 4: 7.)
   (2) Never applied to plants. (See Job 14: 8, etc.)

2. THE TRUTH ABOUT THE SOUL.
(Specifically.)
   (a) And Spirit. Gen. 2: 7.
   (b) And Body. Jas. 2: 26.
   (c) And Personality. Isa. 29:24; Rom. 8:16.

N. B. – "The Spirit is the essential foundation of man; the soul his peculiar essential form; the body his essential manifestation."

We take first of all the soul as a term generally and then specifically. The next chapter will be "The Fundamental Powers" of the soul, which means the soul as it is influenced either by a degenerate intelligence, or by the Spirit of God, and we will deal also with the varied powers of the soul. Then "The Fleshly Presentation of the Soul" will be considered, that means as the soul manifests itself and expresses itself in the bodily life; and finally we take the "Past, Present and Future" of the soul, in which we deal with all the theses that have gathered round the doctrines of the soul, and are somewhat scriptural, but yet lead to conclusions most unscriptural.

The word "sour' in the Old Testament is mentioned about 460 times, meaning is "animal soul," and by animal soul, the soul that is present only in this order of beings. In the New Testament the word for soul is mentioned about fifty-seven times, with the same meaning. When the Bible mentions a thing over five hundred times it is quite time that Christians examined the teaching about it with care.

1. The Term Soul. (Generally.)

"We will take the term "soul" generally, used in three distinct ways. First, the term as applied to men and animals alike as distinct from all other creations; then the more particular use of the word as applied to men distinguished from animals; and then the third use of the term as applied to distinguish one man from another.

(a) (Gen. 1:20, 21, 24, 30.) The term "soul" here includes animals and men to distinguish them from every other form of creation.

(The Bible nowhere says that either angels or God have souls. Angels are never spoken of as having souls, because soul refers entirely to this order of creation, and angels belong to another order. The only way in which the soul of God is referred to is prophetically, in anticipation of the Incarnation. Our Lord emphatically had a soul, but of God and angels the term "soul" is not used.)

Then another thing, soul is never applied to plants. Although a plant has life, the Bible never speaks of it as having soul.

"For there is hope of a tree if it be cut down, that it will sprout again, and that the tender branch thereof will not cease. Though the root thereof wax old in the earth, and the stock thereof die in the ground; yet through the scent of water it will bud, and bring forth boughs like a plant. But man dieth and wasteth away, yea, man giveth up the ghost and where is he?" (Job 14:7-10.)

The distinction there is very clear; you can cut a piece from a plant and the "cut off" part will grow again; you can cut off a limb of an animal and plant it, but it will not grow, or you may cut off "your arm and that will not grow. The reason is that the plant has no soul, and the animal has. There is nothing said in the Bible about the immortality of an animal. The Bible does say that in the regenerated earth there will be animals, but the Bible nowhere says that these animals we see now are immortal and animal. The Bible does say that in the new earth there will be animals, but the Bible nowhere says that these animals we see now are immortal and when they (lie are raised again. "What is indicated is that the spirit of entire nature will be restored by God's mighty redemption, that everything that has been partaker of the curse through the fall will be restored by Jesus Christ through cremation and various ways; nothing will be lost; but nowhere does the Bible teach the immortality of animals.

(b) The term "soul" applied to men and not animals.

"And the Lord God formed man of the dust of the ground, and breathed into his nostrils the breath of life, and man became a living soul." (Gen. 2:7.)

"And so it is written, The first man Adam was made a living soul; the last Adam was made a quickening spirit." (1 Cor. 15:45.)

Now what is the soul? Something that is peculiar to men and animals, that angels do not have, that God has not, and that plants have not. Soul is the holder of spirit and body together. Man has soul, and brute has soul. What kind of spirit has a brute? If the soul is the holder of spirit and body together, then there must be a spirit in the brute, otherwise our statement about soul is wrong. There is certainly a spirit in the brute, and the Bible reveals that when the soul of an animal dies, its spirit "goeth down." The spirit of the brute is the spirit of entire nature, and when the brute dies that spirit goes back again into entire nature. What is the spirit of entire nature? A manifest creation of God. Now the spirit in man that holds soul together with his body is something entirely different from the spirit of a brute; it is the human spirit which God created when He breathed into man's nostrils the breath of life. God did not make man a little God, He breathed into his nostrils the spirit which became in man, man's distinct spirit.

Where does man's spirit go when he dies? "The spirit of the brute goeth downward, and the spirit of a man goeth upward." A number of secularists have told us that death is a beautiful "molecular disturbance," and that when we die we are distributed like the animal life into the gases and spirit of entire nature. The Bible does not say so, the Bible says that the spirit of a man goes back to God. That does not imply that man's spirit is absorbed back into God; it is the spirit goes back to God with all the characteristics for judgment or for praise. When we deal more narrowly with this subject later on, we shall find that the whole nature of a man's spirit, whether it be "sensual" or "spiritual," is to make itself expressed in soul. The whole effort is to try and express the spirit through the soul; that is, express it in what we understand as our ordinary physical life.

(c) The term "soul" applied to men individually.

"Say, I pray thee, thou art my sister, that it may be well with me for thy sake, and my soul shall live because of thee." (Gen. 12:13.)

"And it came to pass when he had made an end of speaking unto Saul, that the soul of Jonathan was knit with the soul of David, and Jonathan loved him as his own soul." (1 Sam. 18:1.)

These passages refer to the use of the term "soul," to the individual personal soul as distinct from every other soul. In popular language we speak of a person expressing "soul" in music, or literature, or art; or else we refer to him as being hard and mechanical and "soulless." It is this aspect of soul we are referring to. An individual soul cannot be divided or cut up. "When in the Scripture "demon possession" is referred to (see Luke 8:26 to 39) it is the body that is the location or habitation of the many other spirits besides the man's own soul. (Thought takes up no room, and soul partakes of the nature of thought, so that there is, literally speaking, no limit to the number of spirits a man's body may hold during demon possession.) The phrase "beautiful soul" or "mean soul" refers to this individual aspect of soul.

2. The Truth About the Soul. (Specifically.)

(a) What is the relationship between spirit and soul: where did the soul come from? Soul has no existence until spirit and body come together. It holds its existence in fee entirely by spirit, which statement is the needed opposite truth of what we have already stated, viz.: that soul holds spirit and body together. What is the spirit in a fallen man? (See 1 Cor. 2:11.) Let us approach this subject by making the distinction between "sensual" man and "spiritual" man. The spirit in a fallen or "sensual" man is his mind which has vast capacity for God, to whom, however, he is dead, and the spirit of a fallen man is imprisoned in the soul and degraded by the body. A sensual person may have marvelous ideas, and a wonderful intelligence, but the whole life may also be corrupt and "rotten." For instance, take Oscar Wilde, a more flagrant example of gross immorality would be difficult to find, yet Oscar Wilde could write that most amazing book called "De Profundis" in prison, after a life of unthinkable immorality, which book shows a wonderful grasp of our Lord and His teaching. The spirit in Oscar "Wilde is nothing more than an intellectual spirit that has no life in itself, nothing more than what the Hebrew calls it, a "spiritual capacity," and it is surely enslaved by the body through the soul. Instead of fallen man's intelligence being able to lift his body up, it is exactly the opposite; a fallen man's intelligence more and more severs his intellectual life from his bodily life and produces inner hypocrisy. Read the lives of certain poets and literary men and geniuses; the exception is the man who has a clean life as well as a good mind. You can never judge a man by his intellectual flights. You may get the most magnificent and inspiring diction from a man who is sunk lower than the beasts in moral living. He has a sensual spirit; that is, his soul instead of being able to allow his spirit to lift his body up, has dragged the man down and the man makes a divorce between his intellectual and practical life.

A "spiritual" man is quite different. Jesus Christ was a spiritual personality, because the Holy Spirit filled His spirit, and brought spirit, soul and body into perfect harmony with God. That is the meaning of the atonement in its full application to you and me, that Jesus Christ has power to grant us the Holy Spirit, and that Holy Spirit "has life in itself," and immediately that life is manifested in my soul, it wars against what I have been describing, and slowly and surely if the man will "mind" the Spirit of God, which fills his spirit and re-energizes it, he will find that Holy Spirit will lift his soul, and with his soul his body, into a totally new unity until that old divorce is annulled. In a spiritual personality the "mind of Christ' ' makes the material body of a man show the nature of Christ. The spirit of a man cannot do this, for it has not life in itself. Never judge a man by the fact that he has good ideas, or yourself by the fact that you have stirring visions of things. For instance, it is said that a man cannot teach the doctrine of entire sanctification unless he is entirely sanctified, but he can. The devil can teach entire sanctification when it pleases him. One of the most dangerous powers in your soul and mine is that very power. There is a "sensual" person and a "spiritual" person, and the "sensual" person is the one in whom the great divorce is discernible between mental conception and practical living. The whole solution of the problem is by receiving the Holy Spirit, not complimenting the Holy Spirit, not believing Him only; but receiving Him; because whatever is wrong in my soul or in my body the Holy Spirit has so energized my spirit that it is able to detect all those things that are wrong, and enables me to rectify them if I "mind" them. (This use of the term "mind" is the Scotch use, and means "remember to obey." It carries with it the other Scotch word "lippen," that is, trust.) "Mind" the Holy Spirit, "mind" His light, "mind." His convictions, "mind" His guidance, then slowly and surely the "sensual" personality will be turned into the "spiritual" one.

(b) The Soul and Body. "For as the soul without the spirit is dead, so faith without works is dead also." (Jas. 2:26.) The body has the earth as its ancestor. "The being of man plants its foot on the earth and the being of earth culminates in man, for both are destined to the fellowship of one history." That means what has been insisted on all through these studies, that the body is the chief glory of a man from God's standpoint. "But we have this treasure in earthen vessels, that the excellency of the power may be of God and not of us." (2 Cor. 4:7.) We have "this treasure," the treasure of God's Spirit being manifested in a human spirit. It cannot be manifested in angels, or in animals, or in plants. It is manifested in human earthen vessels. Do not make that mean that God is pouring contempt on the earthen vessels; it is the opposite. Jesus Christ took on Him the nature of the "earthen vessel" type, not of the angelic type. Of the earth, earthy, is man's glory, not his shame, and it is to the earth earthy that Jesus Christ's full regenerating work has its ultimate reach. Regenerated man's body and the earth on which he treads are to partake in the final restitution. Our soul's history cannot be furthered "in spite of our bodies," but because of our bodies. Nothing can enter the soul but through the senses; the way God enters into the soul is through the senses.

"The words that I speak unto you, they are spirit and they are life." Beware of the other type of mysticism, viz.: the quiet vision absorption; it is not presented in the Bible. On the physical side all the soul retains comes through its bodily senses, and when God's Spirit is finding its way into a man's soul, again the senses are acquainted with it. "The Holy Spirit will glorify Me," says our Lord. "Where? In my imagination, in my heart, that is, in and through the intangible part of my body. And again, "He will bring to your remembrance what I have said." How can this be done saving by our material body in brain memory? Beware of all inward impressions. Beware of all instincts that you cannot curb by the wisdom that is taught by God's Book. If you begin to take every impression as a call of the Spirit of God, you will end in hallucinations. (See 2 Thess. 2: 10-12.) Test every such movement by the tests Jesus Christ has given, and they are all tangible, sensible tests. The only way you can test men is, as Jesus teaches, "by their fruit." You say that the fruit of the Spirit has altogether to do with the spiritual, but the spiritual in the Bible must show itself in the concrete physical body. God knows no divorce whatever between the three aspects of a man's nature, spirit, soul and body. They must be at one, and He says they are either at one in damnation, or one in salvation, and if a man has not the Spirit of God energizing his spirit, he will come more and more to be judged by the judgment that is to be passed on his bodily life. Beware of the people who teach that a man's body may sin, but his soul does not. No such distinctions and refinements are taught in God's Word. The three go together in God's judgment, and if a man is not enlivened by the Spirit of God, his intelligence has no power to lift him. People cannot lift themselves by ideas, by intelligent notions, by knowledge. That is why intelligence from God's standpoint is never first spiritual. "If any man will know My doctrine," says Jesus, "let him do the will." Performance of the will before perception of the doctrine always in spiritual matters. Immediately you receive the Holy Spirit and get energized by God, you will find your bodies the first place of attack for the enemy, because the body has been the center before for ruling the soul, and dividing it from intelligent standards, and the body is the last "stake" of Satan. It is the battleground, the "margin of the battle" for you and me. The presentation of such facts produces confusion until it is understood; health simply means the perfect balance of my body to the outside circumstances and the outside world; if anything upsets that balance, I become diseased. The Spirit of God will upset that balance; immediately the Spirit of God comes into my soul through my spirit, the balance is upset, and disturbance – morally, physically and spiritually – occurs. Jesus Christ said, "I did not come to send peace, but a sword," and what balance will He give back? The old? No! You can never get the same old balance of health back again; you have to get a new balance of holiness, which is not only the balance of my bodily life, but the balance of my disposition with God's law, which is holiness. You will find the "choppy waters" come there, and the "choppy waters" show themselves physically. So many people seem to misunderstand why it is that their bodies are attacked now that they are spiritual in a way they never were attacked when they were not spiritual. In connection with this subject of the soul, we shall have to deal later with one or two very important subjects, viz.: the difference between demoniacal sickness and natural sickness. The Bible has a lot to say about both of them. The Bible throws the only revelation light there is on your physical condition, and the Bible is the only book that throws light on our soul condition, and the Bible is the only book that throws light on our spiritual condition. Physical effects, like smelling, seeing, etc., are not used as methaphors only in the Bible; they are identified with the nature of the soul's life, and this explains what people call the vulgar teaching of the Bible.

God has safeguarded us in every way. Spiritualistic people have committed the great crime; they have pushed down God's barriers, and come in contact with forces they never can control. And on the other hand, the Spirit of God can do through me anything He chooses if I give myself over to Jesus Christ and am ruled by His Spirit. "I beseech you, brethren, present your bodies a living sacrifice,"' and bodies means "faculties" as well. "Why should we expect God to deal with less than the devil deals with? A good man is a flesh and blood good man; he is not an impression. The body is the "vessel" of the soul, enabling the soul to turn her inward life into an outward one.

CHAPTER VI.

SOUL: THE ESSENCE, EXISTENCE, AND EXPRESSION. FUNDAMENTAL POWERS OF THE SOUL.

1. CONTRACTION.
   (a) FIRST POWER. Self-comprehending. Deut. 13:7.
   (b) SECOND POWER. Stretching Beyond Itself. Ps. 27: 12.

2. EXPANSION.
   (c) THIRD POWER. Self -living. Job 2: 6; John 10: 11.
   (d) FOURTH POWER. Spirit-penetrated. Isa. 26: 9.

3. ROTATION.
   (e) FIFTH POWER. Stirred Sensually or Spiritually. Ex 23: 9* 1 Pet. 2: 11.
   (f) SIXTH POWER. Speaking the Spirit's Thoughts. Gen. 41: 40.
   (g) SEVENTH POWER. Sum Total in Unity. Jer. 38: 16.

"We mean by "fundamental," the powers that work in the interior of the soul. The existence of the soul has its origin in the spirit, and in its struggle to realize itself. This is the counterpart of the statement made in the last chapter, viz.: that the soul is the holder of the body and spirit together.

By **Contraction**, we mean that the soul is a substance, so to speak, that has power to contract into itself. By Expansion, we mean that the soul has power to strive away from itself, reaching beyond itself, and by Rotation, we mean that the soul has the power of expressing itself by the restlessness of becoming.

(This mechanical division is merely an arbitrary way of presenting a complex truth. All man's scientific laws and regulations are simply the mental work, attempting to explain observed facts. All scientific laws exist in men's heads. It is dangerous and wrong to talk about the law of gravitation as if it were a thing. The law of gravitation is the name given by scientific men in explanation of certain observed facts, and to say that when Jesus Christ walked on the sea or ascended, He "broke the law of gravitation," is a misstatement. He brought in, so to speak, a new series of facts which the so-called law of gravitation could not account for. This view-point will facilitate matters when made familiar to the mind of the student.)

The First Power is called (a) Self -Comprehending: (Deut. 13:6, 7; 1 Sam. 18:1.) The description indicated is the power to comprehend itself as an individual separate from every other. Watch your own experience, and you will at once recognize this soul power. "When a, child begins to be "self-conscious," it is this power that is awakening, the power to contract into itself and to realize that it is different from its father and mother and from all other children, and the tendency increases to shut the life up to itself. This power begins to show itself in a feeling of isolation and separation, and it alternates between pride and shyness. Self-consciousness drags down the harmony of the soul. The more you meditate on that line, the more you will find it revealed in God's Book and in your own life. In some people it lasts a long time; some never get beyond the first manifestation of the power of their own soul life, viz., they realize they have a. power to contract into themselves, a power to be different from everybody else, but they do not have the power to expand, to realize that they can come in contact with other souls -and need not be afraid or timid.

That is this first power in a natural soul; but take it in the spiritual. I mean by spiritual, a soul "born again" of the Spirit of God. How does this first power of the soul express itself? This power of selfcomprehension in a soul that is born again of the Spirit of God shows itself in opposition to sinfulness. "Watch the "swing of the pendulum," as it were, in your own life, and in the life of anybody who is newly born again of the Spirit of God; it goes to the most extreme limit, which corresponds with the other extreme limit it lived in when it was in the "world." For instance, if the soul was given to finery and dress in the world, it will go to exactly the opposite extreme in its first introduction to the new life. This is the first recognizable power an individual soul has.

The Second Power (b) is called "Stretching Beyond Itself." (Psa. 27:12.) You will find that this aspect of the soul always enables the soul first to find the forces and people that are different to it. It does not find the things in favor with it, but exactly the opposite. The things outside are enemies, and the powers outside seem to be against it. (Prov. 23:2.) Then that power of the soul begins to realize that it can do pretty well what it likes with its body – a dangerous moment in a human life. (Eph. 6: 6.) Or again, this second power realizes itself in a way that makes a soul able to know it can deceive everybody else. (Col. 3:23.)

The person is conscious of things against it; other souls seem to be in opposition fro it. The boy who is self-conscious always first realizes that every other, boy is his natural enemy; he is suspicious of every boy who wants to make himself his friend. With that power comes the power to realize that I have a body, and also with it comes the knowledge that I can do what I like with my body. There is no restriction at all when that power first dawns: I can satisfy my bodily appetites as I choose. That is the dangerous moment in a soul's life. It enables me to know that I can cunningly deceive everybody else. If I am a servant, I can easily defraud my master or mistress; if I am a business man, I can easily defraud the public, and the whole question of this power of the soul is worked out to its complete issue in the life of the world.

This second power of the soul in a spiritual nature shows itself in opposition to sinful craving. Jesus Christ says, in effect: "If you are My disciples, you will be defrauded easily, but you will not allow yourself to be defrauded from the simplicity that is in the Gospel." Knowledge of evil broadens a man's mind, makes him tolerant, but paralyzes action. The knowledge of good broadens a man's mind, and makes him intolerant of all sin, and shows itself in intense activity. A bad man, an evil-minded man, may be amazingly tolerant of everything and every one, no matter whether they are good or bad, Christian or not, and his action is paralyzed entirely; he is tolerant of everything, – of the devil, the flesh, the world, sin and everything else. A soul born again of God shows itself at once in intolerance. Jesus Christ never tolerated sin for one moment, and when His nature gets its way in my soul, the same intolerance is shown, and it manifests itself not in eye-service. If I am a servant, I won't serve my mistress or master with this cunning power of my soul, realizing I have power to deceive; but I will use this power of my soul to show that I belong to Jesus Christ. And I won't use this power of my soul to do what I like with my body. This power of the soul will show itself in a spiritual soul in intense opposition to all sinful cravings. When a soul is born again of the Spirit of God, it does everything, from sweeping a room to preaching the Gospel, from cleaning streets to governing a nation, for the glory of God. The whole mainspring of the soul's life is altered, and this power manifests itself in stretching beyond itself in this peculiar manifestation.

2. Expansion.

The Third Power (c) is Self -living. (Job 2: 6; John 10: These two passages refer to the one power in a man that neither God nor the devil can touch without the man's sanction. The devil has power up to a certain point, but he cannot touch my life (see Job), and whenever Jesus Christ presents the Gospel of God to a soul, it is always on the line of "Are you willing!" No coercion. This is at once the most fearful and the most glorious power in a human soul. It can withstand the devil successfully, and it can withstand God quite as successfully. This self-living power is the human spirit, which is as immortal as God's Spirit, whether the human spirit be good spirit or bad spirit; it is as immortal as God, and as indestructible. You will find this is the power in a soul that can make itself on a par with God. It is the very essence of Satan, and the power that can make a man either a compeer of the devil or a compeer of the Lord is the most tremendous and terrible power in the soul. Jesus Christ, speaking of His own incarnation, refers to this self-living power. He says, "I lay down My life of Myself; no man taketh it from Me." God has so constituted us that there must be a free willingness on our part.

How does this power show itself when the soul is born again of the Spirit of God, lifted into the domain our Lord lives in? This power shows itself in opposition to sinful passionateness. Passionateness simply means something that carries everything before it. The prince of this world is intense, and the Spirit of God is intense. When Paul talks about the two working in a man's soul, he mentions the intensity in the word "lust." The Spirit lusteth, intensely, passionately desires the whole soul and life and body for God; and the mind of the flesh intensely and passionately longs for the whole soul and life and body back again to the service of the world. The Bible points out that passionateness in the spiritual realm means something that overcomes every obstacle. When the writer to the Hebrews talks about "Christian perfection," he talks about this very thing, this overwhelming passion that carries the soul right on to all God has for it. "Be filled with the Spirit," this is the key word of life. The way Jesus Christ indicates that we overcome the world is not by passionlessness, not only by the patience of exhaustion, but by passion, by the passion of an intense and allconsuming love to God. This is the characteristic in a born-again soul – opposition to every sinful passionateness. Do insist in your own mind on this thing, that God does not work in vague, gentle impressions when He begins these works in a human soul; but in violent oppositions that rend and tear the soul life from what it was, and make it instead of being a place of harmonious happiness, exactly the opposite for a season. You find this kind of experience in every one of us when we are going on with God. "When we are first introduced to the life of God, there is always that violent opposition to everything that used to be prevalent, and it is not a mistake; it is what God intends, because it is the force of a totally new life.

The Fourth Power (d) is Spirit Penetration. (Isa. 26:9; Jude 19.) I mean by "spirit penetration" the spiritual power in man which, struggles to express itself in soul. The spirit of man, in an unregenerate nature, is the power of mind not energized by the Holy Spirit and having no life "in itself.?" It proves utterly futile in lifting the body, and produces a great divorce between the ideal and real. Every type and kind of intellectual excellence is a snare of Satan unless the spirit of the man has been renewed by the incoming of the Spirit of God. A man's intellect may give him noble ideas and power to express them through his soul in language, but it has no power to carry them out in action. You will find the charge of idolatry is very apt here. For instance, we are apt to ridicule, or pass over with a smile, the descriptions given of idolatry in, say the Book of Isaiah, where the writer refers to a tree being taken, one part of it being used to cook the man's food, and the other part, carved into an idol, to which the man bows, and worships; yet this is exactly what men do with their ideas. The intellect forms ideas for guiding its physical life, and then takes other ideas and worships them as God, and if a man has made his own ideas his god, he is greater than his own god. This is not such a terrible power, perhaps, as the third power of the soul, but it is a power that works havoc, unless the soul is right with God. It is the power that produces internal hypocrisy, the power that makes me able to think good thoughts while I live a bad life, unconvicted.

How does this power show itself in "those who are born again of the Spirit of God? This power shows itself in opposition to secularity. Take your own experience, those of you who are spiritual – spiritual in the Bible sense, identified with the Lord Jesus Christ in a practical way – can you ever make a distinction now between secular and sacred? It is all sacred; but in the first beginnings of this power you will always find the line drawn clearly and strongly between what men call "secular" and what they call "sacred." Jesus Christ had no division of secular and sacred in His life, but when this power begins with us it always manifests itself in that line of cleavage. There are certain things I won't do; certain things I won't look at; certain things I won't eat; certain hours I won't sleep. None of it is wrong, it is the first beginnings of this power of the Spirit of God in a soul, utilizing the powers of the soul for God; but as the soul goes on, it gets to a full-orbed condition where it manifests itself as it did in the life of Jesus and all is sacred. If you obey the Spirit of God, and practice through your physical life what God has put in your heart by His Spirit, when the crisis comes you will find your nature will "stand by you." So many people misunderstand why they fall. It comes from this condition – people say, "Now I have received the grace of God, I am all right." Paul says, "Do not receive the grace of God in vain," and these people do not go practicing day by day, and week by week, working out what "God has worked in," and when a crisis comes, God's grace is there all right enough, but their nature is not; their nature has not been brought into practice, and the consequence is the nature does not "stand by" them, and down they go, and they blame God. You must bring the bodily life into practice, steadily, day by day, and hour by hour, and moment by moment; then when the crisis comes you will find not only God's grace, but your own nature will "stand by" you, and the crisis is passed over without any disaster at all, but exactly the opposite, in building up the soul into a stronger attitude towards God.

3. Rotation.

The Fifth Power (e), Stirred Sensually or Spiritually. (Ex. 23:9; 1 Pet. 2:11.) Remember the soul is manifested itself as the spirit struggles to make itself expressed. Exodus 23:1-9 is a magnificent passage, and the more you read it the more magnificent you will find it to be. It is intensely, movingly practical in every detail, and there this power of the soul is clearly recognizable. It fits itself on with the second power, viz., the power every one of us has to deceive everybody else, to do cunning things, to defraud, and to utilize other people for our own ends; and the warning is, be careful you are not stirred in your soul by the wrong spirit. 1 Peter 2:11 is the corresponding passage. If the soul can be stirred by its own cunning, the cunning of a man's own nature on the inside, it can be stirred by vileness and abominable sensuality through the senses.

How does this power show itself in a regenerated soul? It shows itself in opposition to worldly bondage. You will find in your own experience, and in everybody else's experience that is recorded, that when your life is going on on God's line, God is putting the fear of you on those who are on the outside, because you have a scorn against worldly bondages. The Spirit of God in you will not allow you to bow your neck to any yoke but the yoke of the Lord Jesus Christ. You will see instantly when you stand on this platform of God's grace that the bondage is in the world. The "etiquettes" and standards in the world are absolute and terrible bondages, and those who live in them are abject slaves, and yet the extraordinary thing is that when the worldling sees anybody emancipated, under the yoke of the Lord Jesus Christ, he says "they are in bondage," whereas exactly the opposite is true. True liberty only exists when the soul has gotten this holy scorn in it, "I will not bow my neck to any yoke but the yoke of the Lord Jesus Christ." He was meek to all His Father did, but intolerant to all the devil did. He would not suffer compromise with the devil in any shape or form. This power of the soul, when the soul is born again, manifests itself in opposition to all and every worldly bondage.

The Sixth Power (f), is Speaking the Spirit's Thoughts. (Gen. 41:40.) We are now dealing with Rotation, the restlessness of becoming. This is how all these powers are going to manifest themselves in a fully matured soul. That picture in Genesis is the picture of a soul right with God, but remember that the corresponding picture is true. A man in whom all these powers of the soul are developing will get to a place where he shows literally, not only with his mouth, but with his eyes and every power of his body, who it is that sits on the throne of his life. If it is the "prince of this world," the man is prime minister under the devil, of his own body. When the full power of the soul is developed I am obliged to carry out the behests of the ruling monarch.

When a soul is born again of the Spirit of God, how does this power show itself? It shows itself in opposition to worldly thoughts and customs. Take Pharaoh in Genesis 41:40 as a picture of Jesus Christ, "Only in the throne will I be greater than thou." The soul that is born again of God, and has been walking on with God, identified with Jesus Christ in practical sanctification, and has the full powers of the soul developed and manifested, that soul is prime minister of his own body under Jesus Christ's dominion. That is the ideal distinctly, and not an ideal only, but an ideal that Jesus Christ expects us to carry out, all the powers of the soul working in an express personality through my body, revealing the ruler to be the Lord Jesus Christ.

We now come to the Last Power (g), Sum Total in Unity. (Jer. 38:18.) The sum total is a perfect unity, either a perfect unity of badness, or a perfect unity of goodness. (Gen. 46:26.) The word "sour' there refers to the full maturity of the powers manifested in the bodily life. That is the description of a fullgrown man, whether he is a bad man or a good man, and when a soul gets into full maturity of expression, the chances are he will never alter. In Jeremiah 38:16 the soul is mentioned in the same way. It is not the soul in its beginnings, in its chaotic state; it is the soul manifested, the soul absolutely mastered by the ruling spirit and expressing itself through the body.

How does this perfection of soul life show itself in a born-again man, a man who is thoroughly and perfectly living the life God wants him to live? It shows itself in opposition to all other powers, and manifests itself in its bodily life in the spirit of wisdom which comes from above. It literally means the uncrushable loveliness of a soul manifesting God's rule, all its powers now in harmony. This is not in Heaven; this is on the earth. This is not mental perfection, it is not bodily perfection; it is the perfection of a sours attitude when all the powers of that soul are under the control of the Spirit of God. You will find now all the "corners" are chipped away, all the extreme swinging of the pendulum regulated, all the chaotic turmoil has become ordered, and the soul is now "manifesting the life of the Lord Jesus in its mortal flesh."

In way of revision, you will find these powers of the soul show themselves more or less in every one of us. For instance, you never think of judging a boy or girl by the same standards of judgment that you pass on them when they are matured, because neither a boy nor a girl is in full grip of a character. But once let a soul get matured, and the character manifested meets a severe judgment; there is no excuse made for it now; its powers are consolidated, and the wrong it does is not the wrong of an impulse, it is the wrong of a "dead set." When the soul is consolidated and right with God, you find exactly the opposite. The whole character manifests something that has a strong family likeness to Jesus Christ. There is certainly a chaotic attitude in Christian experience. Read the Apostle Paul's earnest, almost motherlike solicitation over young converts; he almost seems to "croon" (to use an old Scotch word) and agonize in heart over the young converts, because of the chaotic state of their souls, and you will find that Jesus Christ commissioned Peter, and the other disciples through Peter, to "feed My lambs. "

CHAPTER VII.

SOUL: THE ESSENCE, EXISTENCE, AND EXPRESSION.
FLESHLY PRESENTATION OF THE SOUL

1. IN EMBRYO.
    (a) Before Consciousness. Ps. 139: 15.
    (b) Breath Consciousness. Gen. 2:7; Isa. 2: 22.
    (c) Blood Circulation. Gen. 9: 4; Lev. 17: 10, 14.

2. IN EVOLUTION.
    (d) "Hub" of Life. Prov. 4:23.
    (e) " Hubbub" of Life.
    (1) Sense of Seeing. Ps. 119: 37.
    (2) Sense of Hearing. Job 12: 11.
    (3) Sense of Tasting. Ps. 119: 103.
    (4) Sense of Smelling. Gen. 8: 21; 2 Cor. 2: 14, 16.
    (5) Sense of Touching. Acts 17:27; 1 John 1:1.

3. IN EXPRESSION.
    (f) Hilarity of Life. Eccl. 11:9, 11; Luke 6:45.
    (g) Himself. Judg. 8: 18; Luke 2: 40, 52; Eph. 4: 13.

We do not mean what the Apostle Paul meant when he used the word "fleshly" in his Epistles; we are using the word to mean this natural body.

The subject is divided under three headings: In Embryo, in Evolution, and in Expression. In Embryo, means in the beginning; Evolution means growth, growth of the human soul; (evolution is a fact both scientific and Scriptural, if by that word is meant that there is such a thing as growth in every; species, but not from one species into another. For instance, there is growth in a plant, there is growth in an animal, and there is growth in a man, and that is the only way we are using the word.) The last division simply means the Expression of my soul in, and through, my body.

1. In Embryo.

(a) Before Consciousness, (b) Breath Consciousness, and (c) Blood Circulation. (Hos. 12:3; Gen. 25:22; Luke 1:41.) In the very beginning of human life, body, soul and spirit are together. (Psa. 139: 15.) Modern tendencies of thought which are doing great havoc, indicate that a child has not a soul until it is born into this world. The Bible says that body, soul and spirit develop together. This may not appear to the majority of us as being of any importance, but it will soon, if you are going to come in contact with the views that are abroad to-day, even among some who call themselves Christians, but who are really wolves among the sheep, and whose teachings come from the bottomless pit.

(b) Breath Consciousness. (Gen. 2:7; Isa. 2:22.) In a multitude of verses in the Bible, the soul life and the breath of the body are identified. You will find the Biblje teaches that it is not the body that breathes, but the soul. The body did not breathe in the beginning, before God breathed into man's nostrils the breath of life, so as far as conscious soul life is concerned, it depends on our breathing, and you will find that all through God's Book the soul life is connected with the breathing, in fact it is incorporated into everybody's idea of life that when breath is suspended life is gone, "the soul is departed" is the popular phrase.

Then take the next (c) Blood Circulation. (Gen. 9: 4; Lev. 17: 10-14.) The whole soul is connected in the Bible and identified with breath and blood, two fleshly, physical things. In Genesis 9:4 blood and soul are alternate terms, they are identified entirely, and the verses that go to prove this in God's Book are innumerable. When the blood is spilt, the soul is gone; when the breath is taken, the soul is gone. The whole life of a man, physically, consists in his breath and in his blood. The soul, in working itself into the blood, never fails to impart to it the peculiar character of its own life. This psychologically is brought out very clearly by our Lord's statement in John 6, "Unless ye eat My flesh and drink My blood, ye have no life in you." The ruling disposition of the soul will show itself in the blood, the physical blood. In all our languages, and meanings, and statements, we speak about good or bad, merciful or tender, hot or cold blood. This is all based on Scriptural teaching, and Jesus Christ's teaching reveals that the fact that men are His disciples is shown in the blood, the physical life. The old soul tyranny and disposition, the old selfish determination to seek my own ends, manifests itself in my body, through my blood, and when that disposition of soul is altered it shows itself at once in the blood also. Instead of the old tempers and the old passions being manifested in my physical blood, the good temper reveals itself. It never does to remove Jesus Christ's spiritual teaching into the domain of the inane and vague, it must come right down where the devil works, and as the devil does not work in vagueness, but through flesh and blood, neither does the Lord, and the characteristics of the soul for better or for worse are shown in the blood. The first fundamental reference in the verse, "Without shedding of blood, there is no remission of sins," is unquestionably to our Lord, yet it has a direct reference to ourselves. Do we begin to know what the Bible means by the "blood of Jesus Christ"? Blood and life are absolutely inseparable. The two experimental statements of salvation and sanctification are never separated as we separate them; they are separable in experience, but God's Book always speaks in terms of entire sanctification when it talks of being "in Christ." "Whenever Paul deals with personal experience he begins to show where people have gone wrong. When we refer to the blood of Jesus Christ, we are apt to look upon it as a kind of magic-working thing, instead of its being an impartation to us of the very life of the Lord Jesus Christ. The whole meaning of being "born again" and identified with the death of the Lord Jesus Christ, and with His life, is that His blood may flow through my mortal body. Literally then, the tempers, and the affections, and the dispositions, that were manifested in the life of the Lord will now be manifested in some degree. Our present day "wise talk" is to push all the teaching of Jesus Christ into something that is remote; yet the New Testament drives its teachings straight down to the essential necessity of physical expression of spiritual life, that just as bad soul life shows itself in the body, the good soul life shows itself there too. There are always two sides to Jesus Christ's atonement in my life – not only His life for me, but His life in me for my own; no Christ for me if I do not have Christ in me. All through, there is this strenuous, glorious practicing in my bodily life, the changes which God has wrought in my soul through His Spirit, and the only test that I am in earnest is that I "work out what He works in." Let us apply this truth to ourselves, and you will find in practical experience this, that God does alter passions, God does alter nerves, God does alter breathing, God does alter tempers, God alters every physical thing the devil has used, God alters every physical thing a human being can use, and we can use these bodies, as Paul says, as slaves to the new disposition. We can make our eyes, and ears, and every one of our bodily organs express, as slaves, the altered disposition of our soul. Remember, then, that blood is the manifestation of the soul life, and you will find all through God's Book that God applies moral characteristics to the blood – "innocent blood," "guilty blood" – that rerefers to the soul, and the soul life must show itself in this physical connection.

2. In Evolution.

(d) The "Hub of Life." (Prov. 4:23.) The "hub" literally means the center of the wheel, and the center of my soul life, my personal life and my spirit life, is mentioned in Proverbs 4: 23. We will deal with this fully when we come to the chapters on " Heart."

The Bible has placed in the heart everything that the modern psychologist puts in the "head."

(e) "Hubbub of Life. " By "hubbub " is meant exactly what the word says, a tremendous confusion. This confusion in the soul life is brought about by the exercise of our senses. "In the Bible, psychological terms are not merely metaphors, but reflect the organic condition of the soul." The body makes itself inward by means of the soul, and the spirit makes itself outward by means of the soul. The soul is the binder of these two together. There is not one part of the human body left out in God's Book; every part, inside and outside, physically, is dealt with and made to have either a direct connection with sin, or a direct connection with holiness. That is not an accident, it is part of the Divine revelation. The senses of sight, hearing, smelling, tasting, and touching, to the majority of us do not seem to have any meaning whatever spiritually; but in the Bible they have. In the Bible they are dealt with in anything but a slight manner; they are dealt with as being expressions of your soul life. The Bible teaches that every part of man's physical life, inside and out, is either closely connected with sin or with salvation and anything that sin can put wrong, Jesus Christ can put right. "We are dealing with soul as it expresses itself through the body. The organs of the body are not used as pictures, but as indicators of the state of the spiritual life. We mentioned before, in connection with breathing, that the internal part of a man's nature is affected by his spiritual connection. If his spiritual connections are not right with God, his bodily condition will follow, sooner or later, the disorganization. It is proved over and over again in mental diseases. In most insane persons a bodily organ is seriously affected, and the old method of dealing with insanity was to try and get that organ healed. The modern method is simply to leave the organ alone as far as trying to get that right, and concentrate on the brain. "When the mind is right, the disease in the organ goes.

Take first of all (1), the sense of seeing. (Psa. 119:37.) That is not a figure of speech; it is the literal things we look at. How am I going to have those things, called my eyes, kept from beholding vanity? By having the disposition of my soul altered. God controls the whole thing, and you find that you can control it too, when once He gives you the start. That is the marvelous impetus of the salvation of Jesus Christ. Our eyes record to the brain what they look at, but our disposition makes our eyes look at what it wants to look at, and soon it will pay no attention to anything else. "When your disposition is right, you may place the eyes, literally the body, where you may, and the disposition will guard what it records. So this is not a figure of speech; it is a literal experience. God does »alter the desire to look at the things we used to, and we find that we can guard our eyes, because He has altered the disposition of the soul life.

Then take (2), hearing. (Job 12:11.) Jesus Christ Himself continually refers to hearing. "He that hath ears to hear, let him hear." We always say He means the ears of our heart, but that is very misguiding. He means these physical ears which are trained by the disposition of your soul life. For instance, God spoke to Jesus once, and the people said it thundered. Jesus did not think it thundered. His ears were trained, by the disposition of His soul, to know His Father's voice. You can elaborate that endlessly for yourself all through God's Book. I will always hear what I listen for, and my disposition determines what I listen for, just as the ruling disposition of the soul either keeps the eyes from beholding vanity, or makes them behold nothing else. When Jesus alters your disposition, He gives you the power to see things as He sees them, and to hear as He hears. A telegraph operator does not hear the ticking of the machine which we do. "Why? The ears are trained; the disposition detects the message; we cannot; we detect the jingle and the tapping of the machine and make nothing of it. When God speaks, some people say, "Thank God, I heard His voice!" How did they hear it? The disposition of the soul enabled the ears to hear something that the soul interpreted at once. Isaiah 55:1, "Who hath believed our report?" That literally means, "Who hath believed the things we are talking about, to whom is the arm of the Lord revealed?" You have a disposition of soul that can discern the "arm of the Lord," or you are just like the beasts of the field who take things as they happen, and nothing more. The Psalmist said, "O Lord, I am even as a brute before you." I live without any spiritual intelligence. The disposition of my soul determines what I see, and the disposition of my soul determines what I hear.

(3), Tasting. (Psa. 119:103.) We are getting still more and more remote, and difficult to understand, from our ordinary unspiritual experiences because we have divorced entirely, tasting and smelling, seeing and hearing, and touching, from spiritual conditions, because the majority of Christian workers have never been trained in what the Bible has to say about ourselves. It can be proved over and over again, not only in personal experience, but all through God's Book, that He does alter the tastes. Not mental tastes merely but taste in physical things. He alters the physical taste for foods and drinks, but something far more practical than that, the blessing of God on our soul life gives us the sensible feeling akin to taste, or akin to sight, or akin to hearing.

(4), Smelling. (Gen. 8:21; 2 Cor. 2:14-16.) The Bible has more to say about the sense of smell than any other, and it is the only sense we make nothing of. This sense of smell to the majority of us has only the meaning, viz., an olfactory nerve that makes me conscious of pleasant things, or exactly the opposite; but the Bible deals with the sense of smell in another way. Read this quotation from a book written by Helen Keller, entitled "The World I Live In," the chapter she calls "Smell, the Fallen Angel." Remember, she writes as one who cannot see, nor hear, nor speak.

"For some inexplicable reason the sense of smell does not hold the high position it deserves among its sisters. There is something of the fallen angel about it. "When it woos us with woodland scents and beguiles us with the fragrance of lovely gardens, it is admitted frankly to our discourse. But when it gives us warning of something noxious in our vicinity, it is treated as if the demon had the upper hand of the angel, and is relegated to outer darkness, punished for its faithful service. It is most difficult to keep the true significance of words when one discusses the prejudices of mankind, and I find it hard to give an account of odor-perceptions which shall at once be dignified and truthful.

"In my experience, smell is most important, and I find that there is high authority for the nobility of the sense which we have neglected and disparaged. It is recorded that the Lord commanded that incense be burnt before Him continually with a sweet savor. I doubt if there is any sensation arising from sight more delightful than the odors which filter through sun-warmed, wind-tossed branches, or the tide of scents which swells, subsides, rises again wave on wave, filling the wide world with invisible sweetness. A whiff of the universe makes us dream of worlds we have never seen, recalls in a flash entire epochs of our dearest experiences. I never smell daisies without living over again the ecstatic mornings that my teacher and I spent wandering in the fields, while I learned new words and the names of things. Smell is a potent wizard that transports us across a thousand miles and all the years we have lived. The odor of fruits wafts me to my Southern home, to my childish frolics in the peach orchard. Other odors, instantaneous and fleeting, cause my heart to dilate joyously or contract with remembered grief. Even as I think of smells, my nose is full of scents that start awake sweet memories of summers gone and ripening grain-fields far away."

* Helen Keller's sense of smell takes the place of sight. That is a case which brings the Bible idea more home to us. Let this subject be revised in all our Bible study and enable us to see whether we are leaving whole tracts of our sense-life indifferently, not understanding that we can develop and cultivate eyes, and nose, and mouth, and ears, and every organ of the body to manifest the disposition Jesus Christ has put in us. Not one that has been disorganized, but can be reorganized; not only these senses that we are dealing with, but the senses we cannot deal with, every

one of them, internal and external, is mentioned in God's Book, and is either regulated by the Spirit of God, or by the spirit of Satan. Paul, when he refers to lust, never places it in the body; he places it in the disposition of the soul. "Let not sin reign in your mortal bodies, that ye should obey it in the lusts thereof." Jesus Christ had a fleshly body like I have, but lust resides in the ruling disposition of the body, and when God changes that ruling disposition, the same body that was used as the instrument of sin to work all manner of uncleanness and unrighteousness, is now used as the slave of the new disposition. Not a different body; the same body, but a new disposition.

* The most fascinating and literary of such unscriptural peculations is found in "The Child of the Dawn" by A. C. Benson.

Now last, take (5), the sense of touch. (Acts 17:27; 1 John 1:1.) There the reference is not to a mental feeling, but to real, downright bodily feeling. The disciples had felt God incarnate in Jesus Christ. That is where the issue is so strong between Unitarian teaching and the New Testament teaching, and you will find that God does not ignore feeling. God does not ignore the sense of touch, He elevates it. The first effort of the soul, with its new disposition, towards bringing the body into harmony is a dark effort of faith. It has not yet gotten the body under way, therefore feeling has to be discounted. When the new disposition from God has entered the soul, it takes its first steps in the dark of faith, without feeling. But immediately it has gained control, all these bodily organs are brought into physical harmony with the ruling disposition.

3. In Expression.

(f) "Hilarity of Life." (Eccl. 11:9; Luke 6: 45.) Both these passages have reference to the full physical hilarity of life. Remember, a bad man whose life is bad has a hilariously happy time, and a good man whose life is right has a good and hilarious time.

All in between are diseased and more or less sick, there is something wrong somewhere: but the healthy pagan and the healthy saint are the two that are described all through God's Book as hilarious. The New Testament and especially the apostle Paul is intense on this hilarity of life. Enthusiasm has the idea – intoxicated with the life of God. Watch human nature. If men do not get thrillings in the right way, they will get them in the wrong way. If they do not get thrilled by the Spirit of God, they will try to get thrilled with strong drink. "Be not drunk with wine, wherein is excess," says Paul, "but be filled with the Spirit." We have no business to be spiritually half dead, to hang like clogs on God's plan; we have no business to be sickly unless it is only a preparatory stage for something better, unless God is nursing us through some spiritual illness; but if it is the main characteristic of life, there is something wrong somewhere. Psalm 73 describes the bad man as having all that heart can desire; this is the expression of the soul satisfaction without God; yet in another Psalm, the Psalmist says his "bones delight themselves in marrow and fatness." He is talking about the physical bones, which are affected amazingly by the condition of the soul life. Luke 11 gives a description of the bad man: "When the strong man armed guardeth his palace, his goods are in peace." The context there refers to the prince of this world, when Satan guards this world, his goods – the souls of men – are in peace; they 'are quite happy, quite hilarious and full of life. One of the most misleading statements to make is that worldlings have not a happy time; they have a thoroughly happy time. The point is that their happiness is on the wrong level, and when they come across Jesus Christ, who is the enemy of all that happiness, they experience annoyance. People have to be persuaded that Jesus Christ has a higher style of life for them, otherwise they feel they had better not have come across Him. When a worldly person who is happy, moral, upright, cornea in contact with Jesus Christ, who will destroy the whole thing, and put him, and his happiness and peace, on a different level, he has to be persuaded that He is a Being worthy to do it, and instead of the Gospel being attractive, it is the opposite. Immediately the Gospel is presented to a healthy, happy, hilarious unsaved person, there is violent opposition straight off. "No, thank you; we will agree with you if you will agree with these things; but if you are going to tell us we have to be made all over again, no thank you!" The Gospel of Jesus Christ does not present what men of the world want, but exactly what they need. As long as you talk about being happy and bright, they like to listen to you-, but talk about having the disposition of the soul altered, and that the garden of the world has to be turned into a wilderness by God and afterward into a garden of the Lord, then you find the opposition.

Lastly (g), "himself." I mean by "himself" not God, but man. (Judg. 8:18; Luke 2:40, 52; Eph. 4:13.) There is the description splendidly given of a fullorbed man, bad or good. A full-orbed man or woman bad (bad in God's sight) may be a wonderful being to look at, and full-orbed men and women right with God may also be wonderful beings to look at. The rest of us are simply beings in the making. There is a tremendous fascination about a completely bad man; there is nothing more desirable for this world than a thoroughly well-trained bad man or woman, but they are the opponents of Jesus Christ, they hate Him with every power of the soul; I mean the Jesus Christ of the New Testament.

God grant that we may get the ruling disposition of our souls so altered that we will practically work it out. How many of us have had experimental touch with the grace of God? how many of us have received the Spirit of God? Are we working it out? Is every organ of the body enslaved to that new disposition? Or are we using our eyes for what we want to see, using our body for our right to ourselves? If so we are receiving the grace of God in vain. God grant that we may be Christian men and women who are determined to work out through these bodies the life that Jesus Christ has put in by His Spirit.

CHAPTER VIII.

SOUL: THE ESSENCE, EXISTENCE, AND EXPRESSION.

PAST, PRESENT, AND FUTURE OP THE SOUL,

1. PRE-EXISTENCE.
   (a) Spurious Speculations. Deut. 29:29; Rev. 5:3.
   (b) Startling Scriptures. Jer. 1:5; Mat 3:1; Rom 9: 11, 13;
   Luke 1: 41.
   (c) Steadying Scriptures.
   (1) No "Soul" before Body. Gen. 1, 2.
   (2) No "Soul" Destiny pre-Adamic. Rom. 5: 12.
   (3) No "Soul" but by Procreation. Gen. 5.

N. B. Note the pre-existence of our Lord Jesus Christ. John 17:5.

2. PRESENT EXISTENCE.
   (a) Satisfaction of the Soul. Ps. 66: 9, 12, 16; Isa. 55: 3.
   (b) Sins and Surroundings of the Soul. Prov. 18: 7; Psa. 6;
   Ezek. 18:4; 1 Pet. 1:9.
   (c) Supernatural Setting for the Soul. Luke 9: 54, 56; Eph.
   6: 12; 1 Cor. 10:20, 21.

N. B. " Spiritualism" is the great "Soul" crime. Sickness, natural
and demoniacal, will be examined.

3. PERPETUAL EXISTENCE.
   (a) Mortal Aspect of the Soul. Job 14:2; Jas. 4:14.
   (b) Immortal Aspect of the Soul. Luke 16: 25, 26; 23 : 43.
   (c) "Eternal Life" of the Soul, and "Eternal Death 7 ' of
   the Soul. Matt 10: 28; Rom. 5: 21; 6: 23.

N. B. The peculiar error of "Soul Sleep" will be examined.
Also "Larger Hope" and "Conditional Immortality" will be
considered.

N. B. Facts of sleeping, waking and dreaming will be presented
and analyzed.

In concluding our general survey of the great theme of the Soul, we purpose to sketch in outline the past, present and future state of the soul.

1. Preexistence. The speculation that souls existed in a former world. The student cannot be too careful about (a) speculation, for there is no book which lends itself more readily to speculation than the Bible, and yet the Bible warns against speculation. By speculation we mean taking a series of facts and weaving all kinds of fancies round them. In Deuteronomy 29:29 and Revelation 5:3 the bounds where human knowledge goes with regard to Bible revelation and where it stops, are fairly well marked. For instance, what is revealed in God's Book is for us; and what is not revealed is not for us; speculation means we go into what is not revealed, and the whole subject of pre-existence, as it is popularly taught to-day, is not revealed in God's Book; it is speculation based on certain things said in God's Book. Theosophy largely lends itself to this sort of thing, and theosophy and occult speculations are all ultimately dangerous to the mental, moral and spiritual balance. Speculate if you care to, but do not teach it as a revelation contained in the Bible.

It has already been said that the Bible does not teach pre-existence, yet we have (b) some startling Scriptures which appear to contradict that statement. (Jer 1:5; Mal. 3:1; Rom. 9:11-13; Luke 1:41.) We have called these startling Scriptures for the obvious reason that they look as if the Bible did teach pre-existence. There is what we may term a false and a true pre-existence. False pre-existence, as already stated, is that we existed as human souls before we came into this world. The true pre-existence is in God's mind. This is not an easy subject to state, but it is a subject which is revealed in Scripture – the pre-existence in God's mind of what appears in this order of things, not only in a general way, not only by the great big fact of the human race, but right down to individual lives. Individual lives are expressions of a pre-existing idea in the mind of God. That is the true preexistence. You may call it ideal, or call it what you like, but there it is revealed in God's Book. In the few passages given, and in a great many more, the true pre-existing idea is clearly manifest in the divine mind.

One more thing with regard to individual spiritual experience, and that is, that our individual lives ought to be, and can be manifest answers to the ideas in God's mind. "Man's goings are of the Lord; how then can he understand his ways?" and it gives a lofty dignity, as well as a great carefulness to human lives. "We have it beautifully expressed in the life of our Lord in a way that is becoming very familiar to us – He never worked from His right to Himself, He never performed any miracle because He wanted to express what an able Being He was; He never spoke any doctrine because He wanted to show how wonderfully able His insight into God's truth was; He never did anything from Himself; He always did it from His Father. [At the foot of the outline is a note about the pre-existence of our Lord. (John 17:5.) That pre-existence is quite different from the phase of pre-existence just mentioned. This is the existence of the Being known before He came here, and the reason of His being here is explained by what He was before He came here. This is the only case of the pre-existence of a person in a former life. The Bible, then, nowhere teaches that individuals existed in a world before they came here. The true existence is the existence in the Divine mind.]

Then take (c) the steadying Scriptures, by which I mean those that hold our minds to some steady line of interpretation.

(1) No "Soul" before the body. (Gen. 1 and 2.) The Bible reveals that the soul in the CREATION of man came second, not first. The body existed before the soul in creation, so you cannot trace the history or the destiny of a human soul before the human race. That is the first main general line of revelation. There you have a splendid example of the pre-existence that is true God de-

liberately said what was in His mind before He created the body of man – "Let us make man in our own image," the pre-existence of Adam in the mind of God.

(2) No "Soul" destiny pre-Adamic. (Rom. 5:12.) The soul destiny here begins with the human race, not before it. Some may say we believe that there was no soul before body in the first creation; but what about ourselves? Take any passage that deals with individual destiny – Ezekiel 18, for instance – and you will find that destiny is determined in the life-time of that individual soul. Transmigration speculations are all alien to the Bible teaching.

(3) No -"Soul" but by pro-creation. That is that we are not created direct by the hand of the Almighty as Adam was. We are pro-created, generated, and our body, soul and spirit come together in embryo, as related elsewhere.

All these speculations come right down to our lives In a very enticing manner. Telepathy is the especially enticing way that this speculation of transmigration and pre-existence introduces itself to our minds. Now telepathy simply means being able to discern some one else's thought by my own. Immediately you get there, you have the line of auto-suggestion, and if one man can suggest thoughts to another man, then Satan can do the same thing, and the consciousness of it on the human side opens the mind to it diabolically. Why we mention telepathy is because all these things come right down to us in the most harmless phases. Spiritualism comes to us in the way of palmistry, reading fortunes in teacups, or in cards, planchette, etc. People say there is no harm in that. There is all the harm and "backing up" of the devil behind the whole thing. Nothing awakens the curiosity quicker than reading fortunes in tea-cups, and nothing will awaken insatiable curiosity like reading fortunes by cards. The same thing with all these theosophic speculations; they come right down on the line of things that have been wrongly called by the name of "psychology."

2. Present Existence. Here we come down on to plain, simple ground where we are at home. In the last chapter you remember we dealt with something of the nature of the complex characteristics of the soul, perplexing and whirling and confusing the more you think of them. When you begin to think of the possibilities of the human soul, there is no clear thought possible, at first. We come now to all the possibilities and capacities of the soul. Can these be satisfied here? The Bible says they can; the whole claim of the salvation of Jesus Christ is that the Spirit of God can satisfy our human soul's last aching abyss, and not hereafter only, but here and now. Satisfaction does not mean stagnation; it means the knowledge that I have gotten to the right type of life for my soul.

(a) Satisfaction of the Soul. (Psa. 66:9, 12, 16; Isa. 55:3.) These are simply indications of innumerable passages in God's Book which go to prove that the complex soul which we have been facing can be satisfied and placed in perfect harmony with itself and with God in this present existence. To think that the human soul can fulfill the whole predestined purpose of God, is a great thought. It can be stagnated by ignorance; when we begin we are content to be ignorant; we do not know the capabilities of our lives; when we begin to get conviction of sin, we understand the awful, unfathomable depths of our lives; and the claim of the Bible is that God can satisfy this abyss; and every one who knows first of all, what his human soul is capable of, the possibilities and terrors of it, and knows also that Jesus Christ can satisfy that soul, will bear equal testimony with the written Word of God that He can satisfy the living soul in the present. Isaiah 55:3 is our Lord's message to the age we live in. "We must bear in mind that the devil does satisfy, for a time. Read Psalm 73: "Their eyes stand out with fatness, they have all that heart can desire." "They have no changes, and they do not fear God," says another Psalm.

(b) Sins and Surroundings of the Soul. (We are not taking all the passages given in the chart, only one or two to indicate the line of thought.) Psalm 6; this refers to the surroundings of the soul with regard to bodily sickness and perplexity, and the inward results. The first degree of prayer is, "Heal me for my bones are vexed." The second degree is, "Heal me for my soul is also sore vexed," and the third degree is, "Save me for Thy mercy's sake." There are three degrees of pain in the soul arising from its sur-roundings, (1) perplexity because of pain, (2) because its mental outlook is cloudy, and (3) because God has not said a word. When you get the body perplexed (and you certainly will if you are going on with God – because you are a mark for Satan), and when the sudden onslaught comes, as it did for instance in Job's life, you will cry, "Heal me because of my pain," and there is no answer. "Heal me, not because I am in pain, but my soul is perplexed, I cannot see any way out of it why this thing should be;" still no answer. "Heal me, Lord, not because of my pain, not because my soul is sick, but for Thy sake." These surroundings of the soul, the scenes that arise from our doings, produce perplexity and danger to the soul; you cannot separate your soul from your body, and the bodi-ly perplexities produce difficulties, and the difficulties go inward and at times intrude right to the very throne of God in your heart.

(Ezek. 18 : 4.) In this passage the connection of the soul life and sin that is punished, is clearly stated. The disposition of sin inherited is to be cleansed, but every sin I commit I am punished for. (1 Pet. 1:9.) That word salvation refers to the whole " gamut 7 ' of a man, spirit, soul and body; Christ the firstfruits, with the ultimate reach in the hereafter of spirit, soul and body like His in a totally new relationship. The soul in the present life is satisfied in all perplexities, and in all onslaughts and dangers is kept by the power of God. Sins destroy the power of the soul to know its sins, punishment brings awakening, and self-examination brings chastisement and saves the soul from sleeping sickness, and brings it into healthy satisfaction. (1 Cor. 11:31.)

Now about (c) the supernatural side of the soul's life. (Luke 9:54-56.) These men had known enough of the Lord Jesus Christ to know that He had intimacy with supernatural powers, and it is quite possible to scathe sin and serve your own self at the same time, as they did, doing right in the wrong spirit. [These were the very men who, a little while afterwards, asked that they might be placed one on the right hand and the other on the left; and one of them (see Acts 8) was sent down by God to Samaria, where he realized what the fire was that God was going to send, the fire of the Holy Ghost.]

(Eph. 6:12.) That has not to do with what we consider our body side of things, it has to do with the supernatural. We are surrounded immediately by powers and forces which we cannot discern physically.

(1 Cor. 10:20, 21.) You will always know your spiritually minded Christians by their attitude to the supernatural. For instance, the modern attitude to demon possession is instructive. So many take the attitude that there is no such thing as demon possession, inferring that Jesus Christ Himself knew quite well that there was no such thing; not seeing that by such an attitude they put themselves in the place of the superior person, and claim to know all the private opinions of the Almighty about iniquity. Jesus unquestionably did believe in the fact of demon possession. The New Testament is full from beginning to end of the supernatural. Jesus Christ continually looked on scenery we do not see; He continually saw and understood supernatural forces and persons at work. "Test the spirits whether they be of God or men." The soul of man may be vastly complicated by interference from the supernatural, but Jesus Christ can guard us here.

Sickness, natural and demoniacal. "We mean by natural the sickness that has come about by natural causes, not by the interference of any supernatural force. The second arise when certain organs of the body are infested by demons. Read the records of our Lord casting out demons. He said sometimes, "Come out, thou dumb and deaf demon;" again He said nothing about demons to other deaf and dumb people as He healed them. You will find all through God's Book references to demoniacal sickness, where certain organs of the body are possessed, and Jesus in addressing them mentions the particular organ. The third kind of sickness is instanced in the man of Gadara who was possessed by a legion of demons, not only in organs but all through his body. (How much room does thought take up? None! How many thoughts can I have in my brain? Why, countless! How much room does a spiritual personality take up? How many personalities may be in one body? Take the man of Gadara, Jesus said, "How many are ye?" "Legion!") The other case is that of Judas, the identification of a human soul with the devil himself. Just as a man may become identified with the Lord Jesus Christ, so he can be identified with the devil. Just as a man can be born again into the kingdom where Jesus lives and moves and has His being, and become identified with Him by entire sanctification, so a man can be born again, so to speak, into the devil's kingdom, and can be entirely consecrated to the devil. "Satan entered into Judas." Jesus said, "Have not I chosen twelve, and one of you is a devil?" The subject awakens tremendous terrors, but these are facts revealed in God's Book. There are natural sicknesses and supernatural sicknesses of the human soul and body in this present life, and Jesus Christ can deal with them all, natural or supernatural.

3. Perpetual Existence.

(a) The Mortal Aspect of the Soul. (Job 14:2; Jas. 4: 14.) "We mean by mortal, only in this order of things. You will find all through God's Book that the soul and the presence of a man as he appears just now is described as mortal in one aspect. The soul is the holder of the body and spirit together, and when the spirit has gone back to God who gave it, the soul goes with the body. But in the resurrection there is another body, a glorified body, a body impossible to describe in words, either a glorified or a damnation body, and instantly you have the soul life manifested again. (See John 5:28,29.) We have a picture of the resurrected damned body, yet our Lord states the fact. We have a picture of the resurrected glorified body of the saints in the resurrected body of our Lord. (Phil. 3:21.) The soul life, then, is entirely dependent on the body. The indelible characteristics of the individual are in his spirit, and our Lord, who became the firstfruits, was spirit, soul and body. Therefore resurrection is not of spirit – personality – (that never dies) but of body and soul. God raises an incorruptible glorified body like unto His own, "every man in his own regiment" and Jesus Christ leading. Just as during those forty resurrection days, our Lord's glorified body could materialize, so will ours be able to in the "day" yet to be. In Luke 16:25-29, reference is made to the resurrection of damnation, and the resurrection to eternal life. If the mortal aspect is strong in the Bible, the immortal aspect (b) is just as strong. The annihilationists build all their teaching on what we have said just now; they give proof after proof that the soul and body are mortal, and that the only person who is everlasting is the person who is born again of the Spirit; but the Bible says there is everlasting damnation as well as everlasting life. Nothing can be annihilated. "Destroy" never means "annihilate" in Scripture language. Our soul is mortal in this present bodily aspect, but it is immortal in another aspect of God's truth, for He sees soul in its final connection with spirit in resurrection. Luke 16:25, 26 and Luke 23:43 both have reference to the state immediately after death, and reveal that the spirit of a man, the personality of a man, never sleeps, and never dies in the sense that his body and soul do. Here the "soul sleep" heresy creeps in. The Bible nowhere says the soul sleeps. The Bible referring to this order of things reveals the body as asleep, but never the personality. The Lord Jesus emphatically showed that the second after death, unhindered consciousness is the state.

(c) Eternal Life and Eternal Death. (Matt. 10: 28; Rom. 5:21; 6:23.) We have no more ground for saying there is eternal life than we have for saying there is eternal death. If Jesus Christ meant by eternal life, unending conscious knowledge of God ever increasing, then eternal death is never-ending conscious separation from God. The destruction of a soul in Hades or Hell is the destruction of the last strand of likeness to God. Mark uses a very strange word, he says "salted by fire," preserved in eternal death. Romans 8:6 tells us what eternal death is – "carnal mindedness." Those verses on death and life are easily solvable. The people who say that eternal damnation is not personal, but that eternal life is, have put themselves in a most ridiculous position. We know no more about the one than we know about the other, and we know nothing about either saving what the Lord Jesus Christ has told us. Probably the greatest book that ever was written, outside the Bible, on "Human Personality and Its Survival of Bodily Death" was written during the last few years by a great man, and he tries to prove, outside God's Book, simply by speculation, that the human soul is immortal, and he ends exactly where he begins, viz., with his intuition. All we know about "Hell," all we know about damnation and eternal life, the Bible alone has given to us, and if we go "off" and say "God is unjust" because He teaches perennial "death" (and say therefore He can never have taught it), we have put ourselves exactly under the condemnation that God gives in those passages in Deuteronomy and Revelation. The mortal aspect is that the soul, as merely the expression of spirit, disappears, as we know it, when the body dies. These things transcend reason, but they do not contradict the nature of reason; they are simply divine revelations of our Lord Jesus Christ, and He is the only being who is the final authority.

All we can have hoped to do in these studies of the human soul is to have suggested lines of research for the Bible student.

CHAPTER IX.

HEART: THE RADICAL REGION OF LIFE.

1. CENTRE OF THE PHYSICAL LIFE.
    (a) "Lifeless" Objects. Deut. 5: 11; Matt. 12: 40; Jon. 2: 3;
    Ezek. 26: 4, 25-27.
    (b) Lowest Life-Power. Gen. 18: 5; Judg. 19: 5.
    (c) Life-Power. Ps. 38: 10, 11; Luke 21: 34.
    (d) Life of the Whole Person. Acts 14: 17; Jas. 5: 5.

2. CENTRE OF PRACTICAL LIFE.
    (a) Emporium. Ps. 5:9; 49:11; 1 Pet. 3:4.
    (b) Export. Mark 7:21, 22; Esth. 7:5.
    (c) Import. Acts 5:3; 16:14; 2 Cor. 4:6.

N. B. The relative position of Head and Heart in the Bible and Modern Thought will be explained. "The head is to the external appearance what the heart is to the internal agency of the soul."

1. Centre of Physical Life.

We will deal first with, the N. B. on the chart. In the Bible the heart is made to be the centre of thinking, not the brain, and for a long while mental science has differed from the Bible. It has maintained a steady opposition to the Bible standpoint. But modern psychologists are coming round slowly now to find that the best way to explain the facts of conscious life is to revise previous unbiblical " findings."

Physically, remember that the heart is the first thing to live, and the Bible finds in the heart all the active factors that we have been apt to place in the brain. The brain is simply the head-piece, the true indicator of what the heart is. In the mystical body of Christ, Christ is not called the heart; Christ is called the head. (Eph. 5:23; Col. 2:19; 1 Cor. 11:3.) Now, if the head is to be the exact outward expression of the heart, how can sin have any part in the mystical body of Christ? That is, how can people who are not rightly related to God, whose inward disposition has not been changed, how can they be part of the body of Christ, if Christ is the head and true expression of what that body is, especially in the centre of its life?

The head has the prominence of all blessings in the Old and New Testaments, simply because it is the outward expression of the condition of the heart. (Gen. 48:14; 49:26; Prov. 10:6; Ps. 132:2; Lev. 8.) You find also statements about the countenance; which does not only mean the face and front of the head; but the whole carriage of the person that is external in expression: and the countenance becomes the true mirror of what the heart is like, when the heart has had time enough to manifest its true life. (With regard to the countenance being the mirror, see Ex. 34:29; Matt. 17:2; 2 Cor. 3:13; Isa. 3:9; 2 Sam. 17:11.)

The Bible does not put the head in the central position, it puts it in the prominent position, on the top; the head is the final finish off, the manifestation of what the heart is like. The head is the outward expression, as the tree is the outward expression of what the root is like. That is the relationship between head and heart in the Bible.

The materialistic scientists say that "the brain secretes thinking like the liver does bile." They have made the brain the centre of thinking. The Bible makes the heart the centre of thinking and the brain merely the machinery the heart uses to express itself. That is a very vital point in our judgment of men. For instance, Carlyle represents the judgment of men who do not accept the Bible standpoint. He judged men by brains, and consequently said the majority of the human race were fools.

God never judges men by brains; they are judged by heart.

The heart, then, is the true centre of living, and the true centre of all vital activities of body, soul, and spirit.

When the apostle Paul refers to believing with the heart, he means a great deal more than we are apt to mean. The Bible always means more than we are apt to mean. The Bible term "heart" means the particular centre on which everything turns, in every way and in every detail. The human soul has the spirit in and above it; the body by and about it; but the vital centre is the heart.

The passages under section 1 simply mean that the Bible points out that the centre of everything is its heart. "When we speak of the heart, either figuratively or really, we speak of the mid-most part of a person. "Where we differ in our Bible teaching from secular mental science is, that we make the heart the soul-centre and the spirit-centre also.

One of the greatest dangers in dealing with the Bible is to exploit it, that is, to come to it with a preconceived idea, and take things out of it only what agree with that idea. If you try, as has been tried by psychologists, to take out of it something that agrees with modern psychology, you will find that you always have to omit everything the Bible says about the heart. The heart is the centre, the centre of the physical life, it is the centre of memory, the centre of damnation and the centre of salvation, the centre of God's working, and the centre of the devil's working, the centre from which everything works that moulds the human mechanism.

(c) Life Power. (Ps. 38:10, 11; Luke 21:34.) These passages are typical of many more where the heart is made the centre of all life power, physical and otherwise. Anything that makes the heart move or beat quicker physically always works towards higher or lower manifestations, and you will find our Lord Jesus Christ produces the kind of influence that alters the heart life at once. Some people you come in contact with freeze you (so to speak), you cannot think, things do not "go", you feel everything "tight" and "mean"; you come into the zone of other people and all those "bands" have gone, you are surprised at how clearly you can think, everything seems to "go" better. You feel better and you take a deep breath and say, "Why, I feel quite different; what has happened?" The one personality brought an atmosphere that "froze" the heart not only physically, but psychically, kept it cold, kept it down, kept it back; the other gave it a chance to expand, and develop, and surge again throughout the whole body. (Take it in the lowest physical domain. If people knew that circulation of the blood and the quickening of the heart life would move distempers from the body, there would be a great deal less medicine taken and a great deal more walking done.)

The heart is indeed the centre for all the physical life and all the imaginations that the mind works. Anything that keeps the physical blood in a good condition and keeps the heart circulating in a proper way, will always benefit the soul and spirit life as well. That is why Jesus Christ says, "Be careful that you do not get your heart (that includes physical heart as well) surfeited by the wrong things." Whenever certain kinds of sins are mentioned they are called idolatry. "Covetousness" is called idolatry because every drop of blood in a covetous man's life is drawn away from God physically, and spiritually. The same thing with sensuality, with drunkenness, and with vengeance (vengeance is probably the most tyrannical passion of the carnal mind). The first wonderful thing done by the new life given to us by the Holy Spirit is to loosen the heart, and as we obey the Spirit in the life, it leads in each detail nearer and nearer to what God has for us, and the manifestations become easier. Satan, however, is as subtle as God is good, and he will counterfeit everything God does, and, if he cannot counterfeit it, he will limit it. Do not be ignorant of his devices!

(d) Life of the "Whole Person. (Acts 14:17; Jas. 5:5.) There is indication given of the power of our heart-life. If our hearts are right with God, we are able to realize what is mentioned in the first passage, that everything nourishes and blesses the whole life all through. The other indicates the bad side. "We can develop in the heart life what we will, if we only put our hearts in the right condition, or the wrong one. There is no limit to the growth and development. If we give over to meanness and to Satan, there is no end to our growth in devilishness; if we give ourselves over to God openly, there is no end whatever to our development and growth in grace. Our Lord has no dread about consequences, when once the heart is open towards Him. No wonder the Bible counsels us to "guard our heart," for out of it are the issues of life; no wonder Solomon prayed for "enlargement of heart," and no wonder Paul says that the peace of God will "garrison our hearts. "

2. Centre of Practical Life.

The Emporium, The Export, and The Import.

(Ps. 5:9.) The phrase "inward part" there is simply a translated phrase for heart.. (Ps. 49:11.) There again the "inward thought" is heart entirely. (1 Pet. 3:4.) That is the "great exchange and mart" in your life and mine; words and expressions are simply the coins we use, but the shop resides in the heart, the emporium, where all the goods are, and that is what God can see and no man can. That is why Jesus Christ's judgment always confuses us until we learn how to receive, recognize and rely on the Holy Spirit. The way people judged Jesus in His day is the way we judge Him to-day. The way the critics judge the Bible and the way the critics judge Jesus is an indication of what the heart is if any man has not received the Holy Spirit. When once we receive the Holy Spirit, what happens to you and me is that we get to the condition of the disciples after the resurrection; their eyes were opened and they discerned things, that is, they had power to discern what they saw before. Before they received the Spirit they could not perceive correctly. They simply recorded physically, they simply saw that Jesus Christ was a marvelous being whom they believed to be the Messiah, but when they received the Holy Ghost, received the Spirit life, they discerned what they saw, they discerned what they heard, they discerned what they had been handling. Why? Because the heart had been put right, the whole shop inside had been renovated and restocked by the Spirit of God.

Notice the characteristic of a man who makes his head the centre, and the characteristic of the New Testament being who makes the heart the centre. The man who makes the head the centre becomes an intellectual being, that is he does not estimate things at all like the Bible characters do; sin, to him, is a mere defect, something to be overlooked and grown out of, and the one thing he despises is an enthusiast. Take the apostle Paul, or any New Testament character, you will find the characteristic of the life is enthusiasm; the heart is first, not second, the antipodes of modern life, if the modern life is intellectual. Intellectuality leads to bloodlessness and passionlessness and stoicism and un-reality; you will find that the more and more intellectual a person becomes the more and more hopelessly useless he becomes, such degenerate into mere critical faculties, and they pass the strangest and wildest verdicts on life, on the Bible and on the Lord Jesus Christ.

(b) Export. (Mark 7:21.) This passage is detestable to an intellectual person, it is in absolute bad taste, and nine out of twelve people do not believe it, because they are grossly ignorant about their heart. Jesus Christ says, to put it in modern language, " There has no crime ever been committed that every human being is not capable of committing." Do I believe that? do you? If not, remember we pass a verdict straight off on the Lord Jesus Christ, we say He does not know what He is talking about. Jesus said He "knew what was in man," meaning He knew his heart, and the apostle Paul emphasizes the same thing. "Don 't you trust any man," he says in effect, "only the grace of God in yourself and in other people." No wonder Jesus Christ pleads with us to give the charge of our hearts over to Him so that He can fill them with a new life, and every characteristic seen in Jesus Christ's life becomes possible in mine when once I have handed my heart over to Him to be filled with the Holy Spirit. "We are not capable of guarding our own hearts, the Bible says we are not.

(c) Import. (Acts 5:3.) That is a terrible statement, a statement with a shudder all through, viz., a Pentecostal liar, a lie that has never been mentioned before in that particular profundity, but it is mentioned here because it is the part of the heart to actually try to deceive the Holy Ghost. Peter says, "You have not lied to men; you have lied to God. Satan hath filled thine heart." In 2 Corinthians 4 : 6, our Lord undertakes to fill the whole region of the heart with light and love and beauty and holiness. Can He do it? First of all, do I realize that I need it done? Or do I think I can "realize myself" (that is the phrase to-day, it is growing in popularity, "I must realize myself")? If I want to know what my heart is like, let me listen to my mouth (in an unguarded frame), for five minutes!

Thank God for everyone of us who has been saved from that perilous path by yielding ourselves over to the Lord, and asking Him to give us the Holy Spirit and obeying the light He gives!

CHAPTER X.

HEART: THE RADICAL REGION OF LIFE.

THE RADIATOR OP PERSONAL LIFE.

1. VOLUNTARY.

(a) Determination. Ex. 35:21; Esth. 7:5; Eccl. 8:11; 2 Cor. 9:7; Rom. 6: 17.

(b) Design. 1 Kings 8:17, 18; 10:2; Ps. 21:2; Prov. 6: 18; Isa. 10: 7; Acts 11: 23; Rom. 10: 1.

2.VERSATILITY.

(a) Perception. Deut. 29:4; Prov. 14:10; Isa. 32:4; Acts 16: 14.

(b) Meditation. Neh. 5:7; Luke 2:19; Isa. 33:18; Ps. 49: 3; Ps. 19: 14.

*This includes deliberation and reflection.

(c) Estimation. Prov. 16: 1, 9; 19: 21; Ps. 33: 10, 11.

(d) Inclination. Deut. 32:46; Josh. 24:23; Deut. 11: 18; Prov. 3: 3.

3.VIRTUES AND VICES.

(a) All Degrees of Joy. Isa. 65: 14; 66: 5; Acts 2: 46.

(b) All Degrees of Pain. Prov. 25: 20; Ps. 109: 22; Acts 21: 13; John 16: 6.

(c) All Degrees of Ill-will. Prov. 23: 17; Deut. 19: 6; Acts 7: 54; Jas. 3:14.

A radiator is "a body that emits rays of light and heat." I have used a purely mechanical term, because it exactly pictures what the heart is, it is the centre that emits rays of light and heat in the physical frame, in the soul and in the spirit. The heart physically is the centre of the body; the heart sentimentally is the centre of the soul; the heart spiritually is the centre of the spirit.

A word about the three divisions in the chart. 1, Voluntary, simply means acting by choice; choice is made in the heart, not in the head. By 2, Versatility, is meant the power to turn easily from one thing to another, and by 3, Virtues, moral excellencies, and by Vices, immoral conduct.

1. The Voluntary Division.

The act of choice springs from the heart the Bible says, and there are two things we must look at – one is determination, and the other is design, (a) Determination means to fix the form of the choice. (Ex. 35:21; Rom. 6:17.) These passages are an indication of hundreds that prove from the Bible revelation that the act of choice is in the heart and not in the brain. Determination is not impulse. Impulse in anybody but a child is dangerous; it is always the sign of an unstable and unreliable person. Determination is to fix the form of my choice. Now that means, both in praying and action, I have the power in my heart to fix the form my choice is to take, and God demands this of us when we pray. The majority of us waste our time by mere impulses in prayer. Meditate on that and you will find many verses in God's Book which refer to this power of the heart to choose voluntarily. Impulse is not choice; impulse is very similar to instinct in an animal. It is the characteristic of immaturity that ought not to be your character-istic or mine. "We may take it as a safe guide in spiritual matters never to be guided by impulse in anything; to always take time to curb your impulses and bring them back and see what sort of form the choice would make based on that impulse.

When the phrase, "Bringing every thought and imagination into captivity" is taken in the full meaning, it means practically the harnessing of impulses. Thank God we have the power in our hearts to fix the form of our choice either for good or bad. No wonder the Bible tells us to guard our hearts, for out of them are the issues of our life. We never get credit for giving, impul-sively, spiritually. If we suddenly feel we ought to give a shilling to a poor man, and do it, we get no credit from God for it, there is no virtue in it whatever. The majority of that sort of giving is a relief to the feelings, and is not an indication of a generous character, it is rather an indication of lack of it. God never estimates our gifts on the line of impulse. It is what we determine in our hearts to do that we get credit for; giving that is governed by a fixed determination. The Spirit of Go*d revolutionizes our philanthropic instincts. The majority of philanthropy is simply this impulse to save myself an uncomfortable feeling, by giving to the poor people. The Spirit of God alters the whole thing. My attitude to the poor, as a saint of God, is, "Give, for His sake," not any other motive. So with regard to everything, this power of voluntarily choosing in determining the form of our choice is the power in the human heart that God holds us responsible for using or not using.

Then take (b) Design. Design means more than determination. Design means to plan in outline. 1 Kings 8:17,18 is a typical case, and there are other verses that prove that God gives us credit for the design of our heart, not for the impulses of our hearts. He may never allow that design to be carried out, but He credits us with having the design. Sometimes when you have had a very good dinner and feel remarkably good, you say, "If I only had a thousand pounds, what would I do with it!" You do not get credit for that, until what you do with what you have got, is considered. The proof that the design for the thousand pounds would be worked out is what you do with what you have got. We cannot have designs in outline to please God, unless we have been working out in lesser degrees through our bodies, what God works in us to do. David had planned out in his heart what he would do for God, and, although God did not allow him to do it, God credited him with having the desire and design and the plan in his heart. Thank God we have a God who deals with the designs of our hearts both, for good and for bad! Character is the whole trend of the man's life taken together, not an isolated act here and there. Remember, then, these two voluntary powers of the heart, viz., I have a power to fix the form of my choosing! "Delight thyself in the Lord; and He will give thee the desires of thine heart." Desire embraces both determination and design. God deals with us on the line of character building. Some people, when they read that verse in Psalm 37, behave before God like people do with a wishing-bone over a Christmas dinner. They say, "Now I have read this verse, I wonder what I shall wish for?" That is not desire. Desire is what you have determined in outline, in your mind, and planned out and settled in your heart, that is the desire God will fulfill if you delight in Him.

2. Versatility.

We describe that as being the power of turning from one thing to another. Now that, in the natural world, is called humor. The power to turn easily from one thing to another is owing to a sense of proportion. A "self-righting" lifeboat gives the idea. This is the power that sin destroyed in the spiritual people of God. Read Psalm 106: "Our fathers have sinned and we have sinned with them." How did they sin? They forgot what God did before; they had not any power of turning from their present trying circumstances to the time when the circumstances were not trying, and consequently they sinned against God. We have a power to turn from deep anguish to deep joy in times of trial. Psalm 42:6: "My soul is cast down within me," therefore will I turn and remember something else. There are some people who have the characteristic of being merry, and they think they must always keep up that "role." There are some people who have taken on the character of being great sufferers, and, having taken up that "role," they never turn from it. In the life of our Lord Jesus Christ, you will always find the basal balance of this quality; also take the apostle Paul's argument in Romans 8: "All these things work together for good." You have to take all these things when put "together," not in bits.

If your circumstances are trying just now, remember the time when they were not trying, and you will find that the " self-righting " power is given all through, and you will be surprised when once you realize the enormous power of turning from one thing to another in the human heart. How much misery a human heart can stand, and how much joy! but if you lose the power of turning, you will upset the balance. God's Spirit restores and keeps this balance. (a) Perception. That means the power of discernment, I wonder how many of us have the power of perception! (Deut. 29:4; Prov. 14:10.) In the first ease the power of perception is in the heart. Perception means the power to discern what I hear, what I see, and what I read; the power to discern the history of the nation I belong to, and the power to discern my personal life. How many of us have the power to "hear with our ears" according to Jesus Christ's statement? Jesus said, "He that hath ears to hear let him hear." You have got to have the power of perception to interpret what you hear in God 's light. Isaiah puts it very strongly in chapter 53: "Who hath believed the thing we are all saying and to whom is the arm of the Lord revealed?" That is, "Who has the power to discern the arm of the Lord?" We all see the common occurrences of our daily life, but who amongst us can perceive the arm of the Lord behind them, who can perceive behind the thunder, the voice of God? Remember Jesus Christ (John 12). The people said it thundered, but Jesus said His Father spoke to Him. "What is the difference? The One had perception, the others had not. The light that smote Saul on the way to Damascus staggered and amazed the other men, but they saw nothing in it. Saul knew it was the Lord, and said, "Who art thou, Lord?" Why? The one had the power of perception and the others had not. The characteristic of a man without the Spirit of God is that he has not the power of perception; that is, he cannot perceive God's working behind the ordinary occurrences. That is the marvelous, uncrushable characteristic of a saint.

You may put the saint in tribulation, you may put the saint amid an onslaught of "principalities and powers/ ' you may put the saint in peril, pestilence, under sword, you may put the saint anywhere you like and Paul says he is more than conqueror. Why! Because his heart being filled with God can always turn in the perceiving way to understand that behind all these things "working together for good" is God! How many of us have our ears open?

"Keep mine eyes from beholding vanity." That does not mean "keep my eyes shut," but "give me a power of perception to direct my eyes aright." A sheet of white paper can be soiled, a sunbeam cannot, and God keeps His saints like light.

Oh, the power of full-orbed righteousness! Thank God for the sanity of His salvation! He gets hold of us in our hearts, not our heads! (b), Meditation means getting to the middle of a thing. Meditation does not mean to be like a pebble in a brook letting the water of thought go over you, that is reverie, not meditation. Meditation is the most intense spiritual activity that brings every part of the body into harness, and concentrates its powers to profit. This includes deliberation and reflection. Now deliberation means that I am able to weigh well what I am thinking of, conscious all the time that I am deliberating and meditating. Neh. 5:7: "I thought within myself," is exactly the meaning of meditation. Luke 2:19 is the meaning of meditation also.

Please note, meditation is not prayer! A great many delightful modern people mistake meditation for prayer. Meditation is simply the power I have in my natural heart to get to the centre of a thing, and all this talk in pseudo-scientific circles about prayer being a reflex action is foolish. Meditation has a reflex action, but that is not prayer.

Prayer is definite talk to God, about which God has put an atmosphere, and by which I get answers back. Meditation very often accompanies prayer, but meditation is not prayer. Men can meditate who have not an ounce of the Spirit of God in them, and. this fundamental distinction is obscured over and over again, by teachers to-day. We read that Mary meditated, she got right to the centre of all the thought about her Son, and she never said a word about it to anybody as far as we know; yet read John's Gospel, and a wonder will occur to you. St. Augustine called John's Gospel the "Heart of Jesus Christ." Recall what Jesus said to John about His own mother, "Son, behold thy mother," and what Jesus said to Mary about John, "Woman, behold thy son," and from that hour John took Mary to his own home. It is quite legitimate to think that Mary's meditations found marvelous expression under the guidance of the Spirit of God to John, and may have found expression in John's Gospel and Epistles.

(c) Estimation. Estimate simply means reckoning the value of. (Prov. 16:1-9.) God alters our estimates, we make our estimates in the heart. Let me put it down practically; those of you who have received God's Spirit and understand and know experimentally God's grace, watch how He has altered your estimate of things. It used to matter a lot what your worldly crowd thought about you, how much does it matter now? You used to estimate highly the good opinion of certain people, how do you estimate it now? You used to estimate that immoral conduct was the worst crime on earth, how do you estimates pride now? "We get horrified at immoral conduct in social life, how many of us get as horrified at pride as Jesus Christ was? How many of us begin to understand what Jesus meant when He said you are "whited sepulchres, a generation of vipers"? To whom was He talking? He was talking to Pharisees! God alters our estimates, and, you will find God is giving you a deeper horror of carnality than ever He gave you of ordinary immorality, a deeper horror of the pride that lifts itself against God and lives clean among men, than any other thing. God alters our hearts all along the line, and God will alter your estimates about honor. Every man has honor of some sort, a thief has an honor, a gambling man has an honor, everybody has an honor of a sort, Jesus Christ had an honor, you may call Him a glutton and a wine bibber, you may call Him licentious, you may call Him mad, you may call Him possessed with a devil, but His mouth is shut, "He made Himself of no reputation;" but once you touch His Father's honor, and all is different. "Watch His first public ministry in Jerusalem, a "whip of small cords" overturning the moneychangers' tables and driving men and cattle out. Why? His Father's honor was at stake. "Where is the meek and mild and gentle Jesus now?

The estimate of my honor measures my growth in grace. "What I will stand up for proves what my character is. If I stand up for my own reputation, it is a sign that it needs standing up for. God never stands up for His saints, they do not need it. The devil tells lies, but no slander on earth can alter a man's character; once let them slander God's honor, and you instantly find something else to deal with in your meek saint. You could not arouse them on their own account, but once you begin to slander God and you have awakened this sense of honor – a new estimate. We are able to have God's estimate. God help us to get to the right perspective, to get to ths place where we will understand and estimate that the things that are seen are temporal, ever holding a right scale of judgment.

3. Virtues and Vices.

(a) All Degrees of Joy. Joy resides in the heart. The Bible nowhere speaks about a happy Christian; happiness depends on what happens, Christian joy does not.

(The Bible talks plentifully about joy, and I want to give you one warning about the effect of Christian Science. Mentally, there is not the slightest objection to what Christian Science does to people's bodies, "but there is a tremendous objection to what it does to people's minds. Its result in people's minds is to make them intolerably indifferent to physical suffering, it produces the antipodes of the Christian character, viz., hard and callous in time.) All degrees of joy reside in the heart. How can a Christian be full of happiness, (if happiness means depending on things that happen,) when he is in a world where people are going wrong, where the devil is doing his best to twist souls, where people are tortured physically, where some people are downtrodden and do not get a chance? It would be the outcome of the most miserable selfishness to be happy under such conditions, but joyfulness is never touched by external conditions, and a joyful heart is never an insult. Beware of preaching the gospel of temperament instead of the Gospel of God. There are any number of people to-day preaching the gospel of temperament, the gospel of " cheer up." Remember, Jesus Christ had joy, He was filled with joy. The word "blessedness" is sometimes translated happiness, but it is a very much deeper word than our word, happiness; it includes all that is meant in joy in its full fruition. Happiness is the sign of a child 's life, and God condemns us for taking happiness out of a child's life, but we should have done with happiness long ago, we are men and women who can face the stern issues of life knowing that the grace of God is sufficient for every problem the devil can present.

(b) All Degrees of Pain. (Prov. 25:20). This is simply what has been stated already, preaching the gospel of temperament, the gospel of cheer up, when a person cannot cheer up, telling him to look on the bright side of things. It is just like telling a jelly fish to listen to an oratorio of Handel's, it cannot, it has to be made all over again first; so to tell a man to cheer up when he is convicted of sin by God, is just as futile. "What he needs is the grace of God inside to alter him so that he can have this wellspring of joy. Pain exists in the heart and not anywhere else. We try to aggregate and measure pain in the mass, we cannot. "When there is a great accident and hundreds get killed, we are horrified, much more horrified than at one man getting killed. There is no such thing as pain in the mass, that mass of pain is individual and nobody can feel more pain than the acme of nerves will give, and the more physical expression through pain, the less pain. It is through refusal to estimate things in the right lights that we misunderstand the direction of pain.

(c) All Degrees of Ill Will. The deepest-rooted vice in the human soul is vengeance; drunkenness and sensuality and covetousness are deep, but they do not go as deep as revenge. It is some such thought as that, that explains Judas. Read the record of Judas, it says that he "kissed Jesus much," and then we read of the remorse of Judas, but there was no repentance, in our sense of the word; the whole end of the man's life was reached, there was nothing more to live for. There are records over and over again that a man who commits murder after a long line of vengeance, dies of a broken heart, not because he is penitent, but because he has no more to live for.

It is the deepest-rooted passion in the human soul and the very impersonation of it is Satan, he has an absolute, clear detestation of God, an immortal hatred of God Almighty. He is at the summit of all sins, we are at the base of all. If it has not reached its awful height in us yet, it will, unless we let God alter the springs of our hearts.

Thank God He alters the heart, and when He puts His new life in the heart, we can work it out through the head, and in the expression of the life!

CHAPTER XI.

HEART: THE RADICAL REGION OF LIFE.
THE RADIATOR OF PERSONAL LIFE. (Continued.)

1. VOLUNTARY.

> (c) Love. 1 Tim. 1:5; Prov. 23:26; Judg. 5:9; Phil. 1: 7; 2 Cor. 7:3.
>
> (d) Hate. Lev. 19: 17; Ps. 105: 25.

2. VERSATILITY.

> (e) Memory. Isa. 65:17; Jer. 3:16; 2 Chron. 7:11; Acts 7: 23; 1 Cor. 2: 9; Luke 7: 66; 21: 14.
>
> (f) Thinking. Gen. 8:21; 17:17; 24:45; Eccl. 1:16; Matt. 24:48; Heb. 4: 12.
>
> (g) Birth of Words. Job 8: 10; Ps. 15: 2; Matt. 12: 34; Ex. 28: 3.

3. VIRTUES AND VICES.

> (d) All Degrees of Fear. Prov. 12: 25; Eccl 2: 20; Deut. 28: 28; Ps. 143: 4; Jer. 32: 40.
>
> (e) All Degrees of Anguish. Josh. 5: 1; Jer. 4: 19; Lev. 26: 36; Ps. 102: 4.
>
> (f) All Conscious Unity. 1 Chron. 12:38; Jer. 32:39; Ezek. 11: 19; Acts 4: 32.

In our studies of the heart, it will be an astounding thing for us to be told, and then to realize, that love springs from our voluntary choice.

(c) Love. (1 Tim. 1:5; Prov. 23:26; Judg. 5:9; Phil. 1:7; 2 Cor. 7:3.)

If the division is made in the Bible between Divine and human love, it is only to sum up, or illustrate, Divine love. Love is the sovereign preference of my person for another person manifesting itself in the self-imposed weakness of pity and compassion.

Take it in the highest meaning, and you will find that love never springs naturally, that is, it does not spring naturally out of the human heart. Therefore it is open to every one to choose whether he or she will have this love rooted in them by the gift of God's Holy Spirit.

What we are emphasizing is the need of voluntary choice; there is practically no use praying, "O Lord, for more love! Give me love like Thine; I do want to love Thee better," if one has not begun at the first place, and that first thing is to choose to receive the Spirit that will shed abroad that love. (Rom. 5:5; Luke 11:13.) "We must beware of one tendency in ourselves, and that is to try to do what God alone can do, Und then to blame God for not doing what we alone can do. For instance, .. we try to "save" ourselves, but God only can do that, and then we try to "sanctify" ourselves, but God only can do that, then, after He has done those sovereign works of grace, we have to work that grace out in our lives. (Phil. 2:12, 13.)

We have, then, to make the voluntary choice of receiving the Holy Spirit, who will "shed abroad" in our hearts this wonderful love, and create in us the sovereign preference for Jesus Christ, and if I have this sovereign love in my heart, then my love for all other people will be relative to that centre. Paul, you remember, brings that out very clearly when he says, "We do not preach ourselves, we preach Jesus Christ as Lord, and ourselves your servants, for Jesus' sake." (2 Cor. 4:5.)

The great mainspring, then, is this love, and I, by voluntary choice, can have it created and shed abroad in me, and the Spirit sheds abroad that love which will go on (unless I hinder by disobedience) developing and disciplining and manifesting the perfect love mentioned in First Corinthians, chapter thirteen.

(d) Hate. (Lev. 19:17; Ps. 105: 25.)

The exact opposite of love is hate. Hate is a subject we do not hear much about in connection with Christianity nowadays. The two passages quoted are chosen from an innumerable number in the Bible.

Hatred is the supreme detestation of my personality for another, and that other person ought to be the devil. You will find the Word of God is clear all through about the wrong of hating our brother men, and Paul shows us why it is wrong, that bad men are simply the manifestation of Satan's power. Paul says, "You do not battle against flesh and blood." (Eph. 6:12.) It is not the bad men we are fighting against, it is not the bad people, but it is the" principalities" and "powers" over and behind them.

The presentation of the love of God as having no hate for the wrong and the evil and the sin and the badness and the devil, would simply mean that His love is not as strong as my love, because the stronger and higher and more emphatic your love the more intense is its obverse, hate. God loves us and loves the world so much that He hates, with a perfect hatred, the thing that is twisting and the being that is turning men away from Him, away from right. The two antagonists, to put it in a crude, brief phrase, are God and the devil.

Probably the best way to use David's "cursing" Psalms is in some such way as this, "Do not I hate them that hate Thee?" What is it that hates God? Nobody you know hates God half as much as the old disposition in you; that is the thing you have to hate. The carnal mind is enmity against God, that is the thing you have to hate. It is the principle that lusts against the Spirit of God, and is determined to have your body and mind to rule them away from God, and the Spirit of God will awaken in you an unmeasured hatred of that power, until you not only get sick of it, but sick to death of it, and gladly make the moral choice to go to its funeral. The whole meaning of Romans 6:6 is just that thing put in Scriptural language, "We know that our old man is crucified with Christ." That "old man" is the thing the Spirit of God has taught us to hate. Make no excuse for it, and you will find the concentration of the love of God in your heart will fix your soul in horror against the wrong thing. So next time you come across those Psalms which sensitive people think so terrible, bring them to bear on the right thing.

One more thing, the Book says that God loves the world (John 3:16), and the Book also says that "if you love the world, you are an enemy of God." (1 John 2:15.) The difference between the loves is simply this; God loves the world so much that He goes all lengths to remove the wrong from it, and God loves me so much that He goes all lengths to remove the wrong from me, and I have to have the same kind of love. The other love simply means I take the world as it is, and am perfectly delighted with it. All your talk about sin and evil and the devil and atonement are all so many Orientalisms, and people say the world is all right and we are very happy in it! This is the sentiment that hates God. The person who is the friend of that is the enemy of God. (Jas. 4:4.) Do I love the world sufficiently to spend and be spent for God to manifest His grace through me, till the wrong and the evil are removed? Thank God that all these voluntary choices in my heart and life will work out those tremendous purposes! Have I made the voluntary choice? Have I settled the account with God? Have I come to the end of myself? Am I really a spiritual pauper? Do I really realize, without any cunning, that I have no power in myself at all to be holy? Do I deliberately choose, then, to receive from Him the sovereign grace that will work those things in me, and when He puts them in, work them out with glad activity?

2. Versatility.

"We explained this in a previous study, as "the power to turn easily from one thing to another." "When you are in difficult circumstances, remember the time when they were not so trying. God has given you the power to turn yourself by remembering, and if you lose that power, you punish yourself, and that way will lead to melancholia and a "fixed idea."

As expressive of this great and surprising power, take (e) Memory, to emphasize again what we said before, is not in the brain, but in the heart. The brain is not a spiritual thing, the brain is a physical thing, and the brain recalls more or less clearly what the heart remembers. Memory exists in the heart because memory is a spiritual thing. When Jesus said to the rich man, "Son, remember" (Luke 16), He was talking to a man not in this order of things at all, to a man not with a physical brain. (Isa. 65:17; Jer. 3:16; 2 Chron. 7:11; Acts 7:23; 1 Cor. 2:9; Luke 1:66; 21:14.)

These passages refer to the marvelous power of God to blot out of memory certain things. Forgetting, with us, is a defect; forgetting, with God, is an attribute. God forgets our sins, "I will remember them no more for ever," and these passages allude to the power God grants of forgetting.

Now look at Luke 1:66 and 21:14. There the memory is placed in the heart, and one never forgets unless by the sovereign grace of God. The problem with us, in this life, is, that we do not recall easily. Tour recalling depends upon the state of your physical brain, and when people say they have a "bad memory," what they mean is they have a bad power of recalling. Paul says, "Forgetting those things that are behind" (Phil. 3:13), but notice what kind of things he does forget; he never forgot what he was before, that is, Paul never forgot that he was a perjurer, a blasphemer and an injurious person. (1 Tim. 1: 13.) That is not what he is referring to, he is referring to his spiritual attainments. "I forget what I have attained to, because I press on to something else." Immediately you begin to "rest on your oars" about your spiritual experience, saying, "Thank God I have attained to this!" that moment you begin to go back. Forgetting to what you attained, keep your eyes fixed on the Lord Jesus, and press on.

Do not confuse those two statements. People say God helps us to forget our past life. Is that quite true ? God's grace every now and again brings you back to remember who you are, and brings you back to remember the "pit from whence you were digged," so that you do understand that what you are is all by the sovereign grace of God, not by our own work, otherwise you would be the most uplifted, the most proud and worst of all creatures.

With regard to people with "impaired memory," as it is termed, some say it is best to remove them; it would be better, if it were legal, to put them into a sleep. Why? Because we estimate wrongly; we estimate according to the perfection of the machine, the condition of the character. Now God looks where we cannot see, God looks at the heart; He does not look at the brain, He does not look as man looks, He does not sum up the way we sum up; and here is the wonderful thing, that, by handing our lives over, by a voluntary choice, to God, and receiving His Holy Spirit, He can purify us down to deeper depths than we can ever think of going. Then -how foolish people are not to hand over the keeping of their lives to Him, for "He will keep the feet of His saints," and keep your heart so pure that you would tremble with amazement if you knew how pure the atonement of the Lord Jesus can make the vilest human heart, if that heart will keep in the light with God walking in the light as He is in the light. (1 John 1:7.)

We use that verse much too glibly. It is simply God letting the plummet right straight down to the very depths of a redeemed heart's experience, and saying, "Now that is how I see you" – made pure by this marvelous atonement of Jesus, the last strand of memory purified by God.

Now take the next thing, (f) Thinking. Thinking is placed in the heart, not in the brain. The real spiritual powers of a man reside in his heart, which is the centre of his physical life, the centre of his soul life, and the centre of his spiritual life. Thinking is in the heart, expression of thinking is referred to the brain and the mouth, because by those organs thinking becomes articulate. (Gen. 8:21; 17:17; 24:45; Eccl. 1:16; Matt. 24: 48; Heb. 4:12.)

Thinking according to the Bible, resides in the heart, and that is the region the Spirit of God deals with. Take this as a general rule, that Jesus Christ never answered any questions that sprang from man's head, because any question that springs intellectually merely from our brains, we have always borrowed from some book we have read, or from somebody else we have heard speak, but the questions that spring from our hearts, the real problems that vex us, Jesus Christ answers those. You will find your problems and mine very difficult to state in words, and those are the problems Jesus Christ solves, those are the questions He came to deal with. He deals with this implicit centre.

The heart is the first thing to live in physical birth, and in the spiritual birth it is the same; and it is a wonderful thing that God can cleanse and purify the thinking of my heart. That is why God says "out of the fulness of the heart the mouth speaketh." The Bible actually says that words are born in the heart, not in the tongue. The heart is (g) The Birthplace of Words. (Job 8:10; Matt. 12:34.) Jesus Christ said about His speaking that He always spoke what His Father wanted. Why? Did His Father write His words out and tell Him to learn them by heart? No, the mainspring of the heart of Jesus Christ was exactly the mainspring of the heart of God the Father, and consequently the words Jesus Christ spoke were the exact expression of God's thought, and the tongue in our Lord got to its right place; He never spoke from His head, He always spoke from His heart.

"If a man seem to be religious, and cannot bridle his tongue, his religion is vain," there is nothing in it. Now this tongue and this brain are under our control, not under God's.

Look at the history of words in different countries of our human race. Take our words to-day, take the words at the head of these studies, they are all technical words, there is no "heart" in them. Very few people speak, in an ordinary way, from their hearts. Take the earlier days, take the language of the "Authorized Version" of the Bible! The Bible was translated into the language the people spoke. To-day our speech is a great aid to inner hypocrisy, and it becomes a great snare, for it is so easy to talk piously and live iniquitously. Remember, speaking from your heart does not mean "refinement " of speech merely; Jesus Christ's speech sounded anything but nice to natural ears sometimes. (Matt. 23.) Some words He used and some applications

He made of His truths were terrible and rugged. Read His description of the heart: "Out of the heart," says Jesus, "proceed" – and then comes the catalogue. The upright men and women of the world simply do not believe it. Jesus Christ did not speak as a man there, He spoke as a master of men, with an absolute knowledge of what the human heart was like. That is why He so continually pleads with us to hand over the keeping of our hearts to Him. There is a difference between "innocent" and "pure"; innocence is the true condition of a child, not of a man or woman; purity is the characteristic of men and women. Purity is something that has been tested and tried, and has triumphed; something that has character at the back of it, that can overcome, and has overcome; innocence has always to be shielded. Jesus Christ, by His Spirit, makes us men and women fit to face the misery and wrong and discordance of this life, but always keeping in tune with Him ourselves.

3. Virtues and Vices.

All degrees of fear, all degrees of anguish, and all conscious unity reside in the heart. (Scripture in the chart.)

Watch, if you have not noticed already, how "natural virtues" break down. God does not build up our natural virtues and transfigure them. You will find, very often, natural virtues in a good, upright worldling; when born again of the Spirit of God, they seem to all go wrong, and confusion is the result of the Spirit of God coming in. Jesus Himself said, "I did not come to sow peace on the earth, I did not come to fling broadcast seeds of peace, I came to do the opposite, I came to send a sword," something that would at once divide people, divide homes, divide a man's own personal unity with himself, and the reason is this, that our virtues naturally are not promises of what we are going to be, they are remnants of what we once were.

There is the difference between modern ways of looking at men and the Bible way. Modern people look at man and his virtues and say, "What a wonderful promise of what he is going to be! Give him right conditions, and he will develop and be all right. " Jesus Christ says, "He must be born again first, he has not the germ of the right nature in him, he is a ruin, and only the Spirit of God changes that." You cannot patch up your natural virtues to come anywhere near Jesus Christ's commands. No natural love can come anywhere near the love Jesus Christ wants, no natural patience, no natural purity, no natural forgiveness, comes anywhere near what Jesus Christ commands. The hymn has it rightly:

> "And every virtue we possess,
> And every victory won,
> And every thought of holiness,
> Are His alone.' '

What we have to learn is that we must bring every bit of this bodily machine into harmony with this new life of God, and He will exhibit in us the virtues that were characteristic of the Lord Jesus; He makes the supernatural virtues natural. That is the meaning of learning how to draw on God's life for everything.

(d) All Degrees of Fear. (Prov. 12: 25; Eccl. 2: 20; Deut. 28:28; Ps. 143:4; Jer. 32:40.)

Fear resides in the heart. If you take a big breath, you encourage your heart to pump the blood better through your veins, and the physical fear will go; that is the physical side, but the soul illustration is the same. God alters and expels all the old fear by putting a new Spirit and a new concern in. What is that concern? The fear lest I grieve Him.

(e) All Degrees of Anguish. (Jer. 4:19; Josh. 5: 1; Lev. 26:36; Ps. 102:4.)

There you get the three, the physical, the psychical, and the spirit, all centered in the heart. All anguish is in the heart. Now what do I suffer* from? "What I suffer from proves where my heart is. What did Jesus Christ suffer from? The anguish of His heart was on account of sin against His Father. What is the anguish of my heart? Can I fill up what remains behind of His sufferings? Am I only shocked at social evils and social wrongs ? or am I as profoundly shocked at pride against God? Do I feel as keenly as Jesus Christ did the erecting of man's self-will against God? The centering of the true anguish is right in the heart of man, and when God gets your heart and mine right, He brings us into fellowship with His sufferings, knowing the power of His resurrection, proving in my life the fellowship of His sufferings, filling up what remains behind.

(f) All Conscious Unity. (1 Chron. 12:38; Jer. 32:39; Ezek. 11:19; Acts 4:32.)

The first and last of these references are to unification. The heart is the place where the unification resides, it is where God works; when once He gets there, He brings spirit, soul and body into perfect unity. There are three other things that can do that besides God – the world, the flesh and the devil can do it. The world will give an all-conscious unification to man's heart, the devil will do it and the flesh will do it.

The man who gives way to sensuality, to worldliness, to devilishness or to covetousness, does not want God; he is perfectly satisfied without Him: God calls it idolatry.

We have to watch our hearts to see what they are getting into unity with; what is my heart bringing my soul and body into line with? " Other lords beside Thee, Lord, have had dominion over us."

CHAPTER XII.

HEART: THE RADICAL REGION OF LIFE, THE RENDEZVOUS OF PERFECT LIFE.

1. THE INNER.
> (a) Highest Love. Ps. 73:26; Mark 12:30, 31.
> (b) Highest License. Ezek. 28:2.
> (c) Darkened. Rom. 1: 21; Eph. 4: 18.
> (d) Hardened. Isa. 6:10; Jer. 16:12; 2 Cor. 3:14.

2. THE INMOST.
> (a) Laboratory of Life. Mark 7: 20-23.
> (b) Lusts. Mark 4: 15, 19; Rom. 1: 24.
> (c) Law of Nature. Rom. 2: 15.
> (d) Law of Grace. Isa. 51: 7; Jer. 31: 33.
> (e) Seat of Conscience. Heb. 10:22; 1 John 3: 19 21.
> (f) Seat of Belief and Disbelief. Rom. 10: 10; Heb. 3: 12.

3. THE INNERMOST.
> (a) Inspiration of God. 2 Cor. 8:16.
> (b) Inspiration of Satan. John 13: 2.
> (c) Indwelling of Christ. Eph. 3:17.
> (d) Indwelling of Spirit. 2 Cor. 1: 22.
> (e) Abode of Peace. Col. 3: 15.
> (f) Abode of Love. Rom. 5: 5.
> (g) Abode of Light. 2 Pet. 1:19.
> (h) Abode of Communion. Eph. 5: 19.

"Rendezvous" means an appointed place of meeting. The heart is the oppointed place of meeting, not only for all the life of the body physically, but for all the life of the soul, and of the spirit. We have made quite clear that the heart is the centre of the bodily life physically, the centre of the soul life, and the centre of the spirit life; and that the Bible places in the heart what the modern thinkers put in the brain.

All through these studies, we have insisted on what the Bible insists on, that our body is the most gracious gift that God has given us, and if we "hand over" the mainspring of our life to Him, we can work out what He works in, through our bodily lives. It is through our bodily lives that Satan works out, and thank God it is through our bodily lives that God's Spirit works out.

God fills us with His grace, fills us with His Spirit, puts all that is wrong right, does not suppress it, does not counteract it, but really readjusts the whole thing. Then begins our work; we work out what He works in, and we have to beware of that snare of blaming God for not doing what we alone can do. When the Bible says, "Be renewed in the spirit of your mind," it is the heart that is referred to, renewed by the Spirit of God. The expression of that mind comes through the mechanism of our brain, and the marvelous emancipation which comes slowly and surely is that when the Spirit of God has altered the heart and filled it with a new Spirit, we have the power to will as God wills, and to do what God wants us to do.

You remember Jesus Christ puts the test that "if any man love Me, he will keep My commandments;" not some of them, but all of them. No man can keep Jesus Christ's commandments unless God has done a radical work in his heart; then, if He has, that is the practical, simple, common-sense test, "You can keep My commandments."

1. The Inner, 2. The Inmost, and 3. The Innermost. Now we come right into the very centre, where we do not know anything but what God reveals. Let me remind you that God's Book counsels, "Guard your heart, for out of it are the issues of life." We are far too difficult to understand ourselves; we must hand the keeping of our hearts over to God. If we think we are simple and easy to understand, we will not ask God to save or to keep us, but if we have come to the condition of the Psalmist in Psalm 139, we will hand the keeping of our souls straight over to Him, and say, "Search me!"

First of all, take (a) Highest Love. (See Ps. 73: 26.) Put the emphasis where the Bible ever puts it, "GOD is the strength of my heart." Mark 12: 30, 31. The highest love of your human heart is not for our kind, but for God. Our Lord distinctly showed His disciples that, if they were going to live the spiritual life, they must barter the natural life for it; that is, they must forego the natural life. Remember what we mean by the natural life, the ordinary, sensible, healthy, worldly-minded life. The highest love is not natural to the natural heart, we naturally do not love God. In this life, we will find out that we are apt to name "God" in thinking by names we ought to apply to Satan. Satan uses the greatest problems in this life to slander God's character to us, and he makes us think of all the calamities and miseries and wrongs in this life as springing from God.

"We have defined love, in its highest sense, as being the sovereign preference of my person for another person. The surest sign that God has done a work of grace in my heart is that I love Jesus Christ best, not weakly, not faintly, not intellectually, but passionately, personally and devotedly, overwhelming every other love of my life.

Another striking verse is Romans 5:5: "The love of God is shed abroad in our hearts by the Holy Spirit which is given to us." Paul does not say the capacity to love God is shed abroad in our hearts, but "the love of God." The Bible only knows one love in this connection, and that is the supreme, dominating love of God. And Jesus Christ taught that, if our hearts, in their inmost centre, have had the work of grace done in them, we will show the same love to our fellow-men that God showed us.

The natural heart, we cannot repeat it too often, does not want the Gospel, it needs it. We will take God's blessings and lovingkindnesses and prosperities, but when it comes down to close quarters, and God's Spirit informs us that we have to give up our rule of ourselves, and let Him rule us, then at once we understand what Paul means when he says the "carnal mind," which resides in the heart, "is enmity against God." Am I willing for God not to suppress or counteract, but to totally alter the ruling disposition of my heart, until the love of God is shed abroad in my heart? These are the wonderful works of the grace of God, that God can take me by His spirit, through the atonement of Jesus, and alter the centre of my life, and put there the supreme love, the supreme, passionate devotion of my heart, to God Himself.

The modern man does not like His commands; he will not have them, he covers them over and ignores the first commandment. Men put first, "Thou shall love thy neighbor as thyself"; the great cry to-day is "love for mankind." Yet the great cry of Jesus is "love for God first," and the highest love, this great, supreme, passionate devotion of my heart and life, springs from the inner centre changed by God. What a rest there is when the love of God is shed abroad in my heart by the Holy Spirit, when I really realize that God is love, not loving, but love; something infinitely greater than loving, consequently He has to be very stern.

There is no such thing as God overlooking sin. That is where people make a great mistake with regard to love, they say that God is love, and of course He will forgive sin; God is holy love and of course He cannot forgive sin. Jesus Christ did not come to forgive sin, He came to save us from sin. The salvation of Jesus Christ is the removal of the sinner in my heart and the planting in of the saint. That is the marvelous work of grace, and to know; whether the natural heart of man wants the Gospel of God, notice the natural enmity of the heart against the working of the Spirit of God. "No, I do not object to being forgiven, I do not mind being guided, I do not mind being blessed, but really it is too much a radical surrender if I have to give up my right to myself, if I have to allow the Spirit of of God to have absolute control of my heart," that is the natural resentment. But oh, the ineffable-, unspeakable delight when made one with God, one with Jesus, and one with every fellow-believer in this great, overwhelming characteristic of love, and when life becomes possible on God's plan!

(b) Highest License. In Ezekiel 28:2, there is the presentation of the personality of sin, not only the person with a wrong disposition, like we all have inherited, but the picture of the very being we know as Satan, who is the instigator behind the wrong disposition, inciting to license; which simply means, "I will not be bound by anybody's laws but my own!" The spirit that resents God's law will not have anything to say to Him. "I will rule my body as I choose, I will rule my social relationships as I like, I will rule my religious life as I choose, and I will not allow any creed or doctrine or God to rule me." That is the beginning of license.

Watch how often the apostle Paul warns, "Do not use your liberty for license." What is the difference? Why, liberty is the ability to perform the law, perfect freedom to fulfill all the demands of the law; license is rebellion against all law. If my heart does not become the centre of this awful trust, the centre of divine love, it will become the centre of diabolical license. Do people believe that? Jesus Christ's statements are not accepted by the majority of us nowadays. Immediately we look at them, the intenseness of them, the profundity of them and the fearfulness of them, make us shrink straight away.

A very profitable, a very solemn, and a very awful study is the study of the connection of the phrase "children of the devil," as used by Jesus. He is not referring to ordinary sinners; He is referring to religious sinners; natural sinners are called "children of wrath," but whenever our Lord uses the phrase, "children of the devil," He is referring to religious disbelievers, viz.: people who have seen the light and refused to walk in it, will not have it. Remember those two alternatives. Our hearts, thank God! may be the very centre of divine love, making us one with God's thoughts and purposes, or they may be the centre of the devil's rule, making us absolutely one with the being who hates God, one with the "prince of this world," one with the natural life which barters the spiritual.

(c) Darkened. (Rom. 1:21; Eph. 4:18.) Those are striking passages, quite at home in the New Testament, but at home nowhere else.

This is not a darkness that is "intensity of light," it is a refusal to allow any light at all. Read John 3:19, to see our Lord's use of that word "darkness," "This is the condemnation," this is the critical crisis "that the light is come into the world, and men loved darkness rather than the light, because their deeds were evil." Jesus said,, on another occasion, "If the light in you be darkness, how great is that darkness." Darkness is "my own point of view;" when once I allow the prejudice of my head to shut down the witness of my heart, I make my heart dark.

When Jesus Christ preached His first public sermon in Nazareth, the place "He was brought up in" ((See Luke 4), the people's hearts witnessed to Him, wonderfully and marvelously, but then their prejudices got in the way, and they closed down the witness of their hearts, and they broke up the service, and tried to kill Him. That is an instance of how it is possible to choke the witness of the heart by the prejudice of the head. That it what Jesus is referring to in John 3. He is talking to a man who is in danger of closing down the witness of his heart because of his Jewish prejudice. Is there any light some of us have been thanking God for? (as the 118th Psalm puts it, "Blessed be God who hath showed us light"), and then is there a prejudice coming in, a closing down the witness of the heart? If so, that is where the darkened heart begins; light does not shine because it cannot. You can only see along the line of your prejudices, until the Holy Spirit has come in; if you will let Him come in with His dynamite power to blow away the lines of your prejudice, then you can begin to "go" in God's light. A darkened heart is a terrible thing, because a darkened heart may make a man happy; a man with a darkened heart may be peaceful, saying, "My heart is not bad, I am not convicted of sin, all this talk about being born again and filled with the

Holy Spirit is so much absurdity." The natural heart does not want the Gospel of Jesus, and will fight against it; it needs it, but it takes the convicting grace of God to bring a man or woman to know the radical work of grace that God does in us.

Then (d) Hardened. (2. Cor. 3:14.) The characteristic of hardening is quite familiar in the Bible, but unfamiliar everywhere else. For instance, the Bible says that God hardened Pharaoh's heart. "Whenever a man gets into an exalted position, it is that in which he may show the marvelous grace of God, or else it will harden his heart away from God. You find it true everywhere of the prejudiced heart and the hardened heart, not so much the darkened heart. There is no witness of the heart that is being crushed down, it is simply hard, it is not touched; when God's love and God's works are abroad, it remains like ice; you may smash and break it by judgments, but you simply break ice. The only way we can alter the hardened heart is to melt it, and the only power that can melt a hardened heart is the fire of the Holy Ghost. The heart is such a truly central thing that God alone knows it, and the illustrations used in the Bible are given in varying changing figures, so that we may get a bit of understanding as to how God deals with us. Thank God, everyone of us may have the first, the highest love!

Now take the second column of the outline, (a) A laboratory is a place where anything is prepared for use. Remember, your heart never dies, your heart is as immortal as God's Spirit, for it is the centre of man's spirit. Memory never dies, mind never dies; our daily machines dies, and the manifestation of our heart and life in this body dies, but the heart never dies. "Son, remember," that was to a man out of the body. The things prepared for use are prepared for use in the heart. (Mark 7:20-23.) These are staggering verses, and they spring from the lips of the Master of the human heart. They are not the shrewd guesses of a scientist, or the simple invitations of an apostle, they are the revelation of God Almighty, through Jesus Christ. Look at them, and see whether they do not awaken resentment in you unless you have received the Spirit of God.

Those verses mean this, there is no crime ever committed by a human being that every human being is not capable of. How many people believe that? "Why," they say, "that is morbid nonsense; absurd." That judgment means that Jesus Christ did not know what He was talking about, and people are accepting willingly and eagerly and all-embracingly, "Christian Science," that popularization of this other thing, as though there were no such things as sin and defilement, no such thing as death; they say they are all imagination. The consequence is, people are preaching the gospel of "temperament," "cheer up and look on the bright side of things." How can a man live on the bright side of things when the Spirit of God has shown him the possibilities of Hell inside him? The majority of us are shockingly ignorant, simply because we will not allow the Spirit of God to reveal to us the enormous dangers that lie hidden in the centre of our lives. Dangers to you and to me, said Jesus, never come from outside, always from the inside. If we will accept His verdict and receive the Spirit of God, He will see that those things never belch up because He will re-relate the whole heart from the inside.

The "Rendezvous of Perfect Life." Remember "perfect life" is not "perfection;" perfect life is a perfect adjustment of every one of the powers of the heart to God. By perfection is meant, perfect attainments in everything. Perfect life means the perfect adjustment of all my relationships to God; nothing out of joint, but all rightly related. Now I can begin to live the perfect life, that is, I can begin to attain. A child is a perfect human being, so is a man; what is the difference? The one is not grown, the other is. Read Phil. 3:12-15, and you will find the two perfections put very clearly. "When you are sanctified, says Paul, you are perfectly adjusted to God, but remember, you have done nothing yet, you have attained to nothing in the perfect life yet, you are simply perfectly adjusted to God. The whole life is right, undeserving of censure, now then begin to attain in your bodily life, to prove that your heart is perfectly adjusted.

(b) Lusts. (Mark 4:15-19; Rom. 12:4.)

What is lust? "I must have it at once!" that is lust. Jesus says that that will destroy every work of grace He ever begins in us. "The lust of other things entering in chokes the Word." Now lust is used once in the Bible of another thing beside wrong. It is used of the Spirit of God, "lusting against the flesh;" that means that the Spirit of God, once He gets in in spiritual new birth, lusts after, must have at once, this body for God, and He will not tolerate for one second "the carnal mind," consequently, when a person is born again of the Spirit, there is a disclosure of the enmity against God. No man knows he has that enemy on the inside till he has received the Spirit of God. Immediately he has, then the carnal mind is aroused, and the carnal mind sneers, and the carnal mind clamors, and the carnal mind says, "No, I will not yield to the Spirit," and there you have the war described in Galatians 5. The "Spirit against the flesh, and the flesh against the Spirit," both of them demanding, "I must have this body at once," while I have to give the casting vote. "Which power am I going to give this body to? Thank God for everyone who has said, "Lord, I give it to Thee; I want to be identified with the death of Jesus Christ until I know that my 'old man' is identified with the cross!"

But watch lust on the bad side; watch where it begins. "You did run well, who did hinder you?" Think what simple things Jesus Christ says will crush what He put in, "the lust of other things," "the cares of this world." Once let a man or woman get worried, and the choking of the grace of God begins. If anyone has really had wrought into heart and head the complete, amazing revelation which Jesus Christ gives, that God is love and that I can never remember anything that He will forget, then worry is impossible, also note how much Jesus Christ talks against worry, and you will find the reason. The "cares of this world' ' produce worry, the "lust of other things" coming in will choke all that God put in. Is the thing that is claiming my attention now the one thing that God has saved and sanctified me for? If so, instantly life becomes simpler, the crowding, clamoring lusts have no life.

(c) The Law of Nature, (d) the Law; of Grace, (e) the Seat of Conscience and (f) the Seat of Belief and Disbelief. They are all in the heart.

Conscience we call the "eye of the soul," and the orbit of the conscience, the orbit of that marvelous recorder, is the heart, "Having our heart sprinkled from an evil conscience," and God puts the law of grace where the law of nature worked, in the heart* Thank God for His sovereign grace, which can alter the mainspring of life! God alters the mainspring of the life, God alters the heart, God purifies the heart, God fills the heart.

The Seat of Belief and Unbelief. (Heb. 3:12.) There the distinction is made perfectly clear. Your heart must never be an agnostic; your head, if you like, may be. The reason people disbelieve God is not because they do not understand things with their heads, there are very few things we understand with our heads; it is because they have turned their hearts in another direction. Why was Jesus Christ so stern against "disbelief"? Because it never springs from the head, but from the wrong direction of the heart. Every Christian is an avowed agnostic in the head. Have you ever thought of that? How do I know God? All I know of God I have accepted as a revelation, I did not find Him out by my head. "No man by searching can find out God." Next time you meet some agnostic friends, say something like that to them, and see if it does not alter the problem for them.

One has to keep one's mind open about a great many things. Can I have the evil heart of unbelief taken out of me, and a heart of belief put in? Thank God, the answer comes "Yes!" (Ezek. 36:26.) Can I have an impure, defiled heart made pure, so pure that it is pure in God's sight? Then comes the answer "Yes!" (1 John 1:7.) Can I be filled with the Holy Ghost, until every nook and cranny is exactly under the control of God? Then comes the answer "Yes!" (Matt. 3:11, 12.)

Jesus Christ's Gospel works down in the centre first, not in the circumference. He works exactly where we work in the natural world. Nobody is capable of thinking about being born before they are born, or how they will live after they are born into this world, we have to be born into this world to live, and some of us never think about it. Jesus says, "Do not marvel that I say unto you, Ye must be born again." You must be born into this new world first, and if you want to know My doctrine, do My will spiritually, a right relation of the heart to God is essential first. How am I going to get a right heart relationship to God? "Why, simply by accepting God's Spirit. Who will put me in the right place to understand how God's grace works? Let any man or woman receive the Spirit of God and see whether the Spirit of God will not lead into all truth.

Now take 3. The Innermost

(a) The Inspiration of God may dwell in the innermost recesses of my heart. Read the passage and you will be surprised at the seeming slightness of it. (2 Cor. 8:16.) There the inspiration for benevolence and philanthropy springs from God, and God's Book has some stern revelations to make about our philanthropy and benevolence. They spring from a totally wrong motive; the inspiration of God does not patch up my natural virtues, but remakes the whole of the being, and I find that every virtue I possess is His alone. God does not come in and patch up my good works, He turns the whole lot out, and puts in the Spirit that was characteristic of Jesus; it is His patience, His love, and His tenderness and gentleness exhibited through me. "If any man eat My flesh and drink My blood." When God alters a man's heart, and plants His Spirit inside, the actions have the inspiration of God at the basis; if they have not, we may have (b) the Inspiration of Satan. (John 13:2.)

(c) The Indwelling of Christ (Eph. 3:17) – an unspeakable wonder! Those two figures are very remarkable, made one in the mystical body of Christ, that Christ may indwell us. There are three pictures of Jesus given in the New Testament; first, the historic; second, God incarnate; and third, the mystical body of Christ, that is being made up of sanctified believers now. By the sovereign work of God and the indwelling Christ in me, I can show through my body, through my eyes, my life, my bodily relationships, the very same characteristics that were strong in the Lord Jesus, so that men may know that I have been with Jesus as He said, "men seeing your good works may glorify your Father in Heaven."

The thought is unspeakably full of glory, that God the Holy Ghost, the marvelous grace of God, can come into my heart and fill it so full with the life of God that it will manifest itself all through this body that used to manifest the other thing. Other things being equal, that means that I am willing to let it out, that I am willing to keep on that line, to keep in the light, I am willing to walk in the light, I am determined to keep in the light and obey the Spirit. Then those characteristics of the indwelling Christ will manifest themselves.

(d) The Indwelling of the Spirit. This is a much more explaining thing. The man Christ Jesus, His Spirit, His soul, and His body, were kept in perfect oneness with God the Father; when the Spirit of God dwells in me the very same thing happens. My spirit and soul and body are made at one with God, that is the meaning of atonement. Study Jesus Christ's life, always right to God; His outlook on men was always right, His prayer life was always right to God, His outlook down on sin and the devil and Hell was always right; He never ignored any of these facts (like a great many modern people are doing), and that Spirit will produce the same characteristics in me, energizing my spirit by the Holy Spirit, lifting me through the marvelous atonement of Jesus Christ, by the sovereign works of grace, into the same at-oneness with God that Jesus Christ had. "As He is, so are we in this world." "That they may be one as we are one," not by absorption, but by identification; not the Buddhist teaching, that is so prevalent nowadays, that we have to be absorbed into one great, big, infinite Being, that is not the teaching here, but one in identity. A disposition just like Jesus Christ's, where we are only interested in the things that would have interested the Lord, and we cannot be appealed to by the line on which the world is appealed to.

(e) The Abode of Peace, (f) of Love, (g) of Light, and (h) of Communion.

This is the peace of God, not peace with God; Thank God, there is a peace with God, but this is a different thing. "My peace I leave with you," says Jesus. The peace that characterized Jesus characterizes His saints. The love of God is shed abroad in our hearts, not the capacity to love God, but the very inward character of the love of God. That is what Paul means when he says those words we are so familiar with, "I have been crucified with Christ, nevertheless I live, yet not I, but Christ liveth in me; and the life I now live in the flesh I live by the faith of the Son of God." Not faith in Jesus, but the faith that was in Jesus is in me; the same faith, peace, love and light that characterized Him, characterize me; I am identified with Him to such a degree that you cannot detect a different spring, because there is not one! "It is no longer my old disposition that rules me," says Paul.

Watch where language fails, and that is where people get confused in the New Testament. If you have not the Spirit of God within you, you find the apostle Paul is trying and straining language beyond its limit, to express exactly what the Spirit of God does; the Spirit of God alters the ruling disposition, and the same man shows himself entirely different. Peace, light and love; that wonderful picture of light, "No shadow and no variableness caused by turning," – nothing to hide, those are the characteristics of God, and Peter and Paul say, "Walk as children of light." John says, "Walk in the light." 1 John 1:7 is a wonderful description of the kind of fellowship we will have. Natural affinity does not count here at all, watch in your life how God has altered your affinities since you were filled with the Spirit; you have an affinity of fellowship with people you have no natural affinity for at all; you have fellowship with anybody else who is in the light, no matter who they are, what nation they belong to, or anything else, a most extraordinary alteration.

CHAPTER XIII.

OURSELVES: I; ME; MINE, OURSELVES AS "KNOWER." I THE "EGO."

1. SOME DISTINCTIONS OF IMPORTANCE.
    (a) Individuality.
    (b) Personality.
    (c) Egoism and Egotism.

2. SOME DETERMINATIONS OF INTEREST. John 3:2.
    (a) The "Ego M is Inscrutable. Isa. 26:9; Ps. 19:12.
    (b) The "Ego" is Introspective. Ps. 139; Prov. 20:27.
    (c) The "Ego" is Individual. Ezek. 18:1-4.

SOME DELUSIONS OF IMPORTANCE. 2 Thess. 2: 7-12.
    (a) The "Ego" in Delusions of Insanity.
    (b) The "Ego" in Delusions of Alternating Personalities.
    (c) The "Ego" in Delusions of Mediums and Possessions.

3. SOME DISCRIMINATIONS OF INTEREST. Heb. 2: 10, 11.
    (a) Independence of the Persons. John 1: 11-13.
    (b) Identification with the Purpose. Gal. 2: 20.
    (c) Incorporation of the Power. 1 Cor. 12: 12, 14.

This last section deals with the Readjustment of Ego in Redemption.

1. Some Distinctions of Importance.

We divide this subject of Ourselves into two – one, the part that knows, the Ego; and the other the known, the Me.

First of all, we will take these distinctions generally – Individuality and Personality, and Egoism and Egotism, and find how the Bible gives wonderful insight into these distinctions.

(a) Individuality is a much slighter term than (b) Personality. "We speak of an individual animal, an individual man, and an individual thing. An individual man simply happens to be one by himself, he takes up so much space, requires so many cubic feet of air, etc. Personality is infinitely more. Possibly the best illustration we can get is a lamp. A lamp not lighted will illustrate the individual; a lamp lighted will illustrate the personality. The personality in its influence goes far beyond the individual lamp; it takes up no more room than the individual lamp, but the light permeates far and wide. "Ye are the light of the world," said our Lord. "We do not take up very much room individually, but our influence goes far beyond our calculation. So when we use the term personality, we are using the very biggest mental conception we can have, and that is why we call God a Person, because "person" is the word that has the largest import we know. We do not call God an individual; we call Him a Person. He may be a great deal more, but at least He must be that. It is necessary to remember this when the personality of God is denied, and God is taken to be a tendency. If He is, He is much less than I am. Our personality is always too big for us. When we come to examine the next sections and trace the Bible teaching, we will find that the Bible says we are much too big will find that the Bible says we are much too complex to understand ourselves. Another illustration for Personality, more often used, is as follows: an island at sea may seem very easily explored, yet how amazed we become when we realize that it is the top of a great mountain, whose greater part is hidden under the waves of the sea, and goes sheer down to deeper depths than we can fathom. That little island represents our conscious personality, the part we are conscious of is a very tiny part; the great underneath part we know nothing about, and consequently there are upheavals from beneath that we cannot estimate. We cannot grasp ourselves at all. We begin by thinking we can, but we have to come to the Bible standpoint that no one knows himself but God. "There is a way that seemeth right unto a man, but the ends thereof are the ways of death." Individuality then is a smaller term than personality. Personality means that peculiar, incalculable being that is meant when you speak of "you" as distinct from everybody else. People say, "Oh, I cannot understand myself," of course you cannot. "Nobody else understands me," of course they don't. There is only one Being who understands us, and that is our Creator.

It is necessary to have the proper distinctions in our minds regarding (c) Egoism and Egotism. "Egotism" is a conceited insistence on my own particular ways and manners and customs. It is an easily discernible characteristic, and fortunately is condemned straightway by all right-thinking people. We are all inclined to overlook it in very young and very ignorant people, but even in them it is of the detestable, vicious order. But of Egoism we can only say good things. It is that system of thinking that makes the human personality the centre. Thinking that starts from all kinds of abstractions is contrary to the Bible way of thinking. The Bible way gets us right straight down to man as the centre. What puts man right and keeps man right is the revelation in God's Book. For instance, our Lord and the apostle Paul continually centre around "I," but there is no egotism about it. It is egoism, everything is related to man, to his salvation, to his sanctification, to his keeping, etc. Every system of thinking which has man for its centre and as its aim and purpose is rightly called Egoism.

2. Some Determinations of Interest

The personality of man is the most internal nature of man, it is distinct from spirit, soul and body and yet embraces all. It is the innermost centre of man's spirit, soul and body, and there are three things about this Ego. It is (a) Inscrutable, we cannot understand it, we cannot search it out. The Bible says that a man is incapable of satisfactorily searching himself out. Isaiah 26:9 says, "With my soul have I desired Thee in the night, yea, with my spirit within me will I seek Thee early." The distinction there is made clearly between the inmost personality called "I" and spirit, soul and body, and the distinction is kept up all through God's Book. I can search, my spirit up to a certain point; I can search my soul and my body, but only up to a certain point. Man begins to find, immediately he comes to examine himself, that he is inscrutable. He cannot examine himself thoroughly. He may get certain arbitrary distinctions and call himself body, soul and spirit, and instantly he finds it is not satisfactory. Those of you who are interested in this kind of reading, will constantly find the word "subliminal" occurring, i. e., below the threshold, something that is below the threshold of my consciousness, and every now and again you will get something emerging from below the threshold of your consciousness that upsets your thought about yourself. Our Lord dealing with His disciples brought them into places where they became conscious of doing things they never knew. In Matthew 16 we read that Christ said to Peter, "Get thee behind Me, Satan." Peter had not the slightest notion that God Almighty lifted him up as a trumpet and blew a blast through him, which Jesus Christ recognized as the voice of His Father; and a little while afterwards Satan took him up and blew a blast through him, which Jesus recognized as the voice of Satan. If you had told Peter that he was capable of denying his Lord with "oaths and curses," he would have been unable to understand how you could think it.

There are possibilities below the threshold in my life and yours which no one knows but God, and Jesus Christ brought His disciples through crises to reveal to them that they were much too big for themselves. There were forces of evil and good within them which played havoc with every resolution and every prayer they made. "Who can understand his errors? Cleanse Thou me from secret faults." (Psa. 19:12.) This is simply a type verse of a revelation which runs all through. God's Book. We cannot understand our selves, we do not know the beginnings of our dreams or our motives, we do not know our secret errors, they lie below the region we can get at.

Then not only am I inscrutable, but I am so built that I am obliged to examine myself, that is the meaning of introspective,

(b) Introspection means the act of directly observing the process-es of my mind. That is the line upon which people go insane. Cut a tree in half and you can tell by the number of rings how old it is, and people try to cut themselves in half psychically, that is, they try to cut their consciousness in half and tell you how it is made; and we are so built that we attempt to do this. Immediately a man gets to feel that he is incalculable, he begins to want to un-derstand himself, begins to introspect. The great chapter on wise introspection in the Bible is the 139th Psalm. That Psalm is Inter-cessory Introspection. Those words are a contradiction in terms, but they exactly convey the meaning of the Psalm. This tendency in me which makes me want to examine myself, and know the springs of my thoughts and motives, in this Psalm takes the form of prayer, "O Lord, explore me." The Psalmist gives a description of the great Creator who knows the beginnings of the morning and the endings of the evening, who knows the fathomless deep and the tremendous mountains, but he does not stop with vague abstractions; these things are all very well, but they are useless for his purpose. He asks that great Creator to come and search him. " There are beginnings of mornings in me and endings of evenings in me that I cannot understand; there are great moun-tain peaks I cannot scale, such knowledge is too wonderful for me, I cannot attain unto it, explore me, search me out." Or, again it means, "Search out the beginnings of my dreams, get down below where I can go, winnow out my way until you have got to understand the beginnings of all my motives and dreams, and let me know that you know me; and the only way I will know that you know me is that you will save from the way of grief, you will save me from the way of self-realization, you will save me from the way of sorrow and twistedness, and you will lead me in the way everlasting." The old Greek philosophers used to tell us to know ourselves, and the whole meaning of Socrates' teaching is exactly the same as in this Psalm, only from another standpoint.

Socrates' wisdom consisted in finding out that he knew nothing by himself, and that is why he was called by the Oracle the "wisest man on earth." About myself I have to be an avowed agnostic. "We begin by thinking that we know all about ourselves, but a quarter of an hour of the "plague of our own heart" will upset all our thinking and we will understand the meaning of the 139th Psalm. "O Lord, search me!" Mark you, God does not search me unless He lets me know it. "The spirit of man is the candle of the Lord, searching all the inward parts of the belly." (Prov. 20:27.) The word there translated by the old Saxon word "belly" means "the innermost part." He makes the man know that He is searching him, and when we come to our Lord and His attitude to the human soul, that line of thought explains Him immediately. "If I had not come, they had not had sin." "If I had not come with My light, and if the Holy Ghost had not come with His light, men had not known anything about sin." It takes an apostle Paul, to use the phrase "sold under sin," to know what it meant. He had been searched clean through by the penetrating Spirit of God. We are inscrutable, but we are so built that we must introspect. Introspection without God leads to insanity. We do not know the springs of our thinking, we do not know; what we are influenced by, we do not know all the scenery psychically that Jesus Christ looked at. For instance, our Lord continually saw things and beings we do not see. He talked about "Satan" and "demons" and "angels." Now we don't see Satan, or demons, or angels, but Jesus Christ unquestionably did, and He sees their influence on us. The man who criticizes Jesus Christ's explanation about demon possession, does not see what he is doing. The people who have no tendency to introspect, are those who are described in the New Testament as "dead in trespasses and sins," quite happy, quite contented, quite moral, all they want is easily within their grasp, everything is all right with them; but they are dead to all the world Jesus Christ belongs to, and it takes His voice and His Spirit to awaken the dead.

By (c) the term "Individual," we mean, first, what we stated at the beginning in distinguishing between individuality and personality; and second, that every man is judged before God as an individual being, that what he has done he alone is responsible for. Ezekiel 18:1-4: "The word of the Lord came unto me again, saying, What mean ye, that ye use this proverb, concerning the land of Israel, saying, That the fathers have eaten sour grapes, and the children's teeth are set on edge? As I live, saith the Lord God, ye shall not have occasion any more to use this proverb in Israel. Behold, all souls are Mine, as the soul of the father, so also the soul of the son is Mine; the soul that sinneth, it shall die." This line of revelation which runs all through God's Book shows the absurdity of a certain amount of cheap criticism, a fictitious conception which was that we are punished for Adam's sin. The Bible does not say so. The Bible says that men are punished for their own sins, that is, culpably punished. The Bible says that "sin entered into the world by one man," but sin is not an act on my part at all. Sin is a disposition, and I am in no way responsible for having the disposition of sin. What I am responsible for, is not allowing God to deliver me from it, when once I see that that is what Jesus Christ came to do. What I am punished for is the wrong things I do, and I will be whipped for them no matter how I plead. I will be inexorably punished for, and suffer from every wrong that I do. The inexorable law of God is laid down in the Old and New Testaments that the wrong I do, I will smart for, and be held responsible for, and punished for, no matter who I am. The Atonement has made provision for what I am not responsible for, viz.: the disposition of sin. John 3:19 sums it up: "This is the condemnation (or the crisis, the critical moment) that light is come into the world, and men love darkness rather than light because their deeds are evil." What is light? Jesus says, "I am the light of the world," and He said to His disciples, "If the light in you be darkness, how great is that darkness." My darkness is "my own point of view."

You will find in the matter of regeneration that God works below the threshold of my consciousness; all I am conscious of is a sudden burst up into my conscious life, but as to when God begins to work no one can tell. That is the meaning of our intercessory prayer. A mother, or a husband, or a wife, or a Christian worker praying for another soul has a clear indication that God has answered their prayer; but outside the people are just the same, there is no difference in their conduct, but the prayer is answered. The work is unconscious yet, but at any second it may burst forth into conscious life. You cannot calculate where God is going to begin any more than you can say when it is going to become conscious; and that is why we have to pray in intercession in the Holy Spirit. The path of peace for you and for me is to hand our case over to God, ask Him to search us – not what I think I am, not what other people think I am, not what I persuaded myself I am or would like to be, but " search me out and explore me as I really am in Thy sight."

3. Some Delusions of Importance.
(2 Thess. 2: 7-12.)

There are supernatural powers and agencies we are unconscious of which can play with us like toys whenever they choose, unless we are garrisoned by God. The New Testament continually impresses that on us. "We do not battle against flesh and blood, but against principalities and powers and the rulers of this world's darkness, and spiritual wickedness in high places" – all outside the realm of our consciousness. When we pray, if we only* look for results in the "earthlies," we are ill-taught. A praying saint performs far more havoc among the unseen forces of darkness than we have the slightest notion of. "The effectual fervent prayer of a righteous man availeth much in its working." We have not the remotest conception, nor the right to try and examine and understand what is done by our praying, all we can. know is that Jesus Christ laid all stress on prayer. "Greater works shall ye do, because I go to my Father . . . that whatsoever ye ask the Father in My name that will I do." It is only when these terrors and speculations are awakened in us that we begin to see what the atonement of Jesus Christ means. It means safeguarding in the unseen, safeguarding from dangers we know nothing about. "Kept by the power of God!" The conscious ring of our life is a mere phase, God did not only die and rise again in Jesus Christ to save that, it is the whole personality that is included.

Those verses in the Second Epistle to the Thessa. lonians 2:7-12 represent the borderland realm of things difficult to trace. The theme is not an isolated one, it runs all through the Bible and indicates the borderland that we cannot step over.

First, (a) Delusions of Insanity. What is insanity? One of the greatest mistakes to-day is the statement that the cases of demon possession in the Bible were insanity. The distinction between them is made perfectly clear in the New Testament; the symptoms are not even the same. Insanity simply means that a man is differently related to affairs than the majority of other men, and is sometimes dangerous. Paul was charged with madness (Acts 26:24,25), and that is the charge they brought against Jesus Christ also – "He is mad." Have you ever noticed the wisdom of the charge? Jesus Christ and Paul are unquestionably "mad" according to the standard of wisdom of this world. That means they are related to affairs differently from the majority of other men, and what the majority of other men must do for self-preservation is to shut them up in lunatic asylums. (Our Lord was crucified, and Paul was beheaded.) "When you get imbued with Jesus Christ's spirit and relation to life, you will find that you are just as "mad" according to the standard of this world.

Another thing we say about insane people which is mainly wrong is that an insane person is one who has lost his reason, that is technically untrue. An insane person is one who has lost everything but his reason. He has lost the relation of the body to the reason, and the relation of the outside world to the reason, according to the common, most universal standard. He can find a reason for everything. If you know anything about the diagnosis of insanity, you will find that this is true. If you want to know some of the cleverest dialectics that have ever been printed, read the expositions of the Sermon on the Mount to-day. They want to make out that Jesus is not mad according to the standards of this world, but He is absolutely mad, and there is no apology* for it. The modern attitude to things has either got to alter or pronounce Jesus Christ mad. "Seek ye first the kingdom of God and His righteousness, and all these things shall be added unto you." Volumes have been written to prove that the Lord did not mean anything like that, but He did, He taught it and proved it. Modern sense says, "It is nonsense, I must seek my living first, and then devote myself to the kingdom of God." Read the apostle Paul's reasonings in the First Epistle to the Corinthians, he says there that in the view of God the other crowd is mad, and a man only gets sane in God's sight when he is readjusted to God through the atonement of Jesus Christ.

Then take (b) the Delusion of Alternating Personalities, that is one body being the arena of more than one personality. This is not demon possession entirely, although the case I am going to take is so. This is not a case of insanity. You wonder first of all who is speaking. A man came to Jesus Christ and bowed down; he knew perfectly well, that Jesus could deliver him. But as soon as he got there, the other personality cried out against Jesus Christ and pled that He would deal mercifully with him.

There are cases of alternating personalities to-day. The annals regarding them are amazing, you will get them from the records of doctors of lunacy, of people suddenly disappearing. Case after case has occurred of people disappearing from one part of the country and living in another a totally different life. Alternating personalities cannot be dealt with by science; but Jesus Christ can deal with them.

Then last (c) Delusions of Mediums and Possessions. Paul was grieved because this girl was a medium. Spiritualistic mediumship is the greatest psychical crime in the world. By psychical we mean the greatest crime against our soul. Drunkenness and debauchery are child's play compared to mediumship. It is possible, according to the Bible revelation, for a man or woman to make himself or herself a medium through whom unseen spirits can talk to seen men and women. (Beware of using that phrase " yield, give up your will." Be perfectly certain to "WHOM you are yielding. No man or woman has any right to yield themselves to any impression, any influence, or any impulse saving Jesus Christ. Immediately you do, you are susceptible to all kinds of supernatural powers and influences. There is only one being I have to yield to, and that is the Lord Jesus Christ, and let me be sure that it is the Lord Jesus Christ. Impressionable people are the most dangerous people of all in religious meetings "When you get that type of nature to deal with, pray as you never prayed, watch as you never watched, and travail in communion as you never travailed in communion, because the soul that is inclined to be the medium between any supernatural forces and himself will nearly always be caught up by the supernatural forces belonging to Satan instead of by God. The Bible says, "If it be possible, even the very elect will be deceived" regarding the false revelation of Jesus Christ. So beware to whom you yield. When once a nature gets hold of the sovereign power of God and recognizes to WHOM he is yielded, then the whole power of the nature is safeguarded forever. Beware of impressions and impulses unless they wed themselves to the standard given by Jesus Christ. Insanity is a fact, demon possession is a fact, and mediumship is a fact.)

"All power is given unto Me." "I will give you power over all the power of the enemy." "For this cause was Jesus Christ manifested that He might destroy the works of the devil."

CHAPTER XIV.

OURSELVES: I; ME; MINE.
OURSELVES AS "KNOWN." "ME.

1. THE SENSUOUS "ME." Eccl. 12: 13.
    (a) My Body. Bom. 12: 1.
    (b) My Bounty. Heb. 13: 15.
    (c) My Blessings. Eom. 12: 13.

2. THE SOCIAL "ME." Eccl. 7: 29.
    (a) My Success. Matt. 5: 13-16.
    (b) My Sociability. John 5:40-44.
    (c) My Satisfaction. Matt. 10: 17-22.

3. THE SPIRITUAL "ME." Eph. 2: 6.
    (a) My Mind. Eom. 12: 2.
    (b) My Morals. Matt. 5:20.
    (c) My Mysticism. Col. 2:20, 23.

1. The Sensuous "Me." (Eccl. 12:13J

"We mean by "Sensuous" our bodily, material consciousness. My "Body" represents one aspect of the "Me." Under the heading of my "Bounty," we consider our "flesh and blood relations"; and under my "Blessings" we consider our home, property, and wealth.

2. The Social "Me." (Eccl. 7:29.)

Under the Social "Me" we consider all that my "set" means; if you insult my "set" you insult "Me"; and it is important to impress on ourselves that God recognizes that this is the way He has made us. Our Lord insists on the "social" aspect of our lives. He shows very distinctly that we cannot further ourselves alone.

3. The Spiritual "Me." (Eph. 2:6.)

This last aspect of our subject is the Spiritual "Me." That means my religious convictions, my mind, my morals.

Now to go back over (a) our first statement. If my body is hurt, I look upon it as a personal hurt; if my home or my people are insulted, it is a personal insult; if my "set" and my society are hurt, I consider it a personal hurt; and if my religious convictions are hurt or upset or scandalized, I consider myself as being hurt and scandalized. This, then, is, in the main, the general idea of what we are dealing with.

The normal "me," from the Scriptural standpoint, is not the average man. "Normal" means regular, erect, perpendicular, everything exactly regular and related. "Abnormal" means irregular and away from the perpendicular; and "supernormal" means that which goes beyond regular experience, not contradicting it, but transcending it. Our Lord represents the "Supernormal." We, by partaking of the salvation of our Lord Jesus Christ by His redemption, partake of the "normal," regular, upright; and apart from the atonement of our Lord we are "abnormal."

We mean by the term "me" the sum total of all a man calls his. That means that there is no real, practical distinction between "me" and "mine." My personality identifies "mine" with myself so much that it is not necessary to make a distinction between "me" and "mine."

1. The Sensuous Me.

"Let us hear the conclusion of the whole matter: Fear God and keep His commandments, for this is the whole duty of man." (Eccl. 12:13.) That verse is the conclusion, from the human-wisdom viewpoint, as to what the whole end of our life is, viz.: "to fear God and keep His commandments."

"Sensuous" means that which is affected through my senses, or that which I get at through my senses. The first thing I get at by my senses is my body. The Bible has a great deal to tell us about our bodies.

One of the main distinctions to make to-day about our body is that the Bible shows that our body is the medium through which we develop our spiritual life. The idea in the Middle Ages was that the body was a clog, a hindrance, an annoyance, a thing that kept us back, that always upset our higher calling; it was a thing that had sin in the very corpuscles of its blood, in the cells of its make-up. This view the Bible disapproves of entirely. The Bible tells us that our bodies are "the temples of the Holy Ghost," not things to be despised. So the body, in the Bible teaching, is placed very high indeed.

"I beseech you therefore, brethren, by the mercies of God, that ye present your bodies." (Rom. 12:1.) The Apostle does not say there, "Present your 'air to God." The hymns of "Higher Life" do, and consequently they are unsatisfactory, for you never can know when you have given your "all." Take it in the light of the last chapter; if our personality is too big for us to understand, how are we going to know when we have presented our "all"? The Bible never says anything so vague as present your "all," but present your "body." There is nothing ambiguous or indefinite about that statement, but something definite and clear. The body means only one thing to us all, viz.: this flesh and blood body.

Let us ask ourselves this practical question: Who is the ruling person that is manifested through my body, through my hands, through my tongue, through my eyes, through my thinking and loving? Is it a self-realizing person, or is it a Christ-realizing person? Our body is to be the temple of the Holy Ghost, and the medium for manifesting that marvelous Christdisposition in us all through; and instead of our bodies being a hindrance to our development, they are exactly the opposite. It is only through our bodies that we are developed; our bodies are the way we express our characters. You cannot express a character without a body. "When we talk of a character, we think of a flesh and blood thing; when we think of a disposition, w;e think of something that is not flesh and blood. God, by Christ's atonement, gives us the right disposition; that disposition is inside our bodies, and we have to manifest it in "character" through our bodies, and by means of our bodies. The whole use of bodily control is to make the body the obedient medium for expressing the right disposition. So the Bible, instead of ignoring the fact that we have a body, exalts the fact. We are told to remember that it is the " temple of the Holy Ghost, and Paul says, "If you defile that temple, God will destroy you." Instead of the Bible belittling laws of health, and bodily uprightness, and bodily cleanliness, the Bible insists on these far more by implication than any modern science does by explicit statement. Go back again to our first subject, viz.: The Making of Man (chapter II.), and you remember that the chief fact of man is not that he was in the image of God spiritually, but that he was made of the "earth earthy." It is not his humiliation, it is his glory, and through that mortal body is to be manifested this wonderful life and disposition – "Christ in us the hope of glory."

Then (b) My Bounty. "By Him therefore let us offer the sacrifice of praise to God continually, that is, the fruit of our lips, giving thanks to His name." (Heb. 12:15.) That verse comes in a chapter which is intensely practical in dealing with our relationship to strangers, and our relationships in some of the most intimate and practical ways of life. The next relationship to my body is my blood relations, my father and mother, my sister and brother, my wife, etc. Have you ever noticed that those are the phrases and those are the relationships Jesus Christ refers to most often? Over and over again in our Lord's talk about discipleship, that is the sphere He deals with. He puts the relationships in that sphere as crucial. If you will read Luke 14:26-35, you will find that our Lord places our love for Him away beyond our love for father and mother; in fact, He uses a tremendous word; He says, "Unless you hate your father and mother you cannot be My disciples." This word "hate" appears to have been a stumbling-block to a great number of people. It is quite conceivable that many persons may have such a slight regard for their fathers and mothers that it is nothing to separate from them, but the word "hate" shows by contrast what love we ought to have for our parents, an intense love; yet your love for Me, says Jesus, is to be so intense that any other relationship is "hatred" in comparison when in conflict with My claims.

Jesus preached His first sermon where He was known, in Nazareth (Luke 4), where He was brought up, and He told His disciples that they were to begin at "Jerusalem." What was the reason? Did Jesus Christ have such great success at Nazareth where He was brought up, where they knew Him? He had exactly the opposite. They "broke up" His service and tried to kill Him. Our Lord insists that we begin at Jerusalem, and our Jerusalem is unquestionably among the bounties of our own particular flesh and blood relations; for our own character's sake. It is infinitely easier for the great majority of us to offer the "sacrifices of praise" and thanksgiving to strangers than amongst, or to, our own flesh and blood. It is a sacrifice there. We would rather testify to anyone than to our own flesh and blood, there is where the real sacrifice of praise comes in, and that is where young converts want to skip. The reason seems to be "Because you will be confirmed in your character and relationship to Me," In the fourth chapter of Luke Jesus says distinctly what maddens His own people. He says in effect, "It is God's way to send His message through strangers before that message is accepted." They would not accept it from Him. "Why? Because they knew Him, land immediately you look at that statement you find how it revolutionizes a great many of our conceptions. "We would naturally say that if Jesus testified amongst His own people, how gladly they would have received Him: the only place they did not receive Him, the place that detested Him, and the place that He could not do many mighty works in, was the place where He was brought up. The place He told His disciples to begin their work in was this Sensuous Me, viz. : my own flesh and blood, my own Jerusalem begins there, and then you will get consolidated and know where your true basis lies. We do not very often put these two words together – "sacrifice" and "praise." Sacrifice means giving the best I have, but it also embraces an element of cost. That is where the sacrifice of praise comes in. My own flesh and blood relationships have to be the scene of the sacrifice of praise on my part, whether they accept it or not.

(c) My Blessings. I mean by "Blessings," our home and our property. "Distributing to the necessity of saints, given to hospitality." (Rom. 12:13.) Have you ever noticed what a great deal the Bible has to say about "hospitality" and "entertaining strangers"? God recognizes the enormous importance of my immediate circle. Not only does this term "blessings" include my home and my property, all that I distinctly look at as mine, but I have to use it with this outlook of hospitality. Immediately you look at these things, you will see how personal they are. If your home is insulted, if any stranger begins to find fault with your home, you will find how intense the resentment is. Our home is guarded in exactly the same way as our body. It is mine, therefore it is part of the very make-up of my personality, and God won't have us keep it exclusive, we have to have it open and be given to hospitality. In the East they know a great deal more about hospitality than we do. "What we mean by home is what we Britishers especially think of when we mention "home," the most intimate relationships; THAT is to be the scene where I am to be given to hospitality. The point is "be given to hospitality" from God's standpoint, not because other people deserve it, but because God commands it. That principle runs all through our Lord's instructions in the New Testament. Then in my body, in my blood relationships, and in my home I have to recognize everyone of them, keep them intimate, and keep them right, but I have to keep them with the first duty in each and all towards all. My body is the temple of the Holy Ghost, not for me to disport myself in, not for me to realize myself. My "blood relationships" are meant unquestionably for me to recognize, but they are to be held in subjection, if I may say so; my first duty is to God. And my "home" is to be given to hospitality. Have you ever noticed how God's grace comes to people given to hospitality if they are His children? Prosperity and growth in home, business and everything else comes from following God's advice in every detail.

2. Now we will take the **Social Me.**

"Lo, this only have I found, that God hath made man upright, but they have sought out many inventions." (Eccl. 7:29.) The word "inventions" is a very quaint one. It means devices from man's self love. It is a strange word. Remember, God made man upright, normal, perpendicular, regular; but he sought out many devices from his self love, many ingenious twistings away from the normal. Now the "Social Me" simply means "recognition by my set," and that has a wonderful influence with us all. For instance, the boy who is good and mild to his father and mother at home, may swear "like a trooper" when he is with the other "set." It is not because he is bad or evil, but because he wants to be recognized by his "set"; and you will find that that goes all through life, and God recognizes it, and regenerates that also. "We must be moulded by the set we belong to, whether we like it or not, and you will find that God very often alters our special setting. We may affect any amount of individuality but it remains true that we either "grovel" or we "strut" according to our realization of how we are recognized by the "set" we belong to, and you will find how insistent God is on this. You cannot develop a holy life alone. It will be a selfish, wrong life, without God in it. Jesus Christ was charged with being a "glutton and a winebibber" because He lived so sociably among men, and in His high-priestly prayer He prays, "I do not ask you to take them out of the world, but to keep them from the evil that is in the world." And the first place He led His disciples to after He said, "Follow Me," was to a marriage feast. Jesus says, "My Father and

I will make our abode with you." That is the "set" God places the Christian in, fellowship with the Trinity. Therefore the greatest concern of your life and mine is that we live according to the recognition of that "set," that we do those things that please God.

Let us now take (a) My Success. (Matt. 5:13-16.) [What is the standard of success as a Christian? Do you know; what success is? Success is to end with advantage. Jesus Christ distinctly recognizes that we have to succeed, and the kind of success is indicated. The advantage we have to end with in our lives, is "preserving salt and shining lights," not losing our savor, but preserving in health. If we get salt into a wound, it hurts, and if God's children get amongst those who are "raw" towards God (every immoral person is an open wound towards God) their presence hurts. For instance, the sun, which is a benediction to eyes that are right, is an agony of distress to eyes that are sore. The analogy holds with regard to a man who is wrong. He is like an open wound when salt gets into it, the pain stirs him to annoyance and distress, then spite and hatred. That is why they hated Jesus Christ. He was a continual annoyance. Or again, nothing is cleaner, or grander, or sweeter than light. You cannot soil light. A sunbeam may shine into a puddle, but it. never gets dirty.

You can soil a white sheet of paper, you can soil almost any white substance, but you cannot soil light. When rightly related to God, one can go down and work in the most degraded slums of the cities, or the vilest parts of heathendom, where all kinds of immorality are practised, but one is not defiled because God keeps us like the light.

Next (b) My Sociability. Sociability means good fellowship. How insistent God is that we keep together in fellowship. In the natural world it is only by mixing with other people that we get the corners rubbed off. That is the way we are made, and God takes that principle and transfigures it. "Do not forsake the assembling of yourselves together" is a Scriptural injunction.

John 5:40-44. In these verses our Lord distinctly indicates that there are certain states of society He will have nothing to do with. He cannot have anything to do with the men who "seek honor one of another." He says, in effect, "It is a moral impossibility for that man to believe in Me." Our Lord is exceeding good company and good fellowship to the saints. It is "wheresoever two or three are gathered in My name, there am I in the midst." Beware of isolation; beware of getting the idea that "I have to develop my holy life alone." It is impossible to develop a holy life alone, you will develop into an "oddity" and a "peculiarism," and unlike anything God wants you to be. The only way we can develop is by getting into the society of God's own children, and we will very soon find how God alters our "set." He does not contradict our social instincts, but He alters them. Jesus Christ says, "Leap for joy when men separate you from their company for My sake" (not for some crotchety notion or some faddy ideas of your own, or some principle you have wedded yourself to, but for My sake). When you are true to Him, your sociability is lifted to a different sphere.

"And hath raised us up together, and made us sit together in heavenly places in Christ Jesus." (Eph. 2:6.) "We are not raised up alone, but together. All through, this social instinct is a God-given one, and whenever a man gets alone, from the Bible standpoint, it is always to fit him for public society. Getting alone with God is very often such a dangerous business that God will very rarely allow you to do it unless you are getting into closer contact with people after. It is contact with one another that keeps us full-orbed and well-balanced, not only as natural beings, but as spiritual beings also.

(c) Then My Satisfaction. All these things are applicable in the natural world and the spiritual world alike. Satisfaction means a comfortable gratification. There are certain peculiar people who say if you like a thing, you must not do it or have it. They are as those who would say, "If you like to go to a prayermeeting, you must not go; if you dislike a ballroom, you must go." These people won't have any satisfaction at all, they think it is a sin. Now satisfaction, and the demand for satisfaction, is a God-given principle in our human life, and Jesus Christ says, "Blessed are they that hunger and thirst after righteousness, for they shall be filled" (satisfied). Satisfaction is a good thing, "comfortable gratification," but it has to be satisfaction in the highest.

Read Matthew 10:17-22. That is an extraordinary passage, and you will wonder why that passage has been taken in connection with satisfaction. The reason is that it indicates the only place where satisfaction is to be found – satisfaction in having done God's will. Those verses are very often taken and applied to the methods people adopt when they speak at meetings. (I have heard a man say at a gathering of Christians, "I have not had much time to prepare for this morning's address, so I am going to give you what the Holy Spirit gives me, but I hope to be better prepared this evening." His justification, he said, was this very passage.) When you go along seeking God's satisfaction in the world of men, you are going to come in contact with "open wounds," and they are going to hate you, you are going to be systematically vexed, persecuted and detested, and hated "for My sake," says our Lord; and "they will put you in all kinds of places suddenly where you will be completely humiliated, but when you are put there, do not be alarmed, I am there, and the Spirit of God will bring to your remembrance what you shall say in those moments." So we end where we began, that the social setting of my life is the highest – the Trinity. That is why, in secret or in public, the one set that I am anxious to please is God the Father, God the Son, and God the Holy Spirit, and the only sort of people I have real communion with are the people who have the same dominant note in their lives. Jesus Christ says, "Whoever does the will of My Father which is in Heaven, the same is My brother, sister and mother."

3. The Spiritual Me.

"And hath raised us up together and made us sit together in heavenly places in Christ Jesus." (Eph. 2: 6.) That verse does not refer to hereafter, but to now. My Mind, My Morals, and My Mysticism. I have (a) My Own Mind, and my particular mind means my particular cast of thought and feeling. You ridicule that, and you hurt me. You may not know it, but immediately a certain type of thought or feeling is ridiculed, someone will feel hurt. So it is quite right to put it under this category. "And be not conformed to this world, but be ye transformed by the renewing of your mind, that ye may prove what is that good and acceptable and perfect will of God." (Rom. 12:2.) One of the most wonderful things in your spiritual experience and mine is the way God alters and develops our sensitiveness. There was a time when our mental acts of thought and feeling made us amazingly sensitive to what certain other people thought and felt; now God has altered that and made us that we are absolutely indifferent to what they think, but we have become amazingly sensitive now to what another set of people think (1 Cor. 4:3, 4); then finally we are only sensitive to what God thinks of our cast of thought and feeling, and right through we are commissioned to be renewed in the spirit of our mind for that purpose, viz.: that we "may prove what is that good and acceptable and perfect will of God."

Then (b) My Morals, my standard of moral conduct. Let us take the great verse, "Except your righteausness shall exceed the righteousness of the scribes and Pharisees, ye shall in no case enter into the kingdom of Heaven." (Matt. 5:20.) The practical outcome of that for our lives is wonderful. My standard of moral conduct must exceed the standard of the moral upright man and woman I know, who lives apart from the grace of God. Think of the most upright man, the most worthy person you know who has had no experience whatever of receiving the Spirit of God,

Jesus Christ says in effect you have to exceed their rectitude. Instead of our Lord lowering the standard of moral conduct, He pushes it to a tremendous extreme. You have not only to do the right things, but your motives have to be right, the springs of your thinking have to be right, you have to be so unblameable that God sees nothing to censure in your holiness. That is the standard of our moral conduct if we are born again of the Spirit of God and are going on to obey Him. What is my standard of moral conduct? Is it God's standard, or the modern one? The modern standard is summed up in one phrase, self-realization. The two are diametrically opposed to one another, there is no point of reconciliation between them.

Then (c) My mysticism, my direct and immediate communion with God. (Col. 2: 20-23.) Everyone has something of that sort whereby he directly goes to God, whether he calls himself religious or not. Mysticism is a natural ingredient in everybody's make-up whether he calls himself "Atheist," or "Agnostic," or "Christian." Jesus Christ by the Spirit of God alters the whole thing. He does not alter the need of our nature, but He puts it on a totally different line. We are so mysterious in personality, and there are so many forces at work about us which we cannot calculate or cope with, that immediately we refuse to take the guidance of Jesus Christ, we may be, and probably will be, deluded by supernatural forces far greater than we are. Jesus Christ's way exalts everything about us, exalts our bodies, exalts our flesh and blood relationship, exalts our homes, exalts our social standing, and exalts all the inner part of our own life: mind, morals, and mysticism until we have at-one-ment with God.

CHAPTER XV.

OURSELVES: I; ME; MINE.
OURSELVES AS "OURSELVES." "SELF."

The passages alluded to in this outline are exclusively from the New Testament; any student can supply Old Testament illustrations for his or her own use.

    1. SELF. Luke 18: 9-14.
        (a) Greatness. Mark 12:31. (Comp. 2 Thess. 2:3, 4.)
        (b) Groveling. Luke 15: 19; Luke 5: 8.

    2. SELF-SEEKING. Rom. 15: 1-3.
        (a) Honor. John 5:41-44; John 8:49.
        (b) Humility. Matt. 18: 4; Phil. 2: 1-4.

    3. SELF-ESTIMATION. John 13: 13-17.
        (a) Superiority. Phil. 2: 5-11.

        (b) Inferiority. Matt. 5:19.

N. B. Important Definitions.
    (1) Self means: – The sum-total of all a man can call "Me" and "Mine."
    (2) Selfishness means: – All that gives me pleasure without considering Christ's interests.
    (3) Sin means: – Independence of God.
    (4) Surrendering myself to anything or any one other than our Lord Jesus Christ and His enterprises is the great human crime.

"My total self includes the whole succession of my personal experiences, and it therefore includes that special phase of my conscious life in which I think of myself." Myself is my conscious personality.

There are three divisions to guide our treatment of this subject: Self; Self-seeking; Self-estimation.

1. Self.

(a) Greatness and (b) Groveling. (Luke 18:9-14.) Both of those attitudes are wrong in a final analysis – one "grovels," and the other swells in "greatness," both are expressions of abnormal conditions. Our Lord does not teach the annihilation of self, but He reveals how self can be rightly centered, and the true centre is perfect live to God. (Read 1 Corinthians 13, with this line of thought in your mind, you will understand it in a practical way. "Perfect love" means perfect love towards God, and it takes no account of the evil that is done it. Until I get myself rightly related there, I either grovel or swell in greatness.) The attitudes of conscious greatness or groveling are both of them untrue and needing to be put right. The true centre for myself is Jesus Christ.

(a) Greatness. (Mark 12:31.) The first commandment is not loving my neighbor, but loving God with all my heart, with all my mind, with all my soul and with all my strength, then I can love my neighbor as myself. You will find that this is at the heart of all the revelation in Jesus Christ. Jesus Christ revealed the right centre for myself, and revealed that true centre to be God, and personal, passionate devotion to Him; then only shall I be able to show the same love to my fellowmen that God showed to me. Until I get there, I will either take the position of the Pharisee, or I will take the position of the publican. I will either thank God that I am not an out-and-out sinner, and point out certain people who are worse than I am; or else I will grovel in the other extreme. Both attitudes are wrong because they have not been truly centred. How could this Pharisee love his neighbor as himself? It was impossible, he had not gotten the true centre for himself. Self-realization was his centre, and every time he compared himself with the publican, instead of loving the publican, it increased his self-conceit. Immediately I get rightly related to God, have perfect love toward Him, then I have the same relationship to my fellowmen that God has to me. I can love my fellowmen as I love myself. That is the thing that keeps a man from taking account of the evil that is done towards him. If I love my God best, base ingratitude to me I take no account of because the mainspring of my service to my fellowmen arises from my love to God. When a man gets rightly related by the atonement of Jesus Christ to God, he begins to understand what the apostle Paul meant when he said, "We do not preach ourselves (selfrealization), but we preach Jesus Christ as Lord, and ourselves your servants for Jesus' sake." The point is very practical and clear, if you will look at it for one moment. If I love a person very much and he treats me unkindly and ungenerously, the very fact that I love him makes me feel it all the more, and yet Paul says, "Love taketh no account of the evil that is done to it." Why? Because self is absorbed, and taken up with love to Jesus Christ, and certainly if you are going to live for the service of your fellowmen, you are going to be pierced through with many sorrows, unless you love God. You are going to meet with more base ingratitude from your fellowmen than you would from a dog, and you will meet with unkindness and "twofacedness," and if your motive is love for your fellowmen, you will be exhausted in the battle of life; but if your motive springs from a central love to God, there is no ingratitude, no sin, no devil, no angel can hinder you from serving your fellowmen, no matter how they treat you, because the mainspring of the service is love to God. Then I can love my neighbor as myself, not from pity, but from the real and the true centering of myself in God.

(b) Groveling. "And am no more worthy to be called thy son, make me as one of thy hired servants." (Luke 15:19.) "When Simon Peter saw it, he fell down at Jesus' knees, saying, 'Depart from me, for I am a sinful man, Lord.'" (Luke 5:8.) This is a stage everyone goes through when convicted of sin, and we always get a wrong estimate of ourselves when we are convicted of sin.

The prodigal's estimate of himself is beyond where the father placed it, and whenever we are convicted of sin by the Spirit of God the same thing happens. The balance is upset, the health of our body is upset, the health of our mind and our heart is upset, the balance is pushed right out by conviction of sin. Sin is a thing that puts man's self out of centre altogether – eccentric – and when the Spirit of God convicts him, the man is wrongly related to everything. He knows he is wrongly related to God and to his own body, and to everything round about him, and he is in a state of abject misery. The other picture is the one we first dealt with, the picture of a man who who is not convicted of sin, and who consequently takes himself to be as God. If you watch carefully the tendencies that are all around us to-day, you will find that that is the characteristic tendency: "ignore sin; deny it ever was; if you make mistakes, forget them; live the healthy-minded, open-hearted, sunshiny life; do not allow yourself to be convicted of sin." They tell you that as you realize yourself to be God, you will attain perfectness. There is no repentance, no conviction of sin, and no forgiveness of sin. The Holy Spirit opens, not only my eyes, but my heart and my conscience to the horror of the thing that is wrong inside, and immediately He does, I get to the groveling stage. Conviction of sin consumes a man's beauty, the Psalmist says, "like the moth." His "beauty" means the perfectly ordered completeness of his whole nature. The Pharisee doesn't grovel, there is a certain beauty of order about a conceited man, a certain conformity with himself. He feels all right, he is of the nature of a crystal, clear and compact and hard. Immediately the Spirit of God convicts him, all the hardness crumbles and he comes to the opposite extreme, in solution, as it were. Jesus Christ's salvation takes a man that has been broken on the wheel by conviction of sin, and been rendered plastic by the Spirit, and re-moulds him and makes him a vessel fit for God's glory. Self, then, is not to be annihilated, it is to be rightly centralized in God.

Self-realization has to be turned into Christ-realization. Our Lord never taught "deeper death to self," He taught deeth, right out, to "my right to myself," to my own self-realization. He taught that the principal purpose of my creation is "to glorify God and to enjoy Him forever," and the whole sum total of my life is to be consciously centered in God.

2. Self -Seeking. (Rom. 15:1-3.)

Romans 15:3 holds the whole thing in explanation. The "reproaches of those that reproached Thee fell on me." What reproaches fell on Jesus? Everything that was hurled against God in slander, hurt our Lord. The slanders that were hurled against Jesus Christ Himself never touched Him, they made not the slightest impression on Him, His suffering was on account of His Father. On what account do you suffer? Do you suffer because men speak ill of you? Read Hebrews 12:2: "Consider Him that endured such contradiction of sinners against Himself, lest ye be weary and faint in your minds." Perfect love taketh no account of the evil that is done unto it. It is the reproaches that hit and scandalize the true centre of Christ's life that He noticed in pain. What was the true centre of Christ's life? Absolute devotion to God the Father's will, and as surely as you get Christ-centralized you will understand what the apostle Paul meant when he said, "Filling up what remains behind of His sufferings." You could not touch Christ on the line of self-pity. The whole practical emphasis here is that service is not from pity, but from a personal, passionate love to God, longing to see many more brought into the centre where God has brought us.

(a) Honor. (John 5:41-44; 8:49.) The whole centre of the honor of our Lord's life was His Father's. He was "without reputation." They heaped every kind of scandal it was possible for them to think of on the name of Jesus Christ, and He never once attempted to clear Himself. But once let a man or woman show any attitude of dishonor toward His Father, and instantly you see Jesus Christ ablaze in zeal; "and as He is, so are we in this world," says St. John. He changes the centre of our self-love. What is my honor? Is my honor God's honor? Are they identically the same, as they were in Jesus Christ? Let the following sentences analyze us: We are scandalized at immorality. Why? Because God's honor is at stake*? Is it not rather because our social honor is upset and antagonized. As saints, we should smart and suffer keenly every time we see pride, covetousness, self-realization, because these are the things that go against God's honor. God's honor and the honor of His saints are one and the same thing. "You have not the love of God in you," said Jesus Christ, and He also pointed out that it was a moral impossibility for them to believe. There is not any man who can believe in Jesus Christ who has another standard of honor. Jesus Christ exalts the standard of honor, and puts it alongside God's throne. Take the eleventh chapter of John. What was the real under-current? "He was moved with indignation" because their attitude accepted the scandal against His Father. As soon as death came on the scene, they accepted its interpretation against all God's goodness. The only thing that ever roused Jesus Christ was the thing that brought His Father's honor into disrepute. In the temple, instead of seeing "a meek and gentle" Jesus, we see a terrible Being with a whip of small cords in His hands.

"Why could not He have driven them out in a gentler way? Because passionate zeal had eaten Him up, the enthusiasm and detestation against everything that dared to call into dishonor His Father's honor moved Him, and you will find exactly the same characteristics in the saints. You cannot rouse them on the line of personal interest, you cannot rouse them along, the line of self-pity, you cannot rouse them along the line of self-realization; but once let a thing go contrary to Jesus Christ's honor, and instantly you will find your' meek and gentle saint a holy terror. The meaning of that phrase in the Bible, "the wrath of the Lamb" is realisable along this line. The obverse side of love is hate.

(b) Humility. (Matt. 18:4; Phil. 2:1-4.) Those two passages in the New; Testament are a wonderful revelation, viz.: that the true disposition of a saint manifested in this order of things is humility. Take the case of the little child. The disciples had been discussing who would be the greater, and Jesus took a very little child in His arms, and said, "Unless you become like that, you will never" see the kingdom of Heaven." Now, did He put that little child up as an ideal? If He did, He destroyed the whole principle of His teaching. If humility is an ideal, this will increase pride. Humility is not an ideal, humility is the unconscious result of life being rightly related to God and centred in Him. Our Lord is pulling down ambition, and if He put a little child as a. standard for men, He simply altered pride's manifestation, that is all. But He did not. "What is a little child? "We all know What a child is. until we are asked, and then we do not know. We can only mention its extra goodness or badness, but neither of those is the child. We all know implicitly what a child is, and we all know implicitly what Jesus Christ meant, but immediately you try to put it into words, it escapes. Language won't bear the strain you have to put upon it to define a little chili We can only come near a description of it. The child works from an unconscious principle inside, and if we are born again of the Spirit of God and follow and obey the Spirit of God, we will manifest this humility unconsciously all along the line. We will easily be the servant of all men, because we cannot help it, not because it is our ideal. Our conscious eye is not on our service, but on our Savior.

There is nothing more awful in this world than conscious humility, it is the most Satanic type of pride. A person who consciously serves you is worse than the Pharisee who is eaten up with conceit. Jesus Christ did not raise humility as an ideal; He presented it, like He did the Sermon on the Mount, as a description of what we will be unconsciously when we are* rightly related to God and rightly centred. Our centre will be God's honor, and our humility among men will never be understood byanybody who is not Christ-centred in the same manner. This attitude is portrayed over and over again. Peter said, "They do not understand why you do not go to the same excess of riot you used to." Jesus says, "Leap for joy when men separate you from their company for My name's sake." The centre of the life is altered, and the worldling is hopelessly "at sea" in trying to find out the centre from which the Christian works, and it ends for the worldling's mind in ridicule.

The end of the analysis of a Christian from a worldly standpoint is not attraction, but ridicule. The apostle Paul said that what he preached was to the Greeks (the people who sought wisdom) stupidity, unutterable stupidity, and you will find the same is the attitude of the dispensation we live in to-day. A saint arouses interest for a little while; when things go ill he arouses deep interest, but when things go well, the interest gradually changes into ridicule, and then into absolute ignoring, because the centre of life is altered, centred in some one the world does not see – God! Immediately the Christian complies to standards of this world, instantly the world recognizes it, but when a Christian works from the real standard, which is God, the world cannot recognize it, cannot understand it, and consequently has to ignore or ridicule it. You will find strong antagonism pointed out by Jesus over and over again, and in the Epistles, by the Spirit, between the spirit of the world and the Spirit of God, a, deeply rooted antagonism, and what we have to realize as Christian people more and more is that if we are going to obey the Spirit of God, we are going to be detested and ridiculed and ignored by the people who are centred in self-realization.

Our attitude in a dispensation like this will manifest itself in humility that cannot sting us into action on our own account. That is the thing that maddens the "prince of this world," but once let the prince of this world and his minions scandalize Jesus Christ, begin to misrepresent Him, and the weakest saint becomes a giant, and will go to martyrdom any time and anywhere all the world over for the Lord Jesus Christ. (You hear it said to-day that the spirit of martyrdom has died out; the spirit of martyrdom is here. Let any scandal arise against Jesus Christ, and where you had one martyr in the past you will have many to-day who will stand true to the honor of the Lord Jesus Christ.)

What is my self-seeking? I have to have selfseeking. If my self is truly centred, my seeking is God's honor. God's honor is at stake by my eyes, by my hands and feet, His honor is at stake wherever I take my body. I am the temple of the Holy Ghost, therefore I have to see that this body is the obedient slave of the disposition Jesus Christ put in to stand for Him. My self-centredness is to be God, and love for Him. Suppos ethis question arises, "I believe that I ought to love God like this, but how am I going to do it? Where am I to begin to let the tremendous flow of love toward God come in? I agree emphatically that I ought to love God, but how; can I?"

Romans 5:5 is a very practical solution: "Because the love of God is shed abroad in our hearts by the Holy Spirit which is given unto us." Have you received the Holy Spirit? If not, Luke 11:13 will help you: "If ye then being evil know how to give good gifts unto your children, how much more shall your Heavenly Father give the Holy Spirit to them that ask Him?" Also the last verse in John 17: "That the love wherewith Thou hast loved Me may be in them, and I in them." Ask God to answer Jesus Christ's prayer. There is no excuse for any person not having the problem answered in his own life. My natural heart is not the lover of God;

the Holy Ghost is the lover of God, and immediately He comes in He will turn my heart into a loving centre for God; personal, passionate, overwhelming devotion to Jesus Christ. (God and Jesus Christ are synonymous terms in our practical experience.) When the Holy Spirit comes in, and sin and self-interest are in the road, He will instantly discern them to us, and we will have to give our consent that He clears them out. He will clear the whole lot out as soon as we give our consent, until the body is incandescent with this love to God. Jude says, "Keep yourselves in the love of God. " That does not mean, keep on loving God, it is infinitely profounder than that. It means, "Keep your soul open to the fact that God loves you," and His love will be continually flowing through you to others.

Two terms of modern psychology are of importance here – "Projective" and "Ejective." Projective means thai I see in another person the qualities I have not got, but want. Ejective means that I attribute my qualities and my defects to the other person. The latter is the most remarkable line of solution for judging. When I come to the ejective method, I go on this line, "Yes, I know exactly what that person meant." "When somebody has trespassed against me, instantly I impute to him every mean motive I would have been guilty of if I had been in his condition. "Therefore thou art inexcusable, thou that judgest." In the sixth chapter of Matthew, Jesus puts the forgiveness of my trespasses on the ground that I forgive the people that trespass against me, and if I go on the ejective method, I won't forgive. I simply attribute to them what I would be capable of doing myself in the way of meanness in similar circumstances. The statement that we only see what we bring with us the power of seeing, is perfectly correct. If you see meanness and wrong and evil in other persons, then take the self -judgment at once – that is what you would be guilty of if you were in their condition. The searching light of the Scriptures comes over and over again on that line, and we find out when we come to the last point, Self-estimation, that there is no room in any Christian for cynicism.

3. Self-Estimation. (John 13:13-17.)

That is an iteration of the same point, viz.: that myself must be truly centred in God. Is it? Is my self Christ-centred or self-centred? When I am in difficult circumstances, does the disposition in me make me say, "Now, why has this happened to me?" That disposition was never in the Lord Jesus Christ. Every set of circumstances He ever got into, whenever His consciousness showed itself, it was His Father's honor, not His own that occupied Him. "Myself" is a human edition for God to glorify Himself by. "Let this mind "be in you which was also in Christ Jesus." (Phil. 2:5.) Could anything be more practical than that statement, or more profound? The mind of man shows itself in his speech and in his actions. The mind of Christ showed itself in His actions and in His speech. Did you ever notice what it was that Satan antagonised in Jesus Christ? God-realization. He wanted to alter that centre. "Do God's work your own way, you are His Son, work from that centre." "I came not to do My will, but the will of Him that sent Me," is our Lord's implied meaning all the way through the temptations; and as He was tempted, so are we when once we are rightly related to God through Him. Take that passage in Revelation: "I have this against you, you have left your first love." All the rest become? of no account. To get eccentric, off the centre, is exactly what Satan wants us to do. He does not goad or tempt to immorality; one thing he makes his business, and that is to dethrone God's rule in the heart. The superiority of Christ's self was that He was God-centered. Is that the superiority of yourself? "He that gathereth not with me scattereth," our Lord said, and all morality, all goodness, all religion, and all spirituality that is not Christ-centered is drawing away from Jesus Christ all the time. All the teaching of Jesus weaves round the question of self. It is, "Oh, to be something, something!" aggressively and powerfully something, uncrushably something, something that stands next to God's throne, on the rock, in whom God can walk and talk and move and do what He likes, because the self is personally in love with God, not absorbed into God, but a personal, passionate love to God.

Look at the "N. B.'s" in the outline. The one we need particularly to notice is " Selfishness." Selfishness means all that gives me pleasure without considering Christ's interest. If you talk about selfishness and its badness, you are going to have the sympathy of everybody; but if you talk about unselfishness from Jesus Christ's standpoint, you are going to arouse the interest of very few and the antipathy of a great many. Have you ever noticed that my sympathy for my fellowmen is quite likely to rouse my antagonism to God? Unless I have my relationship to God right, my sympathy for man will lead me and them astray; but immediately I get right with God, then I can love my neighbor as myself. How did God love me? He loved me to the end of my sinfulness, all my self-will, all my selfishness, all my stiff-neckedness, all my pride, and all my self-interest. Then I can show my neighbor the same love. That is Christianity in practical working order, "Love as I have loved you." The same love, the same overflow and the same outflow that God showed to me shall I show to my fellowmen.

Then we will take Surrender. We have dealt with this subject often enough – surrendering myself to any one or anything other than Jesus Christ and His enterprises is the great human crime.

CHAPTER XVI.

OURSELVES: I; ME; MINE.
OURSELVES AND CONSCIENCE.

CONSCIENCE is the innate law in nature whereby man knows he is known.

N. B. The half truth and half error of such phrases as "Conscience is the voice of God" and "Conscience can be educated" will be carefully dealt with.

    1. CONSCIENCE BEFORE THE TALL. Gen. 2: 16, 17; 3:2, 3.
        (a) Consciousness of Self.
        (b) Consciousness of the World.
        (c) Consciousness of God. Gen. 3: 1-24.
        These three are the several sides of man's personal life.

    2. CONSCIENCE AFTER THE FALL. John 3: 19-21.
        (a) The Standard of the Natural Person. Rom. 2: 12, 15.
        (b) The Standard of the Nations – Pagan. Matt. 25: 31-46.
        (c) The Standard of the Naturally Pious. Acts 26: 9; John 16: 2.

    3. CONSCIENCE IN THE FAITHFUL. 1 Cor. 8:7, 12.
        (a) Conscience and Character in the Saint. Rom. 9:1; John 17: 22.
        (b) Conscience and Conduct in the Saint. 2 Cor. 1: 12.
        (c) Conscience and Communion of the Saints. 1 John 1:7; Eph. 4:13; Heb. 9:14.

"Conscience is the innate law in human nature whereby man knows he is known. " From every standpoint that is a safeguarded definition of conscience.

Look at the N. B. at the head of the outline. If conscience were the "voice of God," it would be the most contradictory voice man ever heard. For instance, a Hindoo mother obeys her conscience by treating her child cruelly, and the Christian mother obeys her conscience by sending her child to Sunday-school, and bringing it up generally in the "nurture and admonition of the Lord." If conscience were the voice of God, great contrasts of that kind would never happen. "Conscience attaches itself to that system of things which man regards as highest." Consequently you will find that what conscience records is very different in different people. The Hindoo mother's conscience attaches itself to the highest she knows, viz. : Hindoo religion; the Christian conscience of the Christian mother attaches itself to the highest she knows, viz.: the revelation in the Lord Jesus Christ.

Probably the best illustration of conscience is the human eye. The eye records what it looks at. Conscience may be pictured as the eye of the soul, recording what it looks at, and it will always record exactly what it is turned towards. One thing we soon lose in human sight is what Ruskin called the "innocence of the eye." By the "innocence of the eye" he means this – that the majority of us know what we look at, and we try to tell ourselves what our eye sees. An artist, records exactly from the "innocence" of sight; he does not use his logical faculties. In training art students in sketching from nature, you will find that in looking at a distant hill draped in blue mist, with little touches of white or color here and there, the beginner will sketch not what he sees, but what he knows those blotches indicate, viz.: houses; while the artist will give you the presentation of what he "sees," not what you know he sees. Now something very similar happens in conscience. The record of conscience may be distorted or perverted, and conscience itself may be seared.

Then, again, if you throw a white light on trees, the eye will record that the trees are green; if you throw a yellow light on trees, the eye will record that the trees are blue; if you throw a red light on trees, the eye will record that the trees are brown. Now, your logical faculties will tell you all the time that they are green (because daylight is white light), but the illustration I am using is that the eye has no business other than to record; and conscience does the same thing.

Let us get back to the illustration of the Hindoo mother and the Christian mother. The Hindoo mother's conscience looks out on what she is taught by her Hindoo religion to be God, and her conscience records exactly what it looks at and she, reasoning on the records of conscience, does the thing that is cruel. The Christian mother looks at God in the "white light" of Jesus Christ, consequently her conscience records exactly what it sees, and reasoning on it, she behaves as Christian mothers ought to behave. So it never can be true to call conscience "the voice of God." The varieties of the records of people's consciences are accounted for by the various traditional religions, etc. It does not matter whether a person is religious or not, his conscience attaches itself to the highest he or she knows, and reasoning according to that, guides the life.

The other phrase that "Conscience can be educated," is again a truth that is half an error. Conscience cannot be educated, strictly speaking. What is altered and educated is a man's reasoning, and a man reasons not only on what his senses bring him, but what his conscience brings him, and immediately you face a man with the white light of Jesus Christ (we call Jesus Christ the white light, for white embraces all the other colors and shades of light; it is the pure, true light), the conscience records exactly, and the reason is startled and amazed. When a man gets rightly adjusted to God, his conscience staggers him, and his reason condemns him from all standpoints.

1. Conscience Before the Fall. (Gen. 2:16, 17; 3:2,3.)

Now, originally in our language the words "consciousness" and "conscience" meant the same' thing; they do not mean the same now. In "Conscience before the Fair' we have to take the three sides, or facts, of a man's personal life – consciousness of self, consciousness of the world, and consciousness of God.

"And the Lord God commanded the man, saying, Of every tree of the garden thou mayest freely eat; but of the tree of the knowledge of good and evil, thou shalt not eat of it, for in the day that thou eatest thereof thou, shalt surely die." (Gen. 2:16, 17.)

"And the woman said unto the serpent, We may eat of the fruit of the trees of the garden, but of the fruit of the tree which is in the midst of the garden, God hath said, Ye shall not eat of it, neither shall ye touch it, lest ye die." (Gen. 3: 2, 3.)

There in both passages the three sides or facts are clear – consciousness of myself, consciousness of the world around me, and consciousness of God. It is the last that has gotten most conspicuously blurred by the Fall. Consciousness of self (a) takes us back to the first subject we dealt with, viz.: the general subject of "Man," and you will find there that when the other creations were passed before man in procession, there was not found a helpmeet for Adam; he had no affinity with the brutes, instantly distinguishing man clearly and emphatically from all the brute creation round about him. There is no evidence that a brute is ever conscious of itself, but man is ostensibly so conscious.

Second, (b) he is conscious of the world. I mean by the world the thing that is not himself; the strict word for it would be "continuum," i. e., that which continues to exist outside of me. It is by understanding how we, as men and women, come into contact with what is not ourselves that we will understand our barriers and our limitations. We can never understand what an angel's consciousness is like, nor what a dog's consciousness is like, because both these creations are constituted differently.

First of all, then, let us look at this question, "How do I come in contact with what is not myself?" By a nervous system. Remember, the body of man is his glory, not his drawback. The body is the thing that makes and manifests his character. The body is not an accident, but is essential to the order of creation we belong to. Consequently we can always say, up to a certain point, how a human being sees things outside. The more you think on that line of things, obvious and common sense as it is, the clearer will become the basis of Christian philosophy.

"How do angels come in contact with what is not themselves?" Certainly not by nerves, therefore we have no possibility of knowing how an angel comes in contact with what is not angelic. Read the record of angelic appearances in the Bible, of our Lord after the resurrection; physical barriers simply did not exist to them. They exist to us by means of our nervous system. Angels seem to come and go through rocks and doors, appearing and disappearing altogether in a way we cannot understand. That is a consciousness which is above mine, different from mine. Jesus did not take on Him the consciousness of a man; that is, Jesus Christ came down where man was, in the same world; He came into the world we are in, and took on Him a body and a nervous system like we have, and saw the world just as we see it, and came in contact with it just as we do. Whenever anybody writes or speculates as to how an angel sees and knows, put underneath it "private speculation," and you will always find that God's Book draws the barrier strong, "Thus far and no farther." We only know consciousness of ourselves and consciousness of what is outside us by means of a nervous system; all our conscious life depends on our nerves. The world "goes out" when we are asleep, we are not conscious at all, what has happened? The nervous system is not working. An anesthetic makes the world "go out." Why we must shut a lunatic up in an asylum is that a lunatic's nervous system differently relates him to the world from the majority of men, consequently a lunatic very often becomes dangerous, he does not record what he sees outside as we do, and the consequence is he becomes so different that we have to confine him.

Now, on the other hand, look at the lower animals. There is a great amount said about the intelligence of dogs and a great amount of insight, falsely so called, into the nature of a dog. A dog seems to be the most human of all animals, but we have no means of knowing how a dog sees what is not itself; we simply take our own consciousness and transfer it to the dog. We have no more means of knowing how a dog sees than we have of how an angel sees. These barriers above us and below us are essential to our knowledge. Spiritualists in all times have denied that they are essential; they say we can know, we can come in contact with and understand how an angel sees things.

"Your body is the temple of the Holy Ghost," and we are held responsible for the way we manifest that through our bodies to the external world. That explains what Paul says in 2 Corinthians 5:17: "If any man is in Christ Jesus, he is a new creation, old things have passed away, behold all things have become new." You will ever find that when a man gets a great alteration inwardly, his nervous system is altered. Whenever the grace of God works effectually in a man's inner nature, it alters his nervous system and he instantly begins to see things differently. The external world around him begins to take on a new guise. Why? Because he has a new disposition. If any man is in Christ Jesus, his nervous system will prove that he is a "new creation," meaning by that, that he begins to see things differently.

> "Heaven above is softer blue,
> Earth around is sweeter green,
> Something lives in every hue
> Christless eyes have never seen;
> Birds with gladder songs overflow,
> Flowers with deeper beauties shine,
> Since I know, as now I know,
> I am His and He is mine."

That is not only poetry, it is a fact.

Then take the last fact of primal consciousness (c) Consciousness of God. In Genesis 2 these three types of consciousness are quite clearly manifest in the way Eve talked to the serpent. She was conscious of the surroundings, she was conscious of herself, and she was conscious of God. In Jesus Christ those three consciousnesses are perfectly clear; in us they are not. This latter consciousness is quite obliterated, and you will find men miscall all kinds of things "God." Any system of things a man considers highest he is apt to call God. The God-consciousness in Adam was quite different from our natural consciousness; it was just like it was in our Lord. Those three facts of a man's personal life are restored by Jesus Christ to their more than pristine vigor; we get into real, definite communion with God through Jesus Christ; we get to a right relationship with our fellowmen and the world outside, and we get to a right relationship with ourselves; we get Christ-centered, and not self-centered.

2. Conscience after the Fall. (John 3:19-21.)

That is where we live to-day, viz.: a mixture of Christian and non-Christian, and a great many in between who are neither one nor the other. John 3:19-21 is the fundamental analysis. "Light is come into the world, and men loved darkness rather than the light, because their deeds were evil." You ask, "What is light?" Jesus says, "I am the light." He said to His disciples, "If the light in you be darkness, how great is that darkness." Darkness in this connection is "my own point of view." Immediately a man sees Jesus Christ and understands who He is, that instant he is criticised and self-condemned; there is no further excuse. Our Lord, then, is the final standard.

(a) The standard of the "natural person," the person without Jesus, who has never seen or heard of Him; (b) the standard of the "nations – pagan." who likewise know nothing about Jesus Christ, and (e) the standard of the "naturally pious."

(a) In Romans 2:12-15, the contrast is drawn very clearly and emphatically between what we may call "religious people" and the irreligious. What is the standard of judgment? The Gentiles knew nothing about Jesus Christ or the law of God in an external standard; so they are judged according to their consciences. Take the grossest case we can think of – there is no case of a cannibal tribe anywhere on record, where they ate a man and thought they were doing right; they always tried to conceal it.

(b) Take the standard of the pagan. (Matt. 25: 3146.) These verses are often applied to Christians, but the primary reference is to the judgment of the nations. The standard for Christians is not the twenty-fifth chapter of Matthew; the standard for Christians is our Lord Jesus Christ. But in the twenty-fifth of Matthew the standard is very clear, and God's magnanimous interpretation of the acts of people is revealed, and they are amazed and astounded – "When did we see you sick? "We never heard of you before." "Inasmuch as ye did it unto one of the least of these My brethren, ye did it unto Me." The standard of the "natural person" is conscience; the standard of the "nations" is conscience.

(c) Then the standard of the "naturally pious." (Acts 26:9.) That was according to his conscience. If conscience is the voice of God, ye have a nice problem to solve! Saul was the acme of conscientiousness. In John 16: 2 there is the same thing: "They shall put you out of the synagogues, yea, the time cometh that whosoever killeth you will think that he doeth God service. Obedience to what is understood to be conscience. Jesus Christ says they will think they serve God in putting you to death. And no one who has read the life of the apostle Paul and his own record also, will ever accuse him of being unconscientious; he was hyper-conscientious. The conscience is the standard for men and wo* men to be judged by until they have been brought into contact with the Lord Jesus Christ. It is not sufficient for a Christian to walk up to the light of his conscience; he must walk in a sterner light, in the light of the Lord Jesus Christ.

3. Conscience in the Faithful. (1 Cor. 8:7-12.)

(1 Cor. 8:7-12.) These verses show us how we can be like "spectacles" for other Christians. In the natural life, when the sight is wrong, "spectacles" are put on the outside to adjust the vision. "We have to be a kind of "spectacles" to other Christian people. So many are short-sighted, and so many are long-sighted, so many have not the right kind of sight. Be "spectacles" to them! A very humble position, but a very good one. There is in this First Epistle to the Corinthians Paul's distinction between "equal rights" and "equal duties," the former being wrong. You will find that they have been criticising Paul, and from the seventh chapter he deals with their questions, and evidently the whole thing is this question of "equal rights," and he says, "No! equal duties, but not equal rights." "We all have duties to perform towards God, but not equal rights. His statesmanlike manner of dealing with this matter is very wonderful. There is a difference between "offence" and "stumbling." The Authorized Version translates indiscriminately "offence" and "stumbling"; the Revised Version corrects this. What is the difference? Giving "offence" is sometimes part of moral character; it is sometimes moral duty to give "offence." Offence means going contrary to some one's private opinion. Did Jesus Christ know that He was offending the private opinions of the Pharisees when He allowed His disciples to eat corn on Sunday? Did He know He was offending the Pharisees when He healed the sick on the Sabbath day? But our Lord never put an occasion of stumbling in anybody's way. (The passage that alludes to Him as "a rock of stumbling and a stone of offence" refers to a different thing.) Stumbling is quite a different thing from offence. For instance, somebody loves you very much, and does not know God as well as you do, but they continually do what you do because they love you, and as you watch them, you begin to discern that they are degenerating spiritually, and to your amazement you find it is because they are doing what

you are doing. There is no offence, but they are stumbling, distinctly stumbling. Then Paul says, "I will never do those things again as long as I live whereby my brother stumbles. I do not insist on my rights, or my liberty of conscience; I do exactly the opposite." You will find he works it out from every standpoint in this First Epistle. "I reserve the right to suffer the loss of all things rather than be a hindrance to the Gospel." "Waive aside your liberty of conscience if it is going to be the means of some one stumbling. The application is the application of the Sermon on the Mount in practical experience. The Sermon on the Mount, to put it very briefly and crudely, simply means that if you are My disciple, you will always do more than your duty. You will always be doing something equivalent to the "second mile." People will say, "What a fool you are! Why don't you insist on your rights?" Jesus Christ says, "If you are My disciple, you will always be doing these things." That is the way we can be spectacles to make other people see.

God educates every one of us from the great big principles down to the little scruples. You find people who are right with God guilty of the most ugly characteristics, and you are astounded that they do not see it; but they don't. But wait; if they go on with God, slowly and surely God's Spirit educates them from the general principles down to the particular items, until after a while they are as careful as can be down to the "jots" and "tittles" of life, whereby they prove their sanctification in the growing manifestation in their physical lives of the new disposition God has given. No wonder the Book of God says we need to be patient with one another!

(a) Character in the Saint. Character is the sum total of a man's actions. You cannot judge a man because he does good things at times; you must take the whole of the times together, and if in the greater number of times he does the bad things, he is a bad character in spite of the noble things he does intermittently.

You cannot judge your character because you once spoke kindly to your grandmother, if the majority of other times you did the other things. The fact that people say, "Oh, well, he does do good things occasionally," means that he is a bad character. The very statement is a condemnation. Any of us who do good things occasionally are sure to be bad. It is only when we do good things almost always and wrong things only occasionally that we are good characters. What are conscience and character in a saint? The disposition of Jesus Christ persistently manifested. You cannot appeal to saints on the line of self-interest; you can only appeal to them on the line of the interests of Christ. Whose honor do you seek? The feeblest, weakest saint will become a holy terror immediately you scandalize Jesus Christ. (b) Conscience and Conduct in the Saint. "For our rejoicing is this, the testimony of our conscience, that in simplicity and godly sincerity, not with fleshly wisdom, but by the grace of God, we have had our conversation in the world, and more abundantly to youward." (2 Cor. 1:12.) The point there is a very important one; the knowledge of evil that came through the Fall gives man a broad mind, but paralyzes his action. The restoration of a man by our Lord gives him simplicity, and simplicity always shows itself in actions. Do not call simplicity stupidity. Simplicity here means the simplicity that was in Jesus Christ. Paul says, "I am afraid you will be taken away from the simplicity that is in Jesus Christ." You get men and women of the world who know evil, whose minds are poisoned by all kinds of things; they are marvelously generous with regard to their notions of other people, but they can do nothing; every bit of their broadsightedness paralyzes their efforts.

The knowledge of evil, instead of instigating to action and work and good, does the opposite; it paralyzes; whereas the very essence of the Gospel of God, working in conscience and conduct is that it shows itself at once in action. God can make simple, guileless people out of cunning, crafty people; that is the marvel of the grace of God. It can take out the strands of evil and twist-edness out of a person's mind and imagination and make him simple towards God, so that his life becomes radiantly beautiful by the miracle of His grace.

(c) Conscience and Communion of the Saints. The "together" aspect. Nowhere is "enthusiasm for humanity" mentioned in the Bible. This is quite a modern phrase. Enthusiasm for the "communion of saints" is continually mentioned in the Bible, and the argument is very simple and direct, that if we keep our consciences open towards God as He is revealed in Jesus Christ, we will find God bringing hundreds of other souls into oneness with Him through us. In 1 Corinthians 4:3,4, Paul shows three standards of judgment which he has left behind:

(1.) Standard of the "special set" judgment – "It is a small matter that I am judged of you. ' '

(2.) Standard of the universal human judgment – "Or of man's judgment."

(3.) Standard of conscience – "Yea, I judge not mine own self."

And the standard he accepts as his final one is the Lord.

One of the greatest disciplines in spiritual life is the darkness that does not come on account of sin, but that comes when God's Spirit leads you from walking in the light of your conscience to walking in the light of the Lord. When the latter is learned, bitterness and contention are an impossibility. Defenders of the faith are always bitter till they have walked in the light of the Lord.

CHAPTER XVII.

SPIRIT: THE DOMAIN AND DOMINION OF SPIRIT.
PROCESS OP THE TRINITY.

N. B. "The entire province of life, both in its lowest forms or stages and in its highest, is the province of spirit."
  (1) An Instructive Parallel – God and Man. 1 Cor. 2: 9-11.
  (2) What the Bible says about Godhead. John 4: 24.

THE ESSENTIAL NATURE of God the Father, God the Son, and God the Holy Ghost.
  1. WILL. Ex. 3:14; John 10:17, 18; 16:8-11.
  2. LOVE. 1 John 4: 8; Rev. 1:5; Rom. 5: 5.
  3. LIGHT. 1 John 1:5; John 8:12: John 16:13.

The Spirit is the first power we practically experience anything of, but it is the last power we understand anything about. The whole working of the Spirit of God is much easier to experience than it is to try and understand. The chief reason of this is that we only form our ideas out of things we have seen and handled and touched, and when we come to talk about the Godhead and the Spirit, language is strained to its limit. We can only use pictures to try to convey the ideas that make us think; yet, in spite of this difficulty, it is very necessary that we should think, and learn to think as Christians; it is not sufficient to experience the reality of the Spirit of God within us, it is not sufficient to experience His wonderful work, but we must bring our brains into line, so that we can think and understand along Christian lines, and it is because so few Christians do think along Christian lines, that it is easy for wrong teaching and wrong thinking to get in, especially along the line of the Spirit.

An Instructive Parallel. (1 Cor. 2:9-11.) "What Paul is referring to here is the basis of how to think. He is quite simple and clear and logical. The way you understand the things of a man, he says,

, is by the spirit of man; and the way you understand the things of God is by the Spirit of God, and the spirit of a man cannot understand the things of God, the Spirit of God alone can understand the things of God. That is the first principle he lays down, and we must see that it is clearly grasped and understood by us. The next step is very clear, viz.: that you cannot expound the things of God unless you have the Spirit of God, and you can only expound the things of God to others who have His Spirit. He says there is an analogy; there is a spirit in the natural world whereby you can compare and think and argue about natural things, but it is not the same law which runs through the spiritual world; as there is a law in the natural world, so there is a law in the spiritual world; and you will find Paul says that we cannot discern the spiritual law by our spirit, but only by the Spirit of God, and if we have not received the Spirit of God, we will never discern it, nor will we understand it; we will be continually moving in a dark world, and we will come slowly to a conclusion that the language of the New Testament is put very exaggeratedly and very wrongly; whereas immediately after receiving the Spirit of God, we learn to think along the line of the Bible; we compare spiritual things with spiritual, and we do not speak of the things of God in the "words which man's wisdom teacheth," viz.: we cannot expound the things of God by the spirit of man, but only the Spirit of God.

Verse 14. Again the point is quite clear in Paul's mind, he says that naturally our heart does not understand the things of God, and not only does it not understand, but when it hears them expounded, it says they are "foolishness." Take for instance the attitude of the "master in Israel" to Jesus Christ. He held strongly that the germ was there in him, and in all who were like him, and Jesus Christ brought this view (that Paul is expounding) to Nicodemus; He said, "Marvel not that I say unto you, You must be born from above; that which is born of the flesh is flesh, and that which is born of the Spirit is spirit."

So let us get that plain, fundamental distinction clearly in our minds; we cannot penetrate the things of God by intelligence, we cannot understand them; the only way we can penetrate and understand and practice and fairly grasp and think about the things of God, is by the Spirit of God. I would like to emphasize in this connection that Paul states emphatically that we must be agnostic mentally about God. Every Christian is unquestionably agnostic, mentally, for all we know about God we accept by revelation, we did not find it out ourselves, we did not worry it out by thinking, we did not work it out by reason, we did not say, "Because so and so is true in the natural world, therefore it must be in the spiritual." You cannot find out God that way, and we find practically what Jesus Christ meant when He said, "If you would know My doctrine, My logic and My reasoning and My thinking, do My will, first believe in Me, commit yourself to Me, obey Me, receive the Spirit, then you will get to thinking along the way I reason."

Verse 15. Paul here is at the very fundamental heart of everything, as he nearly always is, because he is not only inspired by the Spirit of God in the way we all understand inspiration, but he is moved in a thoroughly special manner to expound the whole basis for Christian intelligence and Christian thinking.

You will find the teaching abroad to-day that we have the Spirit of God in us, and all that is needed is to develop that germ; if you will put people in the right conditions, put them into the right understanding of things, that Spirit will develop and grow, and they will grasp and understand God. That is contrary to Jesus Christ's teaching, and quite contrary to the New Testament all through. There has to come a stage in your life and mine, when we are "paupers" in our own spirit; we have no power of our own, we cannot grasp God, we cannot begin to understand Him; if we are going to understand Him, we must have the Holy Spirit, and He will begin to expound to us His mind; if we will put our machines, our bodily machines, into line with the Spirit which He gives, we will begin to understand. The way we understand the things of the world is by our natural intelligence, and the very same thing is true spiritually, viz.: the way we understand spiritual things is by our spiritual intelligence.

What the Bible says about the Godhead. (John 4:24.) Jesus Christ in saying "God is Spirit," does not imply therefore I must worship Him sincerely. The term "Spirit" there has nothing whatever to do with human sincerity, it has to do with His Spirit in me; I must have the same Spirit in me, or I cannot worship Him.

Now what is the Spirit? Instantly you find insuperable barriers to thought. Did you ever try for one minute to think of God? "Why, you cannot think of a Being who has had no beginning and has no end, consequently men without the Spirit of God make God out of ideas of their own. It is a great moment in your life and mine, when we do realize we are agnostics, when we realize we cannot get hold of God unless Jesus Christ is able to do for us what He said He was able to do, give us the Holy Spirit, and lift us into a new life whereby we will be able to understand what He reveals, and live the life He wants us to live.

The first thing we have to deal with is the Trinity, the Godhead itself. We have called it the "Process of the Trinity," Father, Son, and Holy Ghost. The first thing to notice is this, that what is true of the Father is true of the Son, and also of the Holy Ghost. There are three main characteristics in God the Father, there are three main characteristics in God the Son, and three main characteristics in God the Holy Ghost, because they are one. The three characteristics of God the Father are will, love, and light. Now we know nothing about God the Father saving as Jesus Christ has revealed Him. "Philip saith to Him, Show us the Father." "Have I been so long time with you, and yet hast thou not known Me, Philip? He that hath seen Me hath seen the Father." And the characteristics in the Lord Jesus Christ are- those three, will, love, and light. So in like manner take the Holy Spirit, the Holy Spirit is the Godhead manifested now. He is not an ethereal influence, we do not see God the Father, we do not see God the Son nowadays, but

God the Holy Ghost is here, and the three characteristics of God the Holy Ghost are, will, love, and light; for these Three are one.

Take the records of God the Father. He entered into His Sabbath rest, and men despised Him; God the Son entered into His Sabbath rest, and men despised Him; God the Holy Ghost has not yet entered into His Sabbath rest, and men are despising Him. The point to convey is this, that the essential nature of one is the essential nature of the others and if you understand the Spirit of God, you understand Jesus Christ, and you understand God the Father, consequently the first thing to do is to receive the Spirit of God.

Now we will look at the essential nature of the Father. In order to show how difficult it is to get this in words, ask yourself this: "How much room does thinking take up?" No room at all, so it is with your spirit whereby you understand the things you come in contact with. Now, God is a Spirit, and if I am going to understand God, I must have the Spirit of God, and because my thinking and because God's Spirit take up no room they act very easily, work and inter-work with one another in my body, and what the Spirit of God does when He comes into me by the atonement of the Lord Jesus Christ is to re-energize my spirit. My spirit in itself has no power to get hold of God; God's Spirit comes into my spirit and re-energizes that, then the rest depends on me; if I do not obey, if I do not bring into the light of the Spirit of God the dark and the wrong things in my soul, and get them dealt with by the light of the Spirit of God which He gives, then I shall grieve the Spirit of God, and grieve Him away. The first fundamental characteristic of God the Father, or God Almighty, is given in Exodus 3:14. There is the description of pure will as being the basis of God Almighty. Now there is no such thing as pure will in a man, God Almighty is the only Being who can have an act of pure will, and the Bible reveals that the essential nature of God is this tremendous power of will. By His will He created what His breath sustains.

What is the main characteristic of Jesus Christ? (John 10:17,18.) There again that is not a man's power, no man has the power to lay down his life in the way Jesus Christ is referring to. Jesus Christ, remember, is God incarnate, and the basal nature of God is the basal nature of Jesus Christ. "I lay down My life because I choose to, and I take it again because I choose to; I am not here by any haphazard choice, I am here by the direct, determined will of God. "

Then take the characteristic of God the Holy Ghost. (John 16:8-11.) There again the basal characteristic, of the Godhead is will, no man has that.

Now with regard to the free will of man. Free will is a most limited subject; human free will is nearly always understated, or overstated, no man has the power to make an act of pure free will. There is a pre-determination in a man's spirit that makes him will along certain lines. You will find when we come to deal with man that Jesus Christ teaches that when the Spirit of God comes into him, the Spirit of God brings His own generating will power, and consequently causes the man to will on lines with God Almighty, and you have this amazing fact, that the saints' free choices are God the Father's pre-determinations.

That is one of the most wonderful things in Christian psychology, that a saint chooses exactly what God determines he should choose. It is beyond the limits of language. If you have not received the Spirit of God, that is one of the things the apostle Paul says sounds so foolish, but when you have received the Spirit, and if you will obey Him, you will find that the Spirit of God puts your spirit into complete harmony with God's, and the sounds of your goings, and the sounds of God's goings are one and the same thing.

We have dealt with the physical world, and you will find that everything is leading back to what the Bible reveals, viz.: that at the back of everything is spirit force, not matter; not material things. What is that tremendous force? The Bible tells you, the force behind everything is this great Spirit of God.

"New Theology," "Christian Science," and "Theosophy." are all the same; they teach this, that God, in order to help Himself to realize Himself, created something called His Son. If you read their statements, you will find they say in effect, "The Son of God is not only Jesus Christ, the Son of God is the whole creation of man and God is all, and the whole creation of men and women is helping God to realize Himself." The practical outcome of this line of thinking seems logical, but logical conclusions bring the mind to saying, "It is absurd to talk about 'sin'; sin is only a defect; and to talk about the need of an 'atonement' by Jesus Christ is an old Orientalism, it is absurd to talk about there being a 'fall.'" The Bible never anywhere says that God created the world to help Him to realize Himself. The Bible reveals that God was absolutely self-sufficient, that the manifestation of Him as God the Son was for another purpose altogether, not for Himself at all, but for the solution of a gigantic problem, and the whole marvel of this new creation is that it is made of the earth earthy, and the great Spirit of God allows the enemy to be at work on this creation in a way he cannot work in any other creation. God overthrows the rule of His spiritual enemy by a being that is a little lower than the angels, viz.: man, and when God came into this order of things He did not come as an angel, He came as a man, and took on Himself human nature, that is the marvel of the incarnation, and the characteristics of the great God are mirrored in the Lord Jesus Christ, and if we want to know what God is like, study Jesus Christ. Let us thank God that the basis of the mighty nature of God is will, consequently when His Spirit comes into my spirit, I can will to do what God wants me to do. Will simply means the whole nature active; will is not a faculty. We talk about people having a "weak will" or a "strong will"; that is a misleading idea. Will simply means the whole nature active, and by the energizing of the Spirit of God, we are energized, and are able to do what we never could do before; that is, we are able to obey God, if we will.

Then take the next great characteristic – love. (1 John 4: 8.) "God is love." The Bible does not say God is loving, the Bible says "'God is love." The phrase "lovingkindness" is used' often in the Bible, but when the true nature of God is revealed, it does not say God is a loving being, it says, "God is love." The whole great basis of God is active will, and that will is love. Jesus Christ's characteristic is seen in Revelation 1:5; there the basal characteristic of Jesus Christ is love, and instantly the kind of love is shown; not lovingkindness in overlooking sin, but the essential nature of love that delivers us from sin. "Who loved us and washed us from our sins in His own blood."

Now take the essential characteristic of God the Holy Ghost. (Rom. 5:5.) There again the essential characteristic of the active power of God's will is "love." When the Spirit of God, is received by me, the meaning in Romans 5:5 is not that He enables me to have a capacity for loving God but that He sheds abroad in my heart the love of God, a very much more fundamental and marvelous thing; not that He gives me the ability to work out a love for God, but He sheds abroad in me the essential nature of God. Paul tries to put that in Galatians 2: 20, a verse which is perfectly familiar to us all, but none of us will ever fathom it no matter how long we live, nor how much we experience. He is stating this receiving of the very nature of Jesus Christ. Again Paul says, "When it pleased God who separated me from my mother's womb, to reveal His Son in me." That is the true idea, of a saint, a saint is not a human being who is trying to be good, a saint is not a human being who is trying by effort and prayer and longing and obedience to get as many of the saintly characteristics as possible, a saint is a being who is recreated, "If any man be in Christ Jesus, he is a new creation, " and we have to be solemnly careful we do not travesty the work of God, or the atonement of the Lord Jesus. If we belittle it in the tiniest degree, although we may do it in ignorance, we will surely suffer, and the first thing that will make us belittle it, is when we get out of sympathy! with God, and into sympathy with human beings; when we begin to drag down the tremendous truths of God's revelation that the essential nature of God's Spirit is will, and love, and light. It is those characteristics that are imparted to us by the Holy Ghost; we have not them naturally, because, by nature, our hearts are darkened away from God, and we have not the power to generate will within ourselves, we have not the power to make an act of pure will, we have no power to love God when we like; and the number of people who are piously trying to make their poor human heart love God, is pathetic,

Then take the last characteristic, the essential nature of God the Father is light. (1 John 1:5.) That is an amazing declaration, there is no variableness caused by His turning. There is no shadow of a turn. "We are told that wherever there is light and substance, there must be a shadow, but there is no shadow in God, none whatever. What is the characteristic of Jesus Christ? Take it on His own terms, "I am the Light of the world"; no shadow; in Jesus Christ. (John 8:12.)

Then take the Holy Spirit. Active will, pervading love showing itself as light in God the Father; active will, pervading love showing itself as light in the Lord Jesus Christ; all-pervading energy and will and all-pervading love showing itself as light in the Holy Ghost. (John 16:13.) There is the active working again of these fundamental characteristics of the Godhead in God the Holy Ghost. They were the fundamental characteristics of Jesus Christ, and they were the fundamental characteristics of God Almighty as God the Father.

Let us revise again. "God is love." No man ever believes that who is wide-awake naturally, unless he has received the Spirit of God. Why, the thing, as Paul says, "is foolishness," it is absurd. Watch the basal characteristic of the Sermon on the Mount. Jesus 'Christ says, in effect, that the basis in everyone of His disciples, after they have been initiated into the life He is living, will be to find that God is their Father and is love. Then you get the wonderful working out in your life; not "I won't worry," but you will come to the place where you "cannot worry," for you have the Spirit of God shedding abroad in your heart the love of God, and you will find you can never think of anything that God your Father will forget. That is why our Lord talked so much about the great difference in the people who are where He wants them to be, and although great clouds and perplexities may come, as in Job 's case, and as in the case of Paul, and as in the case of every saint, they never touch the secret place of the Most High in your life. "Therefore will we not fear though the earth be removed and though the mountains be cast into the midst of the sea." Why? The Spirit of God has got us so rightly centered that everything now is rightly adjusted.

You cannot give yourself the Spirit of God, that is God Almighty's gift if you will simply become poor enough to ask Him (Luke 11:13), but once He is in, there is something you can do, and God cannot do, I mean you can obey Him. If you don't obey Him, you will grieve Him and He will go. Over and over again we need to be reminded of Paul's counsel, "Work out your own salvation with fear and trembling, for it is God that worketh in you to will and to do of His good pleasure." Thank God it is gloriously and majestically true that the Holy Spirit can work in me the very nature of Jesus Christ, if I will obey Him, until in and through my mortal flesh may be manifested works that will make men glorify My Father which is in Heaven, and men will take knowledge of us that we have been with Jesus.

Light is the most marvelous description of clear, beautiful moral character from God's standpoint. 1 John 1:7: "Walk in the light with nothing to hide." What light? – God. What light? – Jesus Christ. What light? – the Holy Spirit. "This is the condemnation," says Jesus, "that light is come into the world and men love darkness rather than light, because their deeds are evil." What is my darkness? My own point of view, my own prejudices, preconceived determinations; if the Spirit of God agrees with that, all well and good; if He does not, I shall go my own way. That is darkness, and that is the very moment of determination. The weaning that goes on when a soul is being taken out of its own convictions into the light of Christ, is a time of perils in a soul life. When a child is being weaned, it is fractious, and when God is trying to wean us from our own ways of looking at things to get us into the full light of the Holy Spirit, we are very fractious too. We call it conviction of sin, and if I persist in keeping to my own light, I will end in darkness, said Jesus, but if I will keep walking in the light, recognizing and relying on the absolute authority of God the Holy Spirit to expound to me the Bible, to bring me into a complete understanding of His way, then I shall have fellowship with others.

But then comes the wonderful thing, I will have a purity of life that is pure in God's sight; that means too pure for me to begin to understand. Anything less – I say it measuring every word – anything less would be blasphemous. If 1 John 1:7 is not true, if God cannot cleanse me from all sin, if God cannot make me unblameable in holiness in His sight, then Jesus Christ has totally misled us, and His great, mighty work of atonement is not what it pretends to be. Oh, if we would only get into the way of facing God with our limitations, and tell Him He cannot do it, we would begin to see the awful wickedness of unbelief, and why Jesus Christ was so vigorous against unbelief, and why, in the Book of Revelation, unbelief is placed at' the very head of all the awful sins! When the Holy Spirit comes in, that unbelief is turned out, and by obedience, the will, the energy of God is put into us, and He can make us will to do His good pleasure, and He can shed abroad in our hearts the love of God. Then I will be able to show the same love to my fellowmen that God showed to me, and He will make me light. My morality, my religious conduct and my spirituality will exceed the righteousness, the morality and the spirituality of all the naturally pious people, because the supernatural, by God's Spirit, has been made natural in the life I now live.

CHAPTER XVIII.

SPIRIT: THE DOMAIN AND DOMINION OF SPIRIT.
MUNDANE UNIVERSE.
SPIRIT AS PHYSICAL FORCE.

1.   WORLD OF MATTER. Ps. 104:30; 33:6; 2 Pet. 3:5.
2.   WORLD OF NATURE. Gen. 1: 2; Job 26: 13.
3.   WORLD OF SELF. John 6:63; Jas. 2:26; Ezek. 1: 20; Rev. 11: 11.

(1) We deal here with the meaning of some big modern words such as transcendence, immanence, etc.

(2) The student will find that we claim the Bible gives the working explanation there is of all things.

We found in our last chapter that the three fundamental characteristics of God were will, love, and light. That God was the only Spirit who could will pure will, no man can have an act of pure will, and that when we participate in God's Spirit, we have our spirit energized, and we are able to do the will of God. "We found that what was true of God the Father was true of God the Son and true of God the HolyGhost. The present day is the dispensation of the Holy Spirit. That is a phrase we are perfectly familiar with, but do we understand sufficiently who the Holy Ghost is? He is identical with God the Father and God the Son; and being a person He must exercise an influence, and the more pronounced the person, the more powerful His influence. What we have to recognize is, that the majority of people do not know Him as a person, they only know Him as an influence, and that is why the Holy Spirit is most popularly spoken of as an influence.

Now consider the Mundane Universe, i. e., this terrestrial world we exist in, the earthly world we live in, the rocks and trees and people we come in contact with. We have divided this theme into three parts, (a) the World of Matter, (b) the World of Nature, and (c) the World of Self. A great alteration has come over what is called "material" science to-day, and it is coming back to the Bible point of view – that at the back of everything is spirit; the material world holds itself in existence by spirit. Away in the earlier days, when the Greeks tried to explain the material world, they said it was made of "atoms," and then down the ages they got to the place where they found they could split up the atoms-, then they called those split-up elements "molecules," then they found they could split up the molecules, and the split-up molecules are made of "electrons," and they have discovered that the electron is like a solar system and behind it all is "force."

That may be of interest or it may not, but the fact is very significant because it points out the absurd cry that the Bible and modern science do not agree, how could they? If the Bible agreed with modern science, in about fifty years both would be out of date. Every science, at one time, has been modern. Science simply means man's attempt to explain what he knows. Another important aside is this, do not belittle the Bible and say that the Bible has only to do with man's salvation. The Bible has not only to do with man's salvation, the Bible is a universe of revelation facts that explain the world we live in, and it is simply giving a "sop to Satan" to say, what a great many modern preachers are saying, that the Bible does not pretend to tell us how the world came into existence. The Bible does, the Bible claims to be the only expositor of how the world came about, and the only expositor of how the world keeps going, and the only book that tells us how we understand the world. Look at the world of matter. (Ps. 104:30, etc.; Ps. 33:6; 2 Pet. 3:5.) Those three passages simply express what the Bible revelation expresses all through, that God created the world out of nothing. The Bible does not say God "emanated" the world. That is a very clever modern idea; they say that God evolved the world out of Himself. The Bible says that God "created" the world by the breath of His mouth. Meditate for one moment on that word "creation" and see what a supernatural word it is. No philosopher ever thought of it, no expounder of natural history ever imagined such a word. "We can use the words "evolution" and "emanation," but we simply do not know; what "creation" is. There is only one Being who does know, and that is God Himself, and the Bible says that God created the world by the word of His mouth. Now there are some people in this twentieth century who take hold of that statement and make it mean that all the rocks and trees and people in the world are simply manifestations of God. The Bible does not say so, the Bible says that God created the world.

What is the world of matter? For instance, I am looking at this book, I see it is bound in red covers, it is flexible, it is fairly hard, and there are black marks on it. Well, I can account for the "redness" and for the "blackness" and the "flexibility" by my senses, but one thing I cannot describe, what the thing is that awakens these sensations! That is matter, something we do not know. The way we see things depends on our nerves, but the thing in itself that makes us see it that way, what is that? I see that clock and will probably describe it in the same way as you will – it is hard and smooth and brown and white and I can hear a sound and see a face, and so on, everyone of these things can be described as the results of my sensations, but what is the "thing in itself" that makes me have those sensations? The way we see the things depends on ourselves, but what the thing is in itself, we do not know, that is we do not know what matter is. The Bible says it is created by God, the way we interpret it depends on what spirit we have.

(b) The World of Nature. That means the order that material things appear in to me. The way I explain things is by thinking, the way I begin to explain the world outside is by thinking, then if I can explain it by mind, there must have been a mind that made it. That is logical, simple and clear, therefore atheism is exactly what the Bible calls it, the belief of a fool, because an atheist says, I can explain to a certain extent what things are like outside by my mind, but there never was a mind that created it. Now we have to come to this problem, How is it that we all see and coma to different conclusions about the world? How is it that a man can be an "atheist," how is it that he can be an "agnostic," how is that he can see everything "as bad as bad can be"? How is it that another man sees another thing "as good as good can be"? It all depends on the spirit inside him. That is why the world of nature seems such a contradiction.

(Gen. 1:2.) There is the reconstruction of the order of things out of chaos. In the beginning God created things out of nothing, matter did not exist before God created it. It is God who created it entirely out of nothing, not out of Himself. The Bible does not say that God created, the world out of Himself, it says He created it by His breath. But Genesis 1:2 is the reconstruction out of chaos. As we pointed out when we dealt with "Man," there was probably a former order of things that was ruined by disobedience, and produced the chaos that God reconstructed the order of things out of, which we know and which we so differently interpret.

(Job 26:13.) There the Bible says that God made the established order of things. We hear people say that if God created the established order, He is responsible for sin being here. Why the Bible says He is, and what is the proof that He is responsible? Calvary! In Colossians 1:16 there is an allusion to what God created and for what God necessarily made Himself responsible. God created everything that was created, He created the being who became Satan, He created man who became sinner, and God holds Himself responsible for Satan and sin.

Take the next step, God did not create sin, sin is the outcome of wrong relationships between two of God's creations. Sin is a relation set up between the being revealed as Satan, and the being revealed as Adam, it is not a creation at all. Yet God holds Himself responsible for it from the very beginning, He holds Himself responsible for the possibility of sin, and the Lord Jesus Christ's life and death and resurrection are proof that He took the responsibility, and God nowhere holds man responsible for having a wrong disposition in him; you won't find one passage in the Bible where God holds a man responsible for having the heredity of sin in him, but He holds him responsible the moment he sees and understands that God can deliver him from that heredity. (John 3:19.)

God is responsible for the established order of nature. Now there are various conflicting views about the world. If you will read carefully tire Book of Job, you will find that the world of nature is a wild contradiction from beginning to end; you cannot explain it in any satisfactory way at all. Immediately you start out to say that God is good, you will come across some facts that prove He is not. "When a man starts and says there is no God at all, he can prove his position. You may have as many accounts of the order of nature outside you, as you have human beings. The spirit inside the man makes him interpret what he sees outside, and if I do not have the Spirit of God in me, I will never interpret the world outside as God interprets it; I will have continually to shut my eyes, and to deny certain facts: I will have to do what our "Christian Science" friends do, deny that facts are facts.

Now we see the limitations of trying to dispute with a man who is an atheist. He can prove his position, you cannot disprove it to him, but immediately you get him to receive the Spirit, you will alter his logic. Paul says, "The spirit of a man understands the things of a man, but does not understand the things of God." If God created nature and I have not the Spirit of God, I will never interpret the order of nature as God does; I will prove the Bible is simply a "cunningly devised old wives' fable"; prove the whole thing is a piece of idiotic Oriental tradition. If I am to understand the Bible, I must have the Spirit of God.

This is for thinking; we all know about the Spirit of God for practical living, but do we realize the need to have the Spirit of God to think with? So many Christian people use dangerous weapons against the enemies of Christianity, which one and all are really against Jesus Christ Himself, simply because they have not been renewed in "the spirit of their minds"; because they will not think on God's line; because they refuse to make their minds work. We have no business to be fools; we have no business to be stupid; we have no business to be ignorant about how God created the world, and no business to be ignorant as to how we can explain to ourselves the way that discerns the arm of the Lord all through. When I receive the Spirit of God for my practical living, He begins to stir my brain after He has transformed my practical life. Will we bring this machine, the brain, into harmony with the new line of thinking? Take an illustration in the 15th of John. Jesus laid down a remarkable principle for practical living and for practical thinking – "I am the true Vine!" Is the natural vine a false one? No, the natural vine is a shadow of the real one. "I am the Bread." Is the ordinary bread we eat false? No, the ordinary bread we eat is the shadow of the real bread. "I am the Door," and so on. Jesus Christ taught His disciples how to think by "correspondences."

If you have the Spirit of God in you, you will be able to interpret what you see with your eyes, and hear with your ears, and understand with your brain, in the light of God. "The sun shall no more be thy light by day nor the moon by night, but the Lord Himself shall be thy everlasting light." Did you ever ask what that meant spiritually? May it not mean that ordinary days and nights bring facts into your life you cannot explain, but when you receive the Spirit of God you get on the line of explaining them? For instance, we cannot explain life, yet it is a very common-place fact that we are alive; we cannot explain love, we cannot explain death, we cannot explain sin, yet they are all blunt, common-sense facts. When we try to explain them in our own light, we cannot make anything of them; the world, the order of nature is a confusion; there is nothing clear about it; a confusing, wild chaos. Immediately you receive the Spirit of God, He energizes your spirit for practical living, and gets your brain slowly into practical thinking line, and you will begin to see God's order in all that chaos, to "discern the arm of the Lord," the Lord will explain to you the facts of common days and common nights. That is the meaning of our Lord Jesus Christ saying, "The kingdom of God is within you." If I want to understand the world, the order of nature, as the Bible reveals it, let me have the Spirit of God. (Luke 11 : 13.)

(Matt. 11:25.) "I thank Thee, Father, that Thou hast revealed these things to babes." Then He thanked God that He was the only medium the Father had for revealing Himself, and the only way we get to understand God, and God's universe, is by the Spirit of God, and the message is given in the same passage, "Come unto Me." That is a message to His disciples, not to sinners on the outside.

Watch the outlook of your mind when you have been "born again" of the Spirit of God, and you will understand the condition of mind Jesus Christ is alluding to, "laboring and heavy laden," trying to think out what won't be thought out, and Jesus Christ's message is, "Come to Me and I will give you rest." "I am the Way." "Get the Spirit that is in Me, imparted to you from God by Me, and. you will begin to see things as I do. If you don't, you will never know God, and you will never see things as I do. Marvel not that I say unto you, You must be born again." "Born again" for practical thinking as well as practical seeing.

It is a strange thing in our schools and everywhere else, the indiscriminate way we are taught to think like pagans, and to live like Christians. All the thinking explanations taught in every university are pagan, every one of them, and we train our men who teach us to think like pagans, and to live like Christians, and the consequence is what we see. What we have to do is to get our thinking into line with the living Spirit of God, to begin to take the laborious trouble to think, "to meditate on these things" and get ourselves continually harnessed in imagination to Jesus Christ. "Bringing every thought and every imagination into captivity to the Lord Jesus." Never allow your mind to run in wild speculation, that is where danger begins, that is the way the "sin of Eve" begins, when the Christian allows the mind to run off on speculative tangents, "I want to find out this and that." "Come unto

Me," says Jesus, "I am the Way," the only way to live, not only the way to get saved and sanctified, but the way to think, and no man knows God, says Jesus, but the one "to whom I will reveal Him," and I will reveal Him to anyone who will come to Me.

Then take (c) the World of Self. (John 6:63.) Can Jesus Christ speak to me to-day? He can by the Holy Spirit, but if I take His words without His Spirit they are of no avail to me. I can conjure with, them, and do all kinds of things, but they are not life. Immediately the Spirit of God is in me, He brings to my remembrance what Jesus said, and makes it live, and it is the Spirit of God in me making alive the words of Jesus outside me, that enables me to assimilate them. God exercises a remarkable power in taking texts out of the Bible context and putting them into the context of our life. You will often find a verse come to you right out of the Bible setting, and begin a new setting in your life; it has become alive and has become a precious, secret possession to you. See that you keep it a secret possession and do not "east your pearls before swine" – the strong words of the Lord Jesus Christ.

If one may use an ingenious symbol, it would be that Jesus Christ was crucified in the place of a "skull," and that is where He is always crucified, that is where He is always put to shame to-day, viz.: in the heads of men who won't bring their thinking into line with the Spirit of God. If they are inspired by the Holy Spirit, they always build their words on the words of Jesus Christ or of God. That is the way we are renewed in the Spirit of our mind, not by an impulse of the Spirit, not by an impression, but by being gripped by the word of God. The old habit of getting "a word from God" is the right one, and don't give up till you get one, never go on an impression, it will go, there is nothing in it, nothing lasting unless the word becomes living and brings back to remembrance some word of His. That is how the world of self is made just as Jesus Christ wants it to be, that is the way we are able to discern the arm of the Lord; if we do not, supposing myself is ruled by another spirit away from Jesus, then I will explain the world according to that spirit, the spirit that rules myself. If it is I, my right to myself, I will never explain anything like Jesus Christ does, I will begin to patronize Him. If I do not dare to patronize Jesus, I will patronize the apostle Paul, and if I don't patronize Paul, I will begin to sneer at the Pentateuch. Anything to appear up to date, because the spirit that is in man, no matter how cultured, no matter how moral, no matter how religious, if it is not the Spirit of God, must be "scattering" away from Jesus Christ; no matter how sweet and delightful, how favorable it may appear to men, "he that gathereth not with. Me scattereth." "I am the Way;" not only the Spirit of God for living, but the Spirit of God for thinking.

(Ezek. 1:20.) The picture there is that the ultimate working of everything in harmony with God is by the Spirit of God. The cherubim are a true picture of the "mystical body of Christ." You remember that Moses was told to make the cherubim, he was also told previously that he must make no image of anything in Heaven above, or on earth beneath, and the cherubim are figures of nothing like anything in Heaven or earth. Why? Because they are like something that is being made now. the mystical body of Christ. You find it figured in the garden of Eden, the only way back to the tree of life is by the mystical body; salvation and sanctification mean not only possessed by the Spirit for living, but possessed by the Spirit for thinking. Cherubim were guardians into the holiest of all, and when the mystical body of Christ is complete, all the machinery of this earth will be moved and directed by the Spirit of God.

There is a great difference between interpretation by intuition and interpretation by thinking. One is never safe, the other always is. If you bring your mind into captivity to the Holy Spirit, and be renewed in it, you will get to what is termed the "Nous." The "Nous" simply means the responsible intelligence; up to that point in your natural life, and that point in your spiritual life, you get things by intuition, impulse, but there is no responsibility. See to it whenever you get to the point of responsible intelligence, then realize that you have come to a sure line of thinking. That is what the writer to the Hebrews refers to in Hebrews 5: "By this time you ought to be teachers," but you want spooned meat again; by this time they ought to be robust and mature, no longer either children or fools, but men and women able to discern between right and wrong, good and bad, with responsible, thoroughly informed intelligences. How many of us have allowed God to bring us there spiritually? How many of us can think along Jesus Christ's line? How many of us have to say whenever any such subject is taught. "I leave those things for other people"? "We have no business to, we have all to be our best for God. We have not only to be good lovers, but good thinkers, and it is along that line we can test the spirits.

How are we going to test the teaching that is abroad to-day? Immediately you get a real Christian experience in a man or woman and the head not informed, not disciplined, the intelligence becomes a hotbed for heresy. If we would revolutionize our thinking and bring our imaginations back again to the context, back to God's heart, the Bible, which not only explains God, but explains the world we live in; not only explains the things that are right, but the things that are wrong!

If I start out with an idea and say, "Everything is going well, and is bright and happy," then there is a sudden earthquake, someone is killed by lightning, tremendous floods, a volcano, or a shocking murder, or worse crime; every conclusion you like to come to will be flatly contradicted by the world outside, by the facts you see. The Bible and the world outside agree, they are an absolute puzzle until you receive the Spirit of God. When you receive the Spirit of God, you are taken first of all into a new realm, a totally new kingdom, then, if you will bring your mind into harmony, and every thought into captivity, and begin slowly to discipline and educate your character, you begin to discern not only order in the Bible, but your eyes are opened and the secrets are understood and grasped. We read history and begin to find out the way God has been working; we look at our own lives and find not a lot of haphazard chances, but that we are working out some preconceived idea of God we do not know; we begin to find, to our amazement, that our lives are answers to the prayers of the Holy Ghost, and back of everything is the tremendous, wonderful mind of God, until a human being can go to the length of saying what the apostle Paul said, "We have the mind of Christ." That is a good deal more than the Spirit of Christ. Remember, the mind of Christ means thinking like Christ; Jesus never thought from any other centre but God. "The words that I speak to you they are spirit and life." Where did He get them from? He got them from the Spirit that was in Him, He never spoke from the other spirit, from His right to Himself, that is why the tongue in Christ got to the right place, and that is how the tongue and the brain in you and me will get to the right place, when once we learn to obey the Spirit of God for thinking. Thank God there is a line of explanation for everything under Heaven! Jesus Christ does satisfy the last aching abyss of the heart by our reception of the Spirit, and obedience to Him. We do feel that one word ringing all over our life mentally," Obey! Obey!" Those of you who know it in the moral realm, put it into the intellectual. Obey! Is the imagination in captivity to Jesus? Is the thinking along His line, being renewed in the spirit of my mind? Is this in absolute harmony with the Lord Jesus Christ?

The day we live in, mentally, is a day of wild imaginations everywhere, unchecked imaginations in music, in literature, and, worst of all, in Scripture. People going off on the wildest speculations, getting hold of one line and then running clean off on a tangent, explaining everything on that line; that is not according to the Spirit of God. There is no royal road, none of us get there all at once, it is by steady discipline, when I am willing that God should bring my brain into harmony with the Spirit He has put in my heart.

CHAPTER XIX.

SPIRIT: THE DOMAIN AND DOMINION OF SPIRIT.

MAN'S UNIVERSE.
(Job 12: 10; Psa. 51: 10.)

N. B. We deal here particularly with Spirit in the "Natural" Man.

1. SPIRIT AS SOUL-MAKING POWER.
   (a) Particular Form. Gen. 2:7; 6: 17.
   (b) Personal Form. Num. 16:22; 27: 16; Zech. 12: 1; Isa. 19: 3; Psa. 51: 10.
   (c) Physical Form. Job 32: 8, 9; Gen. 7: 22; Hab. 2: 19; Rev. 13: 15; Job 34: 14, 15.

2. SPIRIT IN THE FLESH.
   (a) Independent. 1 Cor. 2: 11, 14.
   (b) Dependent. Psa. 32:2; 2 Cor. 7:1; Jas. 3:15.
   (c) Death. Rom. 7:18, 23; 8:5-7; 1 Pet. 3:19.

We will deal first of all with "Nous." The best way to put it practically is – the moment of responsible intelligence, either in a natural man or a spiritual man. (That is not a definition in any other way than being a working indication of the thing for practical purposes.) Now the point when responsible intelligence begins in a natural life is very different, some people never seem to reach it at all, they live like children and die like children, or rather more like "simpletons" than children. They have impulses and imaginations and fancies, but never seem to come to a responsible intelligence. A child has no responsible intelligence to begin with. In the spiritual domain, the same thing is true. In the beginning of the spiritual life we have the "Spirit of God," but not the "mind of Christ." The "mind of Christ" means that we have formed the same intelligent, responsible outlook on things that the Son of God had, and one of the greatest benedictions of God's grace is this, that some people who do not seem to have any natural "nous" can construct one in the realm of grace by the Spirit of God, and the right use of it in the temple of the Holy Ghost. It is not something with which we can say we are endowed; to begin with, we have the capacity, but the formation of the "nous" depends on how we develop, and allow ourselves to be disciplined.

Spiritually, God always holds us responsible for being deficient in the matter of this understanding of things in a responsible way.

Let us look at the subject of "Nous" under three headings, the Natural Nous, the Spiritual Nous, and the Bewildered Nous. Jesus Christ is the responsible expression of the intelligence of God, Jesus Christ is called the "Logos." We have the same thing in man, we have spirit, and immediately we form a responsible intelligence, our words are responsible, all the things we express, the statements we make, and the thoughts we form are all stamped with responsibility. A child's sphere is not responsible, but with persons of a mature intelligence, their statements are responsible; consequently God judges us by our words. It is quite true there are times in a man's life when he has to say "answer my meaning, not my words," but that is an exceptional thing. We have to remember that the words, the expressions in us, when we have a responsible intelligence, are responsible ones.

Take, first of all, the natural responsible intelligence. There is a capacity in man apart from the Spirit of God, to know that there is a God. (Rom. 1: 20.) I interpret the things outside me by my intelligence. I must come to the conclusion that there was an intelligence that made them, not less than my intelligence, therefore every man when he becomes responsibly intelligent, does know that there must be responsible intelligence behind everything there is. So you find that God holds every man responsible, and the writer to the Hebrews says, "A man must believe that God is, before he can come to Him." "We are talking apart from the work of grace, we are talking entirely now in the natural way.

(Rom. 7:23-25.) Paul is revealing that in the natural make-up of a man the ordinance of God is placed, and when the man becomes responsibly intelligent he is able to discern a great many things, things he calls justice and right, and Paul states that heathen are judged by conscience. We are coming very near to the point where conscience becomes a responsible working power in a man's life. When we dealt with conscience we called it the eye of the soul looking out towards God. Well, this is very nearly the same thing. The nous, the responsible intelligence, begins to discern in the natural spirit the ordinance of God written, consequently the idea of people saying men are not responsible for doing wrong is not true to nature or to revelation. The Bible says that the man knows by the way he is made that certain things are wrong, and as he obeys that ordinance of God written in his spirit he will be judged.

(Heb. 11:3.) There again we have the bridge between the natural and the spiritual. This is not a question of swallowing a revelation of God, this is a question of understanding with a responsible intelligence how the world was made, and it is simply a new emphasis on the thing we have been emphasizing all along, the responsibility of those of us who are Christians in experience for being responsible Christians in intelligence. "We have no business to be ignorant of how the world was made. If we can form responsible intelligence as natural men, we have to form it also as spiritual men. The Bible does not only teach the way of salvation, but the way of spiritual sanity. The Bible world corresponds exactly with the natural world, and the Bible world explains the natural world, and it is the only one that does, and we are held responsible by God for not allowing ourselves to form that spiritual "nous," to understand that the worlds were made by the word of God out of nothing that does appear. That is a different thing from Romans 2:20, which is simply that a man, by his natural intelligence, when he becomes responsible knows that there must be a mind behind the things that are.

Now let us take the spiritual nous. (1 Cor. 2:16.) That is a wonderful passage, it is much more than the' Spirit of Christ, it is the responsible understanding of Christ, "We have the mind of Christ." You will find every now and again that the Spirit of God within us, when we are born again, is struggling to get us to understand as God understands, and we are very stupid, very dark and very silly in the way we mifftake a great many things the Spirit of God is trying to lead us to, but in entire sanctification, when the Son of God is formed in us, we understand with this responsible intelligence, we understand just like Jesus Christ did, and the consequence is this, that I am held responsible for doing through my body the things that I understand God wants me to do. Jesus Christ spoke the things that He knew His Father wanted Him to speak, and He spake nothing else; I must do the same if I have the mind of Christ. Jesus worked with His hands only those works that He knew were the exact expression of His Father. I must do the same. Spiritual nous, then, does not only mean the Holy Spirit energizing my spirit; it means my allowing that Spirit to work out in a responsible intelligence in me.

(1 John 5:20.) That word "understanding" does not mean "necromancy," it does not mean a great big flashing "spiritual intuition," it means that we understand with a perfectly responsible intelligence that which comes from God; and God holds us responsible for not knowing it. It is not the question of an uncanny spiritual influence, it is not the question of getting some tremendously wonderful insight from God, it is the question of having the understanding, the nous, so absolutely obedient to the Spirit of God that we can understand what is of God and what is not.

(Heb. 8:10.) That embraces everything, the full, mature understanding intelligence of the people of God, not being driven about by every wind of doctrine, not being at the mercy of spiritual impulses, but being mature, vigorous, understanding people who know the will of God and do it.

(Rom. 8:6.) "Carnal mind," in this sense, is what we all call" common sense." If you ask yourself what common sense is, it simply means the mature, responsible intelligence of a responsible being, and you will find that over and over again (we are bridging now between spiritual and bewildered nous) you will begin to find how those two things clash before they harmonize. The soul gets thoroughly bewildered. We are not dealing with the "carnal mind" in the deep moral sense, but only on the responsible intelligence side, it sets itself against the spiritual understanding, it won't be reconciled to it, just as it won't be reconciled to it morally, and until the "common sense" becomes "sanctified sense" (not sanctified common sense, that is not a Bible phrase or a Bible meaning), until the responsible intelligence of my mind becomes reformed by the Spirit of God, the antagonism goes on. We are all perfectly familiar with the "carnal mind" in the moral way, it is wrong longings, and seekings and antipathies to God, but it takes a good deal of courage to confess and to face that it is absolutely wrong in its responsible thinking, and it will give verdicts against Jesus Christ as the Pharisees did, it will decide straight off that Jesus Christ 's mind and responsible intelligence are the responsible intelligence of a madman, or the irresponsible intelligence of a mere dreamer. You will find, when you begin to think along God's line, an amazing clash with certain things that were accepted as being inalienable "rights" for everybody, and you will find that Jesus Christ's teaching works from another standpoint, and the clashing brings confusion and bewildering for a time, until we are resolved to remove from ourselves altogether the old habits and ways of looking at things, and look at everything now from the "mind of Christ" standpoint. "If any man is in Christ Jesus he is a new creation," not only spirit and soul, but in every other way, and we slowly see the new creation all through.

Bewildered Nous. Jesus said He came to send a sword, and this always happens; when His Spirit comes in it confuses the responsible intelligence of a man, turns him upside down. This is different from conviction of sin.

(2 Cor. 11:3.) There is the responsible intelligence of a devil being allowed entrance into Eve by subtlety, and bewildering her straight off from understanding God's will or obeying it, and Paul says here he hopes that none will be bewitched in that way. He said to the Galatians, "Who hath bewitched you?" This conflict of responsible intelligence goes on at the beginning of Christian life when people are in danger of becoming "legal." Paul said, "I am afraid of you, lest my labor is in vain," lest you get all wrong, you are now going back again to the old ways of making yourself perfect; the old legal notions; and that is the way sometimes the subtlety of Satan takes away from the power of God, the life that was coming under the dominion of the Spirit of God. Our Lord alludes to the same thing when He says the "cares of this world, the deceitfulness of riches and the lust of other things bewilder you, choke what I put in." So no wonder the first law of a born-again soul is concentration. (We hear a great deal about consecration, but we do not hear so much about concentration.)

The consequence of a bewildered soul is that of doubleness. (Jas. 1:8.) "Switherers," that is a very apt description of a bewildered soul. Responsible intelligence of the world pulling, and the responsible intelligence of the mind of Christ pulling too, and you do not know which to take. "Don't let that man think he shall receive anything" because he will not, he is a "switherer." He has to decide whether he will be identified with the Lord Jesus Christ to the crucifixion of the old type altogether, and to the turning out, not only of the "old man," but of the old responsible intelligence, the old bondage, the old legalism, the old thing that used to guide the life before, and get in the totally new mind. It works this way, in your practical life you will come now and again into crises where there will be two distinct ways before you, one the way of ordinary, strong, moral, common sense, and the other waiting on God until the mind be formed to understand God's way. You will find any amount of "backing" in the first line, you will find the backing of worldly people, and the backing of semi-Christian people, but you will get the warning, the drawing back of the Spirit of God, and if you wait on God, study His Word and watch circumstances, you will be brought to a new decision so that your worldly backers and your semi-Christian backers will fall from you with disgust and say it is absurd, you are getting fanatical. That is the way we begin to form a responsible intelligence, and we must not grieve the Spirit of God in these lines.

1. Spirit as Soul-Making Power – (a) Particular Form, (b) Personal Form, (c) Physical Form.

"We are now dealing with Man's Universe, the Particular Form, the Personal Form, and the Physical Form. Remember, the whole meaning of my soul life is this, to express what my spirit means, and the struggle of spirit is to get itself expressed in my soul. Take it in the natural line, you will find when an immature mind tries' to express itself, there are tremendous struggles and all kinds of physical exertions and efforts. It has not the power of expressing itself, it has not a responsible intelligence, it has not a vocabulary, and you get the exquisite suffering of young lives trying to express the spirit that is in them. Music is run to, theatres are run to, literature is run to, anything to get the power of expressing what is in "longing"; and if I go on too long on the music line, or the art line, or the literature line of things, I will never form a responsible intelligence, I will be the most unpractical of all beings on the face of the earth, and the discipline of the machinery of life is to get the power to express what is in you. That is what language is. The difference in the histories of languages is very wonderful. Take the language of our authorized Bible and the language we use to-day, the difference is enormous. The old Saxon words that the Bible is translated into are the words that express the inward soul for the first time, the words we use now are nearly all technical, borrowed from something else, and our words, our most modern words, are not .those that express the spirit at all, they are those that cloak it up cunningly, no expression. In the natural person, the young person, this kind of thing is often heard, "Oh, I don't understand myself, nobody else understands me!" Why, of course you don't, but you are responsible for not having a responsible intelligence to know where you can be understood. (Read Psa. 139.) If it is true in the natural world that a mind trying to express itself gets all these kinds of turmoils, it is just as true spiritually.

That is the meaning of education, education is not to pack into me something that is alien, but something that gives me the power to "draw out" what is in me. One of the greatest benefits to a young life trying to express itself is to give it something to work with its hands, to model in wax, or to paint, or write, or dig, or form; the power of expression. Take it on the spiritual line, when the Spirit of God comes into me, the same struggles go on, He trying to get me into line, out of the "natural ruts," He tries to get me to obey Him so that He can express Himself through my responsible intelligence, and you have the throes and the pains of the spiritual life when you are Spirit-born, till the mind of Christ is in you, and the old carnal antagonism is no more. That is why we find the value, as Paul says, of spiritual teachers and helpers, because they express to us what we have been trying to express for ourselves, and could not, and immediately some book or person has expressed for me what I have been trying to learn how to express for myself I feel unspeakably grateful, and that is the way I begin to learn how to express for myself. Tribulation will teach you, your circumstances will teach you, difficult things will teach you, temptations of the devil will teach you, all these things will develop the power of expression all through until we get in our words and works to be as responsible in expression of the Spirit of God as Jesus Christ was the responsible expression of the mind of God Almighty.

(a) Particular Forms. All the particular forms of nature – rocks and trees, animals and men – are the outcome of the breathing of the Spirit of God. There is a true law of correspondence between the things we see and the mind behind them. When we have the mind behind the things in us, we begin to understand how these things manifest it, but if we have not the mind behind them, we will never understand them.

Then (b) the Personal Form. That means a man has a distinct responsibility of his own, and he can express in a responsible way either by the spirit of the devil or by the Spirit of God; he can express the spirit of the "prince of this world" in a responsible, intelligent way, or he can express the Spirit of God in a responsible, intelligent way. That is what we mean by a man showing "soul" in his writing, "soul" in his speaking, "soul" in his praying, "soul" in his manner of living; the man has power to express himself and you can feel all the time the personal note coming out. Now, God is called a Person, therefore by His creation He expresses the peculiar stamp of His personal outlook, and when we have His Spirit within us and are forming a responsible intelligence, we begin to think His thoughts after Him, we begin to see what His meaning is, not by our natural intelligence, but by the Spirit of God when we allow the Spirit to form in us "the mind of Christ."

Then (c) the Physical Form, or expression. That simply means that this physical life is meant to express all that is in the spirit. The soul has been struggling in travail of birth, and when it is expressed in the body it has reached its zone of expressions "When children get into "tempers," remember, often it is an attempt to express themselves, the soul has not the birth-pangs strong enough, the spirit cannot express itself. Paul says, "When it pleased God, who separated me from my mother's womb, to reveal His Son in me." That is stating just this idea. To begin with, we have not our "own bodies," probably we have a body very much like our grandmother's or grandfather's or someone's else, but every few years these physical forms alter, and they alter into the shape of my ruling spirit, and slowly and surely we will find a beautifully moulded face may take on a remarkably unbeautiful moral expression as it grows older, or we may look on a very ugly face and see it, as it grows older, take on a remarkably beautiful moral expression. The physical life must express, sooner or later, through the turmoil in the soul, the ruling spirit, and we grow exactly like what our spirit is. If our spirit is the spirit of a man, then we will grow further and further away from the image of God. If we have the Spirit of God in us, then we will grow more and more into "the same image from glory to glory."

2. Spirit in the Flesh – (a) Independent, (b) Dependent, (c) Death.

In this expression of the spirit in my flesh, we have three things. Where it is independent of the flesh, to begin with, you find the divorce between a person who is spiritually born again and the fleshly expression. (Beware of that phrase, we hear over and over again, that there is no difference between the external life of a Spirit-born person and a sanctified person. It is untrue, there is a tremendous difference. It is untrue to God, and untrue to experience) When a person is born again of the Spirit, the flesh does not express anything like to the same degree that it does when sanctification has been reached. Why? Because it has not yet learned obedience to God. When the soul is brought into harmony with the mind of God and is willing to enter into identification with the mind of Jesus Christ, something like the following happens: in the first place, the Spirit works (a) in independence of the flesh and you get the conviction of sin. The Spirit of God produces very great darkness and difficulty in the soul when He comes in, He produces the discernment of the wrong mind, He produces the discernment that makes the spirit pant and yearn and long after being made like God, and there is nothing that can comfort the soul that is born of the Spirit, but God, and the only hope for that spirit is concentration on obedience to the Spirit of God. (2 Cor. 2:11-14.) So when the Spirit of God comes into me, He does not express Himself straight off in my flesh; He works independently of my flesh, and I am conscious of the divorce. I gain slow, sure, steady victories, but I am conscious of the turmoil. The soul is the birthplace of the new spirit and the soul struggles while the spirit tries to express itself through the body.

Then take (b) Dependent. This is quite true but the other thing is true also, that if I won't obey the Spirit, my spirit will become enchained to my flesh and absolutely dependent on it, and clamoring of the flesh through the avenues of the flesh, and the clamoring of the old mind, will gradually crush and grieve the Spirit of God away. (2 Cor. 7: 1.) The Spirit of God is independent in me, just as my spirit is, to begin with, but it is also true, that the insistence of my "flesh," the insistence of the "carnal mind," if I don't obey the Spirit of God, will gradually defile everything the Spirit of God has been trying to do. The Spirit "lusts against the flesh and the flesh against the Spirit," and we can, when the Spirit of God is in us, slowly and surely and victoriously claim the whole territory for the Spirit of God, until, at entire sanctification, the only thing there is the Spirit of God, who has enabled me at last to form the mind of Christ, and now I begin to grow, and manifest that growth in grace which expresses the life of Jesus in my own moral flesh.

Then (c) Death. (Rom. 8:5-7.) That last verse is very direct, it puts an end to all absurd squabbles as to what is spiritual death. "To be carnally minded is death," to be given over to an ordinary, responsible intelligence that has not been reformed by the Spirit of God, is death, and it will grow and develop further and further away from God in its manifestation, until the man who has the mind of death can sink so low that he is perfectly happy without God. Psalm 73 describes it, "No bands in his death, he is not troubled like other men, his eyes stand out with fatness, he has everything heart can desire," and the extraordinary thing is he is the only man the worldly people call alive. If you get persons who have the Spirit of God in them, slowly manifesting by sanctification the mind of Christ in their life, then the world says they are "half dead." Peter says they "think it strange that you do not go to the same excess of riot." No wonder Paul states that, "If any man is in Christ Jesus, he is a new creation, old things have passed away, and behold all things have become new."

"Where are we with regard, to this responsible intelligence? How many of us, as Christians who are in the definite experience of spiritual life, are forming the responsible intelligence and realize we have to be renewed in the spirit of our minds, and for what purpose? That we may be able to discern with a responsible intelligence what the will of God is for us, the thing that is perfect and acceptable and good and right. All the childish clamor of being driven from "pillar to post" by every wind of doctrine must cease altogether, and the mature, sensible, strong, stable life come. Nothing can upset it, neither things present, nor things to come, nor height, nor depth, nor any other creation. Every power it comes against, whether it be material things, or human things, or diabolical things, or spiritual things, simply means another occasion for forming a deeper and more intelligent grasp of the mind of God. As the only way we develop intelligence in the natural world is by coming in contact with things that are irrational and unintelligent, so in the things of God we form the mind of God by subduing all to a, spiritual understanding.

CHAPTER XX.

SPIRIT: THE DOMAIN AND DOMINION OF SPIRIT.

MAN'S UNIVERSE.
(1 Cor. 15:45.)

N. B. We deal here particularly with Spirit in the "spiritual" man.

1. SPIRIT IN ITS FREEDOM FROM FLESH. (EXTRAORDI-
   NARY.)
   (a) Ecstasy. Acts 10:10; 22:17; 2 Cor. 12:2-4; Rev. 4: 2.
   (Sometimes with the body. Acts 8: 39; 2 Cor. 12: 2-4; 1
   Thess. 4: 17; Rev. 12: 5; Matt. 4: 1.)
   (b) Emancipation. Luke 16:25; 23:43; Heb. 12:23. (Death).
   Heb. 4:12; Gal. 5:24; Col, 2:11; Rom. 6: 6; Gal. 6:8; John 3:8;
   20: 22. (Deliverance.)

2. SPIRIT OPERATING IN SENSE. Ex. 6:9; Prov. 15; 13; 2 Cor.
   2: 13; Acts 17: 11-16; John 11: 33.

3. SPIRIT OPERATING INWARDLY. Luke 10: 21; 1 Cor.2:4;
   14: 2, 14-16. (Here we will deal with the"Tongues" question.)

4. SPIRIT OPERATING MORALLY. Ex. 35:21; Acts 19: 21; 20:
   22; Prov. 16: 18; Isa. 11: 2.

The contrast in 1 Corinthians 15:45 is not a contrast of moral
worth, but a contrast of revelation. "Adam" does not mean the
"old man," "Adam" means there, our human nature, in Adam
we are made "living souls"; in Christ we are made "living spirits." Never confound the "old man" and "Adam," and never confound the "old man" and the "devil," they are not synonymous.
The phrase here "the first man Adam was made a living soul,"
refers to the great fact of God's creation; "the second man Adam
was made a quickening spirit," refers to God's regenerating work
in the living soul. The Bible says that man's spirit has not life in

itself; that is, no spirit in man can will pure will, and love pure love; the Holy Spirit has life in Himself, when He comes in He energizes our spirit and enables us to will the will of God.

"We have divided the subject into four parts: 1. Spirit in Its Freedom from the Flesh, under two headings – (a) Extraordinary Ecstacy and (b) Emancipation; 2. Spirit Operating in Sense; 3. Spirit Operating Inwardly, and 4. Spirit Operating Morally.

Spirit in Its Freedom from the Flesh.

We will take the Extraordinary section. "We mean by extraordinary, what the word means, off the ordinary, out of the ordinary, not contrary to the ordinary, or against it, but out of it. Take first of all (a) Ecstacy. Ecstacy means transport, something that lifts a man right out of his ordinary setting; a state of mind marked by temporary mental alienation, and altered consciousness. By that a man's soul gets into the condition of seeing and hearing apart from his bodily organs.

We have to bear in mind there are facts revealed in God's Book that are not common to our experience, and it is a great moment reached in my mental life when I have ray mind opened to the fact that there are states of experience which the majority of us know nothing about, either for good or bad, and ecstacy is one of them. For instance, it is a very easy business to ridicule, but ridicule may be a sign of ignorance. It simply means, "Nobody has ever seen or understood anything that I have not, and if they say they have, they are fools." That means that I put myself in the place of the Lord, and I know everything that everybody can experience, and if they say they have seen things that I have not, then I laugh at them. That is because I am a fool. Paul uses exactly that argument about the testimony for sanctification and the testimony for "Christ crucified;" he says it is foolishness to those that seek after wisdom, they say it is stupid, they tell you point blank to your face no man ever was sanctified, and if you say you are, you are a liar, or you suffer from hallucinations. Do let us see that we do not take the same attitude to these other things as well, it is quite possible that a good many of us may have just this mental attitude to these extraordinary experiences recorded in God's Book.

First of all, ecstacy where the man's soul is taken out of the bodily relationship into an extraordinary state where it sees and hears things without the bodily organs. (Acts 10:10.) The word "trance" there does not mean "faint," the word "trance" means exactly what "ecstacy" means. (Acts 22:17.) Again that refers to ecstacy. If you read the context immediately afterwards you find the exact description given of an ecstacy, seeing and hearing apart from the bodily organs. (2 Cor. 12:2-4; Rev. 4:2.) Each one of these verses refers to ecstacy. Paul, in recounting the experience of fourteen years previous, says, M l do not know whether the man was in the body or out of it." Now remember, that power of a human soul may be for good or bad. Indian necromancy can produce exactly those states, and nothing but ignorance and stupidity makes us say they cannot, they can. Indian necromancers can take a man's personality right out of his bodily setting and put him into another setting where he sees and hears altogether apart from his body.

Take the next thing in ecstacy, where the body is sometimes taken with the spirit in these extraordinary conditions. (Acts 8:39.) There is the taking of the body with the soul by extraordinary transportation, by a supernatural aeroplane, by an ecstasy; something absolutely unusual. (1 Thess. 4:17.) That refers to the instantaneous change of a "material body" into a "glorified" one. (Rev. 12:5; Matt. 4:1.) The very same idea there. After our Lord's resurrection He appeared to the disciples during the forty days, that is, He had power to "materialize" whenever He chose. For instance, after the resurrection Jesus ate fish and honeycomb. In the Millennium we shall have exactly the same power, as saints. We are to reign with Him in the "air." Conceivable to you? If it is, it is not conceivable to me. I do not know how I am going to stay up in the "air" "with the Lord." It is no business of mine, all I know is that revelation says so, and we will do so. What we are arguing for is an open mind about something that we can know nothing about as yet. (The Bible states it, and if I say it does not mean what it says, I put myself in the place of the Almighty. Immediately there is a record of an experience I have never had, and I say it is nonsense, I put myself in the place of the superior person, an attitude I have no business to take.) The marvelous power of the resurrection body, the glorified body is pictured in the Lord Jesus Christ. He could materialize whenever He chose, He proved He could, He could disappear whenever He chose, and we shall do exactly the same. Just think of the time when all your thinking will be in language as soon as you think it! The majority of us who have the idea that we are penned up in a little physical temple, are altogether twisted off the Bible revelation. "We are in this order of things, penned in this temple, for a particular reason, but at any second God can change this temple, in the "twinkling of an eye" into a glorified body.

Another thing, the question of ecstacies and transportation of bodies as well as spirits is indicated in the Bible, does it contradict common sense? It certainly does not, it transcends it. A miracle? It is no more a miracle than that I am alive, not a bit more of a miracle. Why should it be more of a miracle that God can transform me into the image of His Son by resurrection, than the fact that I am alive now? How is it that I am alive now? How is it that this material wood of this table and the material flesh of my hand are different? If we can explain that, we can explain the other, God who made the one made the other. The point I am driving at is that we have to remember that God is a Spirit, and the consequence is that at any moment He may turn upside down man's calculations about what He will do and what He won't do. Scientific men have long reached the conclusion that they dare not produce what they call their "experimental curve" beyond into the "inferential region." Now pseudo-scientific men do, the average scientific men say that according to the common record of common experience such and such is the case; if there is an isolated experience they put it by itself, they do not say it cannot be, they say it does not come into their line of explanation. The false scientists say because the majority of human beings have never experienced this, therefore it is untrue. No real scientist ever said such a thing. It is simply "part and parcel" of the subject of our own personality. As long as we are flippant and stupid and shallow and think we know ourselves, we will never give ourselves over to Jesus Christ. Once we become conscious that we are infinitely more than we can fathom, and infinitely more terrible than we can know, either for good or bad, we will be only too glad to hand ourselves over to the Lord Jesus Christ.

Mystery there must be, but the remarkable thing about the mysteries of the Bible is that they never contradict human reason, they transcend it. Now the mysteries of every other religion contradict human reason. Every one of the miracles (which simply mean the public power of God) transcends human reason, but not one of them contradicts human reason. Water turned into wine, it is done every year all over the world in process of time. Water is sucked up through the stem of a vine and turned into grapes, who does it? When it is done suddenly by the same Being who does it gradually, why should it be considered more of a miracle? The water turned suddenly into wine by Jesus at Cana does not contradict human reason, it transcends it. When Jesus Christ raised a man suddenly from the dead, He simply did what we all believe, in our implicit hearts, He is going to do presently.

Have any of us got sealed minds about facts in Gad's Book that we have never experienced, or do we try to apologize for them, do we try to make out that Philip was not carried away suddenly, do we try to make out that the apostle Paul was not caught up into the "third heaven," do we try to make out that Peter did not fall into a "trance" and see all the things he did see and learn all the things he did learn? That is the danger. Accept them as facts and you will find an enormous illumination to your understanding of how things can happen, marvelously with the great, mighty God.

Take the next thing, manifestation. We are dealing with spirit in its freedom from the flesh. (We mean by flesh, this body we are in, not the "mind of the flesh.") It is possible, then, for the spirit to exist apart altogether from man's body. Take it in (b) Emancipation from the flesh while we are here.

(Luke 16:25.) That refers to the place where the flesh is not, the unseen. (Luke 23:43.) That again refers to the place where the flesh cannot be, the unseen. (Heb. 13:13.) In our own minds we quite agree that the Bible points out that man's spirit is immortal, whether he be energized by the Spirit of God or whether he is not, that is, spirit never sleeps, that instead of sleeping at what we call death, at the breaking away from this body, his spirit is ten thousand-fold more awake. The majority of us in this body have our spirits half concealed. Remember, spirit and personality are synonymous, but man's personality is obscured as long as he is in this body. Immediately he dies, it is no more obscured, it is absolutely awake then. "Son, remember," no limitations now, he is face to face with everything else that is of spirit. That is what the Bible reveals. Soul and body depend on one another, spirit does not, spirit is immortal; soul is simply the spirit expressing itself in the body. Immediately body goes, soul is gone, but immediately body is brought back, soul is brought back. That means spirit, soul and body will be together. Spirit has never died, never can die, in the sense the body dies; the spirit is immortal, either in immortal death or immortal life. There is no such thing as annihilation in the Bible. The suspension of spirit, apart from body and soul, is a mere temporary business. In the resurrection, remember it is the resurrection of the body.

(John 5:29, 30.) The picture of the resurrection body of the bad is not given, but it is stated emphatically by Jesus that there will be a resurrection of the bad. Our Lord never talks about the resurrection of the spirit, the spirit never needs resurrecting. It is the resurrection of a resurrection body for "damnation" and a resurrection body for "glorification." Now we know what the resurrection body for "glorification" is, it is like Jesus Christ and all we know about the resurrection of the bad is that Jesus Christ (who ought to know what He is talking about), says that there will be a resurrection to damnation. The question of eternal punishment is a fearful one, but let no one say that Jesus Christ did not say anything about it, He did, He said it in language we can't begin to understand, and He spoke about it oftener than He spoke about Heaven, and if anybody should know surely Jesus Christ should. The least thing we can do is to be reverent with what we do not understand.

Then take (b) Emancipation in the sense of deliverance. (Heb. 4:12.) That is what the "Word of God does, it discerns between the soul and the spirit. Modern Christians do not, modern Christians say spirit and soul are the same thing; the Word of God discerns all through. Immediately the Spirit of God comes into my mind and heart He divides between the two instantly. That is how He convicts of sin. (Gal. 5:24.) What is flesh? Paul is not talking about disembodied spirits, then he certainly does not mean this flesh, he does not mean mortal flesh, he is not talking to a lot of corpses, he is talking to living men and women. Crucifixion means death. Then he is referring to a disposition on the inside and lie calls it the flesh. Whenever Paul means this body, he speaks of it as mortal flesh; whenever he refers to the old disposition, he calls it the flesh. (Col. 2: 11; Rom. 6:6; Gal. 6:8; John 5:8; 20:22.) This emancipation is deliverance while I am in this flesh, not counteraction, not suppression. In Paul's mind and in the teaching of the New Testament, man can be delivered, from the "old man," and Paul says, "Let God be true and every man a liar." In the majority of human testimonies the contradiction is given to the apostle Paul. Which are you going to side with? It may begin in counteractions, but, blessed be God ! emancipation is possible here and now.

Emancipation does not remove the possibility of disobedience; if it did, I would cease to be a human being. If the removal of the old disposition is made to mean that God has removed my human nature, then it is absurd and false. God removes the wrong disposition, but He never alters my human nature, I have the same body, the same eyes, the same imperfect brain and nervous system, but Paul's argument is, this body that you used to use as obedient slaves to the wrong disposition, you can now use as obedient slaves to the new disposition, and the marvel is that you will find the Spirit operating in sense.

We have been dealing with the emancipation of the spirit from the slavery of sin, now we are going to show how the Bible says the Spirit can operate through the senses, can express through my life that I am delivered, if I am delivered; no "reckoning" and hood winking, no pretending I am emancipated when I am not, but manifestation through every cell of my body that God has done what my mouth testifies He has done.

Exodus 6:9. That is an expression of how the spirit in the children of Israel had distorted their sense, they could not listen. (Prov. 15:13.) When a man is happy, he can't pull a long face in the natural world, he will try to, but it is the face of a clown; when he is happy inside he shows it outside. To hear a Christian with a sad face saying, "Oh, I am so full of the joy of the Lord! I am so happy!" Well, you know it is not true. If I am full of the joy of the Lord, it will pour out of every cell of my body. (2 Cor. 2:13.) All the uses of the term "spirit" in these passages is spirit that instantly shows itself in the flesh. The spirit of wrong shows itself in a man's flesh, and thank God, the Spirit of God does the same thing. (Acts 17:11-16; John 11:33.) The real Greek in that verse is, "He shook Himself violently with indignation."

2. Spirit Operating in Sense.

As soon as you get rightly related to God, the prince of this world has his last stake in this flesh. So many Christian workers do not know that, and he will wear you out to the last cell if you are working for God, but if you know his "trick" and God's grace, you will get supernatural physical recuperation every time you are exhausted in God's work, and the only sign that it is God's work is that you know the supernatural recuperation. As soon as you get right with God, Satan will suck every bit of your physical life out of you if he can. In the natural world, when you are doing work and are exhausted, what have you to do? You have to take a holiday and iron tonics, but if you are exhausted in God's work, all the iron tonics in the world will never touch you, the only thing that will recuperate you is God Himself. Paul, in Acts 20:24, said, "I do not count my life dear unto myself," and when the "dear sisters" and "brothers" say, "My sister, you must not work so hard," simply say, "Get thee behind me, Satan." Remember, Satan's last stake is on this very line, and when once you learn that "all your springs are" in God, you will draw on Him. The Spirit does operate in the flesh. Beware of laying off before God tells you; if you lay off before God tells you, you will rust, and that leads to "dry rot" always.

3. Spirit Operating Inwardly.

As the Spirit operates outwardly through my senses it operates inwardly towards God. (Luke 10:21.) There our Lord is talking inwardly by His Spirit to God, not through His senses. (2 Cor. 2:4.) That is why the preaching of the Gospel is supreme idiocy, that is the meaning of Paul when he says the preaching of the cross is ridiculous to the wisdom of this world. "When you have the Spirit of God in you, you find Paul's preaching is according to the wisdom of God; when you have not the Spirit of God in you, the preaching of Christ crucified is stupid, nothing else.

(1 Cor. 14:14-16.) Now the question of tongues in the fourteenth chapter of First Corinthians is not a foreign-language tongue, but what is called "glossalalia," that means a spiritual gibberish, nothing intelligible in it. Paul tells you how it comes about; as a baby before its human spirit has worked through its soul for expression blethers, so a soul after being born of the Holy Ghost is apt to be carried away with the same emotional ecstacy. Try and understand a baby, you cannot, unless you are its mother, then possibly you may, and Paul deals with these people the same way. Paul says what you have to do is to get your spirit into a spiritual "nous," into an understanding whereby you can express it. For instance, all phrases like "Hallelujah!" and "Glory be to God!" arise from the same thing. When first a soul is introduced by the Spirit of God to the heavenly domain, there is all the tremendous bursting up of new life in the soul, and there is no language for it, but the "lala" of the Corinthians, or the Psalms of David. Paul says, Get to the understanding point as soon as ever you can; this thing will produce disgraceful mockery among the nations if you don't watch what you are doing; if I come into your meetings and see you are jabbering, all I can think is you are giving occasion to the enemy to blaspheme. As long as you are amongst people who know who you are and what you are doing, that you are spiritual babes, all well, but if you begin to parade it abroad, as they had been taught to do, it's not well. May God forgive the teachers, for they were inspired by the devil, and God's blight has been on them.

The first thing we have to note when we are introduced by the Spirit of God into a new domain, is that we have no language; sighings and groanings and tears, but no language, spiritual babyhood. Now Paul says, "Get instructed," and the wisest way you can get instructed is to get the Psalms to express for you; when you are worked up to pitches like that, read some of the Psalms and you will find the Spirit of God gradually teaches you how to have a spiritual "nous," a mind whereby you will understand, and then slowly and surely you will get to the place where you are lifted up into a totally new language. The gift of tongues at Pentecost was not the gift of "glossalalia," it was the gift of new language. The responsibility all through with the modern Tongues Movement is with the teachers. May God have mercy on them!

4. Spirit Operating Morally.

The Spirit working through the senses and working inwardly to God, produces a moral character just like Jesus Christ's, a morality and an uprightness like His. The worthiness of our Lord Jesus Christ is moral worth, in the human and divine sphere, and our moral worth is the same.

God grant that we may ever walk in the Spirit, and thus not fulfill the lusts of the flesh!

N. B. This ends abruptly, but we leave it so. The whole book is merely a verbatim report of the lectures; the task of altering it to make it fit for publication would have been too stupendous. We have therefore decided to let it go for what it is worth – a mere effort to rouse up the average Christian worker to study the wealth of the Scripture, and to become better equipped for dividing the Word of Truth. The lectures are going on week by week and year by year, not in repetition, but in exhaustive detail of all laid down here in such scamped and hasty manner.

God bless all who care to read the book!

INDEX

2. The Pre-Adamic Anarchy.

    (a) Satanic Pretensious.

    (b) Satanic Perversions.

    (c) Satanic Perils.

3. The Punished Anarchists.

    (a) Destitution and Death.

    (b) Division from Deity.

    (c) Divine Declaration.

CHAPTER IV.

Man: His Creation, Calling, and Communion.
Readjustment by Redemption.

1. Incarnation – Word Made Weak.
    God-Man.

    (a) Self-surrender of Trinity.

    (b) Self-same with Trinity.

    (c) Self-sufficiency of Trinity.

2. Identification – Son Made Sin.
    God and Man.

    (a) Day of His Death.

    (b) Day of His Resurrection.

    (c) Day of His Ascension.

3. Invasion – Sinner Made Saint.
    God in Man.

    (a) The New Man.

    (b) The New Manners.

    (c) The New Mankind.

CHAPTER V.

Soul: The Essence, Existence, and Expression.

1. The Term Soul (Generally).

    (a) Applied to Men and Animals.

    (b) Applied to Men, not Animals.

    (c) Applied to Men Individually.

2. Truth about the Soul (Specifically).

    (a) Soul and Spirit.

    (b) Soul and Body.

    (c) Soul and Personality.

CHAPTER VI.

Soul: The Essence, Existence, and Expression.
Fundamental Powers of the Soul.

1. Contraction.

    (a) First Power – Self -comprehending.

    (b) Second Power – Stretching beyond Itself.

2. Expansion.

    (c) Third Power – Self -living.

    (d) Fourth Power – Spirit-penetration.

3. Rotation.

    (e) Fifth Power – Stirred Sensually or Spiritually.

    (f) Sixth Power – Speaking the Spirit's Thoughts.

    (g) Seventh Power – Sum Total in Unity.

CHAPTER VII.

Soul: The Essence, Existence, and Expression.
Fleshly Presentation of the Soul.

1. In Embryo.

    (a) Before Consciousness.

    (b) Breath Consciousness.

    (c) Blood Circulation.

2. In Evolution.

    (d) The Hub of Life.

    (e) Hubbub of Life.

    (1) Sense of Seeing.

    (2) Sense of Hearing.

    (3) Sense of Tasting.

    (4) Sense of Smelling.

    (5) Sense of Touching.

3. In Expression.

(f) Hilarity of Life.

(g) Himself.

CHAPTER VIII.

Soul: The Essence, Existence, and Expression.

Past, Present and Future of the Soul.

1. Pre-existence.

(a) Spurious Speculations.

(b) Startling Scriptures.

(c) Steadying Scriptures.

(1) No Soul before Body.

(2) No Soul Destiny pre-Adamic.

(3) No Soul but by Pro-creation.

2. Present Existence.

(a) Satisfaction of the Soul.

(b) Sins and Surroundings of the Soul.

(c) Supernatural Setting for the Soul.

3. Perpetual Existence.

(a) The Mortal Aspect of the Soul.

(b) The Immortal Aspect of the Soul.

(c) Eternal Life and Eternal Death of the Soul.

CHAPTER IX.

Heart: The Radical Region of Life.

1. The Centre of the Physical Life.

(a) Lifeless Objects.

(b) Lowest Life Power.

(c) Life Power.

(d) Life of the Whole Person,

2.   The Centre of Practical Life.

(a) Emporium.

(b) Export.

(c) Import.

CHAPTER X.

Heart: The Radical Region of Life.
The Radiator of Personal Life.

1. Voluntary.

    (a) Determination.

    (b) Design.

2. Versatility.

    (a) Perception.

    (b) Meditation.

    (c) Estimation.

    (d) Inclination.

3. Virtues and Vices.

    (a) All Degrees of Joy.

    (b) All Degrees of Pain.

    (c) All Degrees of Ill-will.

CHAPTER XI.

Heart: The Radical Region of Life.
The Radiator of Personal Life (Concluded),

1. Voluntary.

    (c) Love.

    (d) Hate.

2. Versatility.

    (e) Memory.

    (f) Thinking.

    (g) Birth of Words.

3. Virtues and Vices.

    (d) All Degrees of Fear.

    (e) All Degrees of Anguish.

    (f) All Conscious Unity.

CHAPTER XII.

Heart: The Radical Region of Life.
The Rendezvous of Perfect Life.

1. The Inner.

    (a) Highest Love.

    (b) Highest License,

(e) Darkened.

(d) Hardened.

2. The Inmost.

    (a) Laboratory of Life.

    (b) Lusts.

    (c) Law of Nature.

    (d) Law of Grace.

    (e) Seat of Conscience.

    (f) Seat of Belief and Disbelief.

3. The Innermost.

    (a) Inspiration of God.

    (b) Inspiration of Satan.

    (c) Indwelling of Christ.

    (d) Indwelling of Spirit.

    (e) Abode of Peace.

    (f) Abode of Love.

    (g) Abode of Light.

    (h) Abode of Communication.

CHAPTER XIII.

Ourselves: I; Me; Mine.

Ourselves as a Known." I the "Ego."

1. Some Distinctions of Importance.

    (a) Individuality.

    (b) Personality.

    (c) Egoism and Egotism.

2. Some Determinations of Interest.

    (a) The Ego is Inscrutable.

    (b) The Ego is Introspective.

    (c) The Ego is Individual.

3. Some Delusions of Importance.

    (a) The Ego in Delusions of Insanity.

    (b) The Ego in Delusions of Alternating Personalities.

    (c) The Ego in Delusions of Mediums and Possessions.

4. Some Discriminations of Interest.

    (a) Independence of the Persons.

    (b) Identification with Purpose.

    (c) Incorporation of the Power.

CHAPTER XIV.

Ourselves: I; Me; Mine.

Ourselves as "Known." "Me."

1. The Sensuous "Me."

   (a) My Body.

   (b) My Bounty.

   (c) My Blessings.

2. The Social "Me."

   (a) My Success.

   (b) My Sociability.

   (c) My Satisfaction.

3. The Spiritual "Me."

   (a) My Mind.

   (b) My Morals.

   (c) My Mysticism.

CHAPTER XV.

Ourselves: I; Me; Mine.

Ourselves as "Ourselves." "Self."

1. Self.

   (a) Greatness.

   (b) Groveling.

2. Self-seeking.

   (a) Honor.

   (b) Humility.

3. Self-estimation.

   (a) Superiority.

   (b) Inferiority.

CHAPTER XVI.

Ourselves: I; Me; Mine.

Ourselves and Conscience.

1. Conscience before the Fall.

   (a) Consciousness of Self.

   (b) Consciousness of the World.

   (c) Consciousness of God.

2. Conscience after the Fall.
    (a) Standard of the Natural Person.
    (b) The Standard of the Nations – Pagan.
    (c) The Standard of the Naturally Pious.
3. Conscience in the Faithful.
    (a) Conscience and Character in the Saint.
    (b) Conscience and Conduct in the Saint.
    (c) Conscience and Communion of the Saints.

CHAPTER XVII.
Spirit: The Domain and Dominion of Spirit.
Process of the Trinity.
1. Will.
2. Love.
3. Light.

CHAPTER XVIII.
Spirit: The Domain and Dominion of Spirit.
Mundane Universe.
1. Spirit as Physical Force.
    (a) World of Matter.
    (b) World of Nature.
    (c) World of Self.

CHAPTER XIX.
Spirit: The Domain and Dominion of Spirit.
Man's Universe.
1. Spirit as Soul-making Power.
    (a) Particular Form.
    (b) Personal Form.
    (c) Physical Form.

CHAPTER XX.
Spirit: The Domain and Dominion of Spirit.
Man's Universe (Concluded).
1. Spirit in Its Freedom from Flesh.
    (a) Ecstasy.
    (b) Emancipation,
2. Spirit Operating in Sense.
3. Spirit Operating Inwardly.
4. Spirit Operating Morally.

www.ingramcontent.com/pod-product-compliance
Lightning Source LLC
Chambersburg PA
CBHW062152080426
42734CB00010B/1654